American Cinema of the 1910s

 AMERICAN CULTURE / AMERICAN CINEMA

DECADES

Each volume in the Screen Decades: American Culture/American Cinema series presents a group of original essays analyzing the impact of cultural issues on the cinema and the impact of the cinema in American society. Because every chapter explores a spectrum of particularly significant motion pictures and the broad range of historical events in one year, readers will gain a continuing sense of the decade as it came to be depicted on movie screens across the continent. The integration of historical and cultural events with the sprawling progression of American cinema illuminates the pervasive themes and the essential movies that define an era. Our series represents one among many possible ways of confronting the past; we hope that these books will offer a better understanding of the connections between American culture and film history.

LESTER D. FRIEDMAN AND MURRAY POMERANCE
SERIES EDITORS

André Gaudreault, editor, *American Cinema, 1890–1909: Themes and Variations*

Charlie Keil and Ben Singer, editors, *American Cinema of the 1910s: Themes and Variations*

Ina Rae Hark, editor, *American Cinema of the 1930s: Themes and Variations*

Wheeler Winston Dixon, editor, *American Cinema of the 1940s: Themes and Variations*

Murray Pomerance, editor, *American Cinema of the 1950s: Themes and Variations*

Barry Keith Grant, editor, *American Cinema of the 1960s: Themes and Variations*

Lester D. Friedman, editor, *American Cinema of the 1970s: Themes and Variations*

Stephen Prince, editor, *American Cinema of the 1980s: Themes and Variations*

Chris Holmlund, editor, *American Cinema of the 1990s: Themes and Variations*

American Cinema of the
1910s

Themes and Variations

EDITED BY

CHARLIE KEIL AND BEN SINGER

RUTGERS UNIVERSITY PRESS

NEW BRUNSWICK, NEW JERSEY, AND LONDON

LIBRARY OF CONGRESS CATALOGING-IN-PUBLICATION DATA

American cinema of the 1910s : themes and variations / edited by Charlie Keil and Ben Singer.
    p. cm. — (Screen decades : American culture / American cinema)
  Includes bibliographical references and index.
  ISBN 978–0–8135–4444–1 (hardcover : alk. paper)
  ISBN 978–0–8135–4445–8 (pbk. : alk. paper)
  1. Motion pictures—United States—History. 2. Motion pictures—United States—Plots, themes, etc. I. Keil, Charlie. II. Singer, Ben.
  PN1993.5.U6A85733 2009
  791.430973—dc22

                   2008016734

A British Cataloging-in-Publication record for this book is available from the British Library.

Visit our Web site: http://rutgerspress.rutgers.edu

Manufactured in the United States of America

CONTENTS

ACKNOWLEDGMENTS

We would like to acknowledge our gratitude to the series editors, Lester D. Friedman and Murray Pomerance, for their valuable input; to Leslie Mitchner and her colleagues at Rutgers University Press for their professionalism and patience; to the contributors for their painstaking scholarship and good humor; and to our families for their perennial forbearance.

Charlie Keil	Ben Singer
Toronto	Madison
March 2008	March 2008

TIMELINE

The 1910s

1910

5 MARCH — The Independent Moving Picture Company launches a concerted campaign to create name recognition for Florence Lawrence.

21 APRIL — Mark Twain (Samuel Langhorne Clemens) dies.

25 JUNE — The Mann Act, which makes illegal the transportation of women across state lines for the purposes of prostitution, is passed into law, designed to halt so-called "white slavery."

4 JULY — By knocking out Jim Jeffries in the fifteenth round, Jack Johnson becomes the first African American heavyweight boxing champion.

27 NOVEMBER — New York's Penn Station opens, acknowledged as the largest train station in the world and an architectural masterpiece in the Beaux Arts style.

1911

FEBRUARY — *Motion Picture Story*, the first film periodical aimed at moviegoers, releases its inaugural issue.

25 MARCH — The Triangle Waist fire kills 146 (almost all female) employees, sparking outrage about labor conditions.

15 MAY — The Supreme Court orders the dissolution of Standard Oil because it violates the Sherman Anti-Trust Act.

NOVEMBER — Irving Berlin's "Alexander's Ragtime Band" is published as sheet music.

1912

15 APRIL — After striking an iceberg, the ocean liner *Titanic* sinks off the coast of Newfoundland, taking 1,523 lives.

8 JUNE — Carl Laemmle and Charles Baumann amalgamate several Independent production companies to form Universal Film Manufacturing Company.

26 JULY — The initial episode of Edison's *What Happened to Mary*, the first motion picture serial made in the United States, debuts in theaters.

12 AUGUST   Trade papers announce the formation of Mack Sennett's Keystone Film Company.

27 SEPTEMBER   W. C. Handy's "Memphis Blues," credited with establishing the blues as a recognized form of American music, is published.

5 NOVEMBER   Democrat Woodrow Wilson prevails in the presidential election, defeating Republican incumbent William Howard Taft and former president Theodore Roosevelt, who was running on a third-party ticket.

1913

15 FEBRUARY   The Armory Show, officially known as the International Exhibition of Modern Art, brings together over fifteen hundred works of modern art in New York City.

8 MARCH   The Internal Revenue Service begins to levy and collect income tax.

1 APRIL   The Pennsylvania State Board of Censors officially begins its activities.

OCTOBER   D. W. Griffith leaves Biograph, a company where he had been the primary director for over five years.

28 OCTOBER   George Herriman's "Krazy Kat" begins its run as a daily comic strip in the *New York Journal*.

1914

7 FEBRUARY   Charlie Chaplin's first appearance as the Tramp character occurs when *Kid Auto Races at Venice* is released.

15 FEBRUARY   Reputedly the first feature film shot in Hollywood, Cecil B. DeMille's filmmaking debut, *The Squaw Man* (co-directed by Oscar Apfel), opens.

12 APRIL   The Strand Theatre, the largest movie house yet built, with a seating capacity of 3,500, opens in Times Square.

26 MAY   The *New York Times* acknowledges the new verb "to film" and the new noun "movie."

28 JULY   Austria-Hungary's declaration of war on Serbia initiates World War I.

5 AUGUST   The first traffic light is installed, in Cleveland.

1915

25 JANUARY   Alexander Graham Bell in New York telephones Thomas Watson in San Francisco—the first transcontinental call.

8 FEBRUARY	*The Birth of a Nation* premieres (with the title *The Clansman*) at Clune's Auditorium in Los Angeles.
23 FEBRUARY	The U.S. Supreme Court rules that First Amendment protections of free expression do not apply to the movies.
7 MAY	A German submarine sinks the British liner *Lusitania* off the coast of Ireland; 1,198 people perish, including 128 Americans.
8 MAY	Regret becomes the first filly to win the Kentucky Derby.
28 JULY	U.S. forces invade Haiti, beginning a nineteen-year occupation.

■ 1916

27 FEBRUARY	Charlie Chaplin signs with the Mutual Film Corporation, beginning an outstanding creative phase in his career.
7 APRIL	Hugo Munsterberg's book *The Photoplay: A Psychological Study*, arguably the first sustained work of film theory, is published by Appleton & Co., New York.
5 JUNE	Louis Brandeis is sworn in as an associate justice of the U.S. Supreme Court.
16 OCTOBER	Margaret Sanger opens the nation's first birth control clinic in Brooklyn.
7 NOVEMBER	Woodrow Wilson wins reelection by a narrow margin over former (and future) Supreme Court justice Charles Evans Hughes.

■ 1917

1 MARCH	An intercepted telegram containing a proposal by German foreign secretary Alfred Zimmermann to ally with Mexico and Japan in an invasion of the United States is released to newspapers, tipping public opinion in favor of entry into World War I.
2 APRIL	Jeannette Rankin of Montana is seated in the U.S. House of Representatives, becoming the first female member of Congress.
6 APRIL	The United States declares war on Germany.
25 APRIL	First National Exhibitors Circuit is incorporated by a consortium of major exhibitors aiming to thwart Paramount's domination of the industry by financing and distributing films themselves.
2 JULY	Racially motivated mob violence erupts in East St. Louis, Illinois, leaving at least forty-eight people dead, nearly all of them African Americans.

1918

19 MARCH   Congress authorizes time zones and approves daylight saving time.

6 APRIL   The Edison Company, the first motion picture studio, releases its very last film.

15 MAY   The first regular airmail service begins, between New York, Philadelphia, and Washington.

20 JULY   Winsor McCay's groundbreaking animated short *The Sinking of the Lusitania* is released by Universal.

11 NOVEMBER Armistice Day—World War I fighting ends at 11 A.M. on the Western Front.

1919

6 JANUARY   Former president Theodore Roosevelt dies at age sixty-one.

17 APRIL   United Artists is incorporated as a joint venture by Charlie Chaplin, Douglas Fairbanks, D. W. Griffith, and Mary Pickford.

13 MAY   D. W. Griffith's *Broken Blossoms* premieres at the George M. Cohan Theater in New York. Tickets cost up to three dollars, the same as the most expensive seats for a Broadway play.

19 OCTOBER   The Cincinnati Reds win baseball's World Series against the Chicago White Sox in a series marred by the infamous "Black Sox" scandal.

19 NOVEMBER The U.S. Senate rejects the Treaty of Versailles and League of Nations.

American Cinema of the 1910s

INTRODUCTION

Movies and the 1910s

BEN SINGER AND CHARLIE KEIL

■ The Birth of a (Modern) Nation

The 1910s represents a turning point for American society, a period that saw many of the key transformations that helped shape the United States into a modern nation. By the decade's close, America's global supremacy as a supplier of commercial goods was secured, in part due to the disruptions caused by World War I. Progressivism, the dominant political movement of the era, guided social policy and legislation with the goal of taming the mayhem of unchecked modernization. An enhanced sense of American identity was promoted by the spread of national distribution and communication networks that disseminated everything from mass circulation magazines to nationally branded consumer items, trends and fads like the wristwatch, the Raggedy Ann doll, and the Ouija board, and—of particular significance for a shared notion of Americanism—the movies. A host of new products, from Oreo cookies to the Frigidaire and the Model T, demonstrated how technological innovation continued to affect daily life. The horrors of World War I, the first highly technologized war, underscored that fact in a grim way. Liberalization within the social sphere brought the introduction of Planned Parenthood and the nation's first no-fault divorce law (in Nevada). In popular culture, ragtime music, the fox-trot dance craze, and lavish revues like the *Ziegfeld Follies* signaled the weakening grip of Protestant moral austerity and the growing importance of amusements emphasizing stimulation and fun. In the realm of high culture, American artists in various fields participated in the modernist experiment, with figures as diverse as painter Joseph Stella and writers Ezra Pound and Gertrude Stein redefining the boundaries of aesthetic expression. Stein, tellingly, related her stylistic innovations to a quintessentially modern and American mode of constant change encapsulated in the moviegoing experience. If the movies were indeed representative of American modernity during this decade, it was arguably the ever-changing nature of motion pictures and the rapid transfiguration of the industry creating them that capture most vividly their representative quality.

For many, the image that comes to mind when thinking about America at this time is of teeming masses and traffic jams in Lower Manhattan or Chicago's Loop. Such pictures convey the strikingly modern experiential milieu of at least some portion of the population. It is important to bear in mind, however, that most Americans still lived in distinctly quieter places. The country's population in the 1910s was one-third of its current size (around 100 million versus 300 million) and, while urbanization was escalating, America remained a predominantly rural society. Quantifying population distribution is complicated due to idiosyncrasies and changes in the categories and methodologies employed by the census bureau, but as a rough approximation one can say that in this period about 60 percent of Americans lived in small towns or rural areas. One person in three worked on a farm, compared with one person in fifty today. Only about one person in four or five lived in a major city (that is, one of the twenty to twenty-five cities with populations over a quarter million).

Given the rural majority, what justifies emphasizing modernization as the keynote of the 1910s? One answer would be that all cultures have centers and peripheries, and it is invariably the centers—hotbeds of expression, innovation, industry, commerce, politics, and civil society—that define an age and rightly attract historical attention. A more compelling answer, the one that informs this volume, is that the 1910s was a time when the center reached into the periphery on an unprecedented scale, due to new technologies and systems of transportation, communication, and distribution. The boundaries between urban and rural America became less distinct. An urban national culture infiltrated the hinterlands as never before, rendering the periphery's consciousness of and contact with the cultural center more extensive and palpable than in previous decades. With ever-expanding transportation networks and the emergence of mass production, mass marketing, and mass communications (especially the cinema), American society became more integrated, more interconnected, and more dynamic in its circulation of goods, images, ideas, and people.

This is not to suggest that a rural/urban divide no longer existed; small-town America was largely buffered from the sensory and heterosocial intensity of the nation's metropolitan centers, and even a casual glance at the period's entertainments will find that popular culture never tired of highlighting comic and moral differences between provincial country folk and urbane urbanites. In the many films focusing on small-town life, country lads and lasses are virtuous, albeit awkward and naive, while city slickers and "vamps" are suave but degenerate. Yet this very motif underscores the fact that the issue of contact and interaction between the two was a timely phenomenon engaging social reflection.

The primary engine driving new forms of interconnection was the tremendous rise of big business during the decade, a force reflecting major technological innovations, a movement toward stringent "rationaliza-tion" (i.e., the implementation of optimally efficient techniques and sys-tems of corporate management, manufacturing, distribution, marketing, accounting, and so on), and access to enormous sums of investment cap-ital to finance large-scale commercial expansion. The growth of big busi-ness is exemplified by the rise of Ford Motors, a company whose stunning success stemmed from quintessential examples of industrial rationaliza-tion (to such a degree that the term "Fordism" is often used as shorthand for "rationalization"). Automobile manufacturing began in the mid-1890s in the United States. In the 1910s, Henry Ford and his engineers trans-formed the automobile from a flimsy plaything of the rich to a rugged, practical machine affordable to mainstream consumers. He did so by focusing on a single simplified and standardized design—the Model T—and innovating ultra-efficient manufacturing techniques, most signifi-cantly the moving assembly line, which, upon its introduction in 1913, cut the labor required to assemble a chassis from 12.5 hours to 1.5 hours. Six thousand Model Ts were manufactured in 1908, its first year of pro-duction. By 1916, that number had increased almost one-hundredfold, to nearly 600,000 cars, while the purchase price had dropped from $850 to $360 (equivalent, in today's dollars adjusted for inflation, to a drop from just over $19,000 to $7,000). During that period, Ford's distribution net-work rose from 215 to 8,500 dealerships across the country (Tedlow 125, 137). Overall, 8 million automobiles (of every make) were registered in the country by the decade's end, up from just under half a million in 1910 (Blanke 3).

To cite a few other examples of the decade's shift toward big business on a national scale, the A & P discount grocery chain expanded from 650 stores in 1914 to 4,600 stores six years later. Mail-order giant Sears, Roe-buck saw its net sales increase from $61 million in 1910 to $245 million in 1920 (adjusted for inflation, the equivalent of $1.4 billion and $2.5 billion today). Sales of Coca-Cola rose from just over 4 million gallons in 1910 to almost 19 million gallons in 1919 (Tedlow 29, 194, 280). Such figures indi-cate not only the upsurge in consumerism that characterizes the decade, but also the degree to which the conveniences afforded by an ever more technologically sophisticated manufacturing sector, delivered through ever more intricate delivery systems, permeated the life of every American who could afford to partake of them. Many could, as the decade witnessed unprecedented increases in economic output and average wages. But balancing the unbridled expansion was increased concern for the social costs attached to that expansion.

With the election of Woodrow Wilson as president in 1912, the continued influence of Progressivism on American politics was assured. Progressivism, sustained through the previous administrations of Roosevelt and Taft, had affected not only government, but the related spheres of journalism, academia, and activism. Committed to battling the excesses of big business and the potentially dehumanizing effects of modern life (largely attributable to the Industrial Revolution), advocates of Progressivism were proponents of efficiency, expertise, social justice, and, above all, the notion that it was the proper role of government to implement them. As the name implies, Progressivism was committed to an ideal of progress, a betterment of living conditions that nonetheless often put its faith in the power of trained authorities and bureaucratic systems to effect the necessary changes. Progressivism accounted for many of the notable achievements and trends of the decade, from the introduction of labor reforms (such as the eight-hour work week, minimum wage guarantees, and the increased acceptance of unionism) to the journalistic tradition of muckraking (dedicated to exposing fraudulent business practices, social inequities, and government corruption) to the reining in of industrial combines through trust-busting.

The Progressive commitment to efficiency often found itself at odds with its own drive for improved social justice and enhanced democracy. For example, Progressives championed the employment of city managers—professionals hired to oversee the daily operations of municipal governments—even though this empowered non-elected officials and potentially opposed the will of the people. Similarly, their zeal to eradicate social problems that they believed interfered with progress, such as prostitution and the consumption of liquor, led them to propose solutions that not only impeded individual liberties, but also were ultimately ineffective, since they tended to attack the symptom without addressing the root causes. Critics would argue that the Mann Act of 1910, prohibiting the transportation of women across state lines for "immoral purposes," may have thwarted so-called "white slave" traffic, but also led to a crackdown on brothels that simply forced many prostitutes onto the streets. Similarly, the passage of the Eighteenth Amendment to the Constitution in 1919, which rendered the production and sale of liquor illegal beginning a year later, created a huge underground economy and inadvertently aided the operations of organized crime in the process.

Even though the Progressive agenda was riven by its own inconsistencies, the movement's achievements during this decade remain remarkable. Aside from the labor reforms already mentioned, the Wilson administration alone was responsible for an extensive list of changes to the operations and influence of the federal government, among them the introduction of a national income tax; the establishment of both the Federal Reserve system and the Federal Trade Commission; changes to tariff laws, loan policies, and, eventually, in 1920, ratification of the Nineteenth Amendment, extending the right to vote to women. Progressive reforms touched many other aspects of public life as well. An emphasis on the value of education led to a substantial rise in funding, so that it reached $1 billion by the end of the decade, with per-student spending vaulting from $4.64 to $9.60 (Blanke 26). Progressives were influenced by John Dewey's child-centered approach to pedagogy, a philosophy that led to curricular reforms, better training of teachers, and more attention paid to the benefits of age-specific learning environments (including the widespread introduction of kindergarten during the decade, and a large increase in the number of high schools). The need for child protection prompted the creation of a wide range of social service agencies, epitomized by the federal Children's Bureau, established in 1912. The Bureau gathered statistics on everything from infant mortality to juvenile delinquency, an endeavor that helped provide the data required to support Progressive legislation. Overall, the Progressive tendency was to educate mothers in the proper raising of their children and to lessen the strain on childrearing (even to the point of providing monetary support, as with the provision of "mothers' pensions" throughout the decade). While Progressive efforts definitely helped ameliorate some of the most pernicious policies of earlier eras (including child labor), they also led to intrusive and moralizing attempts to monitor the lives of the poor and of immigrants under the assumption that professional experts possessed superior knowledge.

While poorer females were often the focus of Progressive initiatives, the burgeoning middle class produced numerous women who helped define the activist dimension of Progressivism, particularly within the domain of social justice. Civic leaders such as Jane Addams set the agenda for aiding urban ills through settlement houses (institutions established to provide support for poor urban women), while crusaders like Margaret Sanger pushed for birth control to be provided to women. The common drive for suffrage proved a unifying issue. Its implicit demand for a rejection of outmoded ways of defining womanhood also contributed to the social phenomenon of the "New Woman." This label attached itself to those who broke with previous traditions by pursuing a more active and independent lifestyle, replete with dancing in public, smoking, and engaging in athletic pursuits. As consumerism increased throughout the decade, advertisers used the image of the New Woman to entice women to embrace a lifestyle defined by indulgence and self-involvement, an aim at odds with the loftier goals of the Progressive impulse.

Despite the expressed Progressive concern for the improvement of living conditions of all Americans, certain groups fared better than others. Poverty continued to be widespread, especially among immigrants, rural inhabitants, and African Americans. Upholding segregationist policies, the Wilson administration did little to aid the plights of Blacks in America during this time, leaving advocacy for their rights to groups like the National Association for the Advancement of Colored People (NAACP), founded in 1909 and dedicated to upholding the Fourteenth Amendment provisions that had expressly ensured equal protection under the law to former slaves. Blacks found themselves subject to sustained and often violent racism during the decade, particularly demonstrated by the recurrence of lynchings and the resurgence of the Ku Klux Klan. By the latter part of the decade, increased dissatisfaction with their situation and better prospects in the North resulting from World War I (as enlisted men vacated jobs and immigration slowed to a trickle) fueled the Great Migration and contributed to major race riots in 1917 and 1919.

Barred from equal access to most of the practices and institutions that define a citizen's daily life, African Americans still managed to influence white society through one means in particular—music. Syncopated rhythms, derived from African musical styles, became popularized through ragtime. Demand for sheet music flourished, due largely to dramatic increases in the sale of pianos for home parlors. Vying with the music of Tin Pan Alley as the popular choice of sheet music consumers, ragtime was played in the parlors of millions of white Americans, raising the hackles of many cultural critics, but also paving the way for the acceptance of other homegrown musical forms created primarily by Blacks, such as the blues and jazz. The broad popularity of music by Scott Joplin, W. C. Handy, and "Jelly Roll" Morton pointed to ways in which black culture could influence the white-dominated mainstream. Irving Berlin appropriated ragtime, for example, for his massive hit "Alexander's Ragtime Band." It also demonstrates how the spread of popular music became increasingly dependent on centralized distribution (mass-produced sheet music and audio recordings) and was fostered by an urban ethos of sophisticated entertainment that motion pictures would also tap into as the decade progressed.

Modernization influenced the fads and leisure pursuits of Americans throughout the decade. Mass production and improved systems of delivery sped the dissemination of prized consumer goods across the nation, and even toys and games capitalized on the fascination with technology that defined the age. The Erector Set, which allowed children to construct their own miniature versions of skyscrapers, the Singer toy sewing machine, and Model T joke books, are different examples of playthings owing their existence to the modern era. Modern marketing also influenced the way goods were sold, with corporate icons (like the Campbell Soup kids, which became the model for a pair of popular dolls) demonstrating the newfound popularity of the tie-in. The omnipresence of advertising is one of the clearest markers of the ethos of modernity that blanketed the country, as advertising revenues soared, doubling to a total of close to $1.5 billion by the end of the 1910s (Lears 162).

The most obvious beneficiary of this additional advertising spending was the mass circulation magazine, including such stalwarts as the *Saturday Evening Post*, *Ladies' Home Journal*, and *Cosmopolitan*. It was not uncommon for half of such a magazine's pages to be devoted to advertising. Since the substantial revenues generated by the sale of advertising space offset production costs, publishers could keep the price of magazines low, maintain high circulations, and, in turn, ensure their attractiveness to advertisers. Inevitably, advertising also helped sell the war to the American public: the single most recognizable image attached to enlistment efforts was James Montgomery Flagg's poster of Uncle Sam soliciting prospective soldiers through the direct "I Want You."

America's involvement in the war was measured at first: when war broke out in August 1914, Wilson issued a formal proclamation of neutrality. However, economic ties with Allied Powers, especially Britain, and a British naval blockade obstructing trade with Germany soon made the United States neutral in name only. The war was a tremendous economic boon to Americans, as the Allies purchased billions of dollars of weaponry and supplies and took out billions more in loans from American banks. By contrast, the Central Powers (Germany, Austria-Hungary, the Ottoman Empire, and Bulgaria) gained virtually no material or economic assistance.

Tensions escalated in early 1915, when Germany announced that it would target for surprise submarine attack all enemy ships in the seas around the British Isles. On 7 May, a German U-boat sank the British passenger liner *Lusitania* off the coast of Ireland (en route from New York to

The film industry's patriotism on display: Fatty Arbuckle in Times Square putting up a poster for the 1917 Liberty Loan drive. National Archives and Records Administration.

Liverpool): 1,198 people perished, including 128 American citizens. Although the incident spurred anti-German sentiment and prompted Wilson and Congress to initiate measures toward increased military preparedness, many Americans still opposed involvement.

Antiwar separatism became an untenable position in March 1917, after U-boats sank seven American merchant ships and after revelation of "the Zimmermann telegram": a secret communiqué from the German foreign secretary to his ambassador in Mexico advancing the idea of a German-Mexican alliance (encouraging Mexico to invade the United States and win back Texas, New Mexico, and Arizona). On 6 April, after exhorting that "the world must be made safe for democracy," President Wilson issued a declaration of war. Domestic opposition receded quickly as America mobilized, in part due to a major propaganda initiative mounted by the government's purpose-created Committee on Public Information. The film industry played an important role in the success of the CPI, especially promoting the sale of war bonds.

In accordance with the Selective Service Act, 24 million men registered for the draft, and 2.8 million were called up for service, joining roughly 2 million volunteers. American forces engaged in their first battles in northern France in May 1918. Helping stop a German offensive, and then fighting a successful counteroffensive, U.S. troops hastened the armistice, which began on 11 November 1918. In all, 52,000 Americans died in battle—a small fraction of the nearly 10 million military casualties suffered in the war overall. Sixty thousand more American soldiers died from an outbreak of influenza that would soon spread around the globe, causing an estimated 50–100 million deaths worldwide. It was by far the deadliest pandemic in modern history (or perhaps recorded history: by some estimates, it claimed more lives than even the Black Plague).

At home, the postwar "return to normalcy" was anything but normal, marked by widespread labor strife, racial conflict, and political repression triggered by terrorist bombings and a resulting Red Scare. Wilson participated actively in the European peace treaty negotiations, calling (ultimately unsuccessfully) for nonvindictive conditions of surrender by the Central Powers. His one great diplomatic accomplishment was the formation of a League of Nations as a mechanism for avoiding future wars. In a bitter defeat at home, however, Congress rebuffed the plan, fearing it would entangle the United States in international conflicts without pressing national interest.

Casting an influence over every aspect of life in America, the war years offered enhanced employment opportunities to Blacks and women, while also bolstering the fortunes of unions that helped support the war effort. Federal bureaucracy increased during this period, including the formation of the Federal Bureau of Investigation in 1917. Popular culture channeled patriotism through songs like George M. Cohan's "Over There" and through the resonant work of magazine illustrators, the most famous of whom was Norman Rockwell; his iconic work for the cover of the *Saturday Evening Post* first appeared in 1916. Rockwell's combination of realism and nostalgia for the simple pleasures of a premodern era remind us again of the transitional nature of this period. By the same token, changes to the ways Americans ate and dressed during the 1910s demonstrate as clearly as any other social shifts the combined influence of modernity and World War I on the decade.

Whereas 1910 still saw women's fashions favoring the hourglass silhouette produced by the constricting corset and layered, ornate clothing, the influence of the New Woman as a model of increased freedom and vitality prompted the adoption of looser, more comfortable garments as the decade wore on. Numerous developments affected fashion trends. The increased popularity of public dancing by mid-decade, spurred by various dance crazes, including the fox-trot and turkey-trot, required female clothing that permitted freedom of bodily movement. Similarly, the growing acceptance of athletics as part of a middle-class existence (encouraged in part by the active lifestyles of celebrities, including movie stars) translated into a more liberal conception of casual clothing. The normalization of automobile travel also dictated the adoption of garments for riding that permitted one to ride in the open air. And the scarcity of materials during the war years led to simpler, more relaxed clothing styles for both sexes and a reduced palette of colors. Advertising played a role in transmitting fashion trends all the more readily to the national populace and certainly led to the popularization of cosmetics and other beauty aids.

A parallel trend toward lighter diets and increased convenience defined the way Americans approached eating and food preparation during the decade. Technological innovations in the realm of kitchen appliances and cookware permitted a wider range of meal choices, while lifestyle changes rendered the eating habits of an earlier era outdated. Breakfast, in particular, became a meal defined by both convenience and lighter foods. Packaged breakfast cereals proliferated during the decade as companies like Kellogg's, Quaker, and Post profited from the assumed health benefits of their products. Of course, not all convenience foods conferred healthiness onto their consumers: snacks of various kinds became popular ways to satisfy appetites between meals, and World War I only increased the appeal of chocolate bars and chewing gum, not to mention cigarettes. Overall, the lifestyle changes introduced during the 1910s are evidence of a nation constantly involved in the process of redefining itself in light of the influence of technology and media, among other modernizing forces.

Struggles for Control, Systems of Efficiency

As American society faced a series of challenges and changes, the American film industry was undergoing its own transformation. The decade began with a relatively new structure imposed by the recently established Motion Picture Patents Company (alternately known as the MPPC or the Trust) in its attempt to monopolize production. Strictly speaking, the MPPC was set up as a patent pooling organization, but it was designed to drive out of business all producers and distributors who were not members. The Trust desired to restrict the market only to those producers who were part of the original cartel, organizing exchanges (small-scale distributors working within defined territories) and exhibitors in the process, by issuing licenses allowing them to show Trust films (and use Trust-produced equipment).

These licensed exchanges and exhibitors were charged fees for the privilege of showing MPPC product, a practice that invited considerable resentment. The Trust also chose to disregard a substantial number of peripheral exchanges and exhibitors that were unlicensed and therefore, they assumed, would wither away. Ignoring this portion of the market would prove to be a fatefully unwise business decision.

Although its chief aim was to profit by eliminating competition, to its credit, the MPPC injected some much-needed supply stability into what had become an industry growing too quickly on the demand side. An estimated 12,000 nickelodeon theaters clamored for films. The Trust initiated numerous improvements that allowed exchanges and exhibitors to plan their own business practices with more confidence. Chief among these was the establishment of a 1,000-foot format standard, regular release schedules, and more attentive control over the quality of prints in circulation. In 1910, the MPPC moved to extend its monopolistic designs by creating the General Film Company, a parallel organization that systematically purchased every licensed exchange, effectively placing a large sector of the distribution sector under its control. The sole holdout among the licensees was the Greater New York Film Company, owned by William Fox (who would subsequently found the Fox Film Corporation).

As vigorously as the MPPC pursued its goal of total market control, it could not keep pace with the burgeoning market. Intense demand for films allowed for the emergence of an opposing faction, the Independents. These producers, who primarily courted those exchanges and theater owners who remained unlicensed (and those licensees who chafed against Trust control), emerged almost as soon as the MPPC made its intentions known, and by 1910 there were several Independents already in operation, including the New York Motion Picture Company, Powers, Nestor, and, most important in terms of later developments, Carl Laemmle's Independent Moving Picture Company, commonly known as IMP. Nineteen ten saw the creation of more Independent firms of substance, including Thanhouser, Reliance, Solax, and the American Film Company. Many of these companies established themselves by hiring away personnel from established Trust firms, particularly the most prized asset, actors. This poaching of acting talent by upstart companies demonstrates that "picture personalities" were fast becoming one of the cinema's most identifiable and promotable ingredients.

The various fledgling Independent producers soon realized that they would need to organize themselves in a manner similar to the Trust if they were to survive. Accordingly, a few of the leaders of the Independent

An example of the Independents' campaign against the MPPC, ca. 1910 (Bowers 63). ("Simoleon" is period slang for "dollar.")

faction, Laemmle among them, established the Motion Picture Distributing and Sales Company in April 1910 to provide unlicensed exchanges with a steady supply of Independent films. The Sales Company was sufficiently successful in its efforts that it managed to provide twenty-one reels a week to its exchanges by June, while the Trust was guaranteeing thirty (Bowser 81).

The basic structure of Trust versus Independents would prevail for several years, and this version of limited competition within a climate of strong demand led to an increasingly powerful production sector. Limiting the presence of foreign films on domestic screens also tipped the balance. While films from France in particular had dominated the U.S. market in the pre-Trust years, the MPPC cannily limited the number of foreign firms allowed to join its cartel. As Eileen Bowser has pointed out, the combination of curtailed access to the American market by foreign film companies and an improving rate of productivity led to a growing percentage of American films circulating within the market: "By the end of 1912, national production accounted for well over 80 per cent of the American market, at least according to the number of film titles released (not copies sold)" (Bowser 85). By the time World War I had decimated foreign production (most pointedly in France and Italy), U.S. control of the world market would follow. American domination of its own market was the economic foundation upon which its subsequent success in many other countries was built. Producers could sell their films at a relatively low price to ensure competitiveness elsewhere.

Ironically, the Independent faction experienced its own internal divisions by the time it had reached parity with the Trust. The Sales Company's domination of Independent distribution was shaken by the formation of the Mutual Film Corporation in 1912, a breakaway firm that soon attracted numerous companies that had previously leased their films through Sales. The success of Mutual forced a reorganization of the Sales Company, renamed Universal Film Manufacturing Company later the same year. Universal would remain a vital force within the industry, much more so than the MPPC, which found itself attacked on numerous fronts. Competition from the Independents eroded the Trust's early domination of the market, and the growing popularity of features caught at least some of its members off-guard. Beset by government legal attacks (for violation of antitrust legislation), the Trust was officially dissolved by court decree in 1915. It was effectively defunct by that time anyway, a victim of ever-changing market forces.

The robust demand for films during this decade spurred producers to find ways to ensure a steady flow of product. The reforms introduced by the MPPC went some way to ensuring supply would meet demand, but changes to the mode of production aimed further at increasing efficiency and, hence, productivity. It is during the decade of the 1910s that one sees concerted efforts toward increased rationalization of production duties, leading to the ascendancy of the producer as the central organizing figure. Investing control in the position of a central producer introduced the concept of managerial oversight to film production: no longer did directors have the same autonomy that previously they had enjoyed. Scripts became blueprints for budget-based decision making and delegation of duties. These changes were prepared for by establishment of the 1,000-foot reel as the standard length for films, a common unit of exchange that defined norms for the production sector, leading to a greater standardization in production procedures. Key craft areas were identified, and labor divided among task-specialized departments. A Vitagraph promotional pamphlet from 1913 depicts a host of departments, ranging from scenic to costume to property to carpentering and upholstering. The company lists its workforce as numbering 400 in its Brooklyn studios alone (exclusive of extras). In describing its managerial structure, the pamphlet notes that "each one of [the company's] branches is governed by its head, and the whole force is under the Studio Manager, who lays out the work, and is responsible for the performance of the work and the fulfillment of the duties apportioned each day. The regular Vitagraph production is one complete picture a day, or six a week. Often it reaches ten a week."

As long as distribution practices favored the delivery of a slate of single-reel films to exhibitors, the overall quality of a producer's output proved more important than the attributes of any individual title. The price of leasing a film was standardized, so there was little incentive for producers to undertake ambitious, expensive productions or multi-reel films. When on occasion a producer did make a multi-reel film, invariably it would be broken up and distributed as a set of single-reel units.

For the first several years of the decade, the dominance of the single-reel format led to a degree of predictability in every sector of the film industry. Within the realm of production, the 1,000-foot length provided the parameters for scenario construction: filmmakers came to know exactly what was required to turn out a story lasting approximately the same amount of time for each title. For distributors, the uniform length ensured an interchangeability of product, so that different titles from different producers could be mixed and matched at will when programs of films were offered to exhibitors. And theater owners easily integrated films of this nature into their preexisting variety programs. An evening's entertainment at a small-scale theater would involve a bill of five to six one-reel films, illustrated song slides (that encouraged audience participation), and a range of live entertainment, typically music or vaudeville performance, depending on the theater's budget, size, and cultural aspirations. The ever-changing bill of fare meant that patrons did not need to worry about start times for the performance: if one walked in during the middle of a film, one could be certain that another would commence in a few minutes. When the single-reel format was displaced by the feature, exhibitors lost control over the organization of their programs; producers assumed that power.

Since fixed receipts and fixed film lengths discouraged individually distinctive productions, some producers focused on strength in particular genres to differentiate their products. For example, Keystone was known almost exclusively for comedy; American for westerns. Other studios relied more on the popularity of familiar actors. Promotion of motion picture actors did not begin in earnest until the start of the 1910s, in part as a tactic by Independent producers to draw attention to their new offerings. The most high-profile defection of a star from an established company to a new concern at the beginning of the decade was that of Florence Lawrence. Previously billed as the Biograph Girl, her fame derived from her presence in that company's films. Lured by Carl Laemmle to IMP, Lawrence was made the focus of an elaborate advertising campaign devised by Laemmle to manufacture controversy and put her name in the news. The IMP ads stressed the falseness of "reports" of Lawrence's death in a streetcar accident and asserted they were planted by unnamed "rivals" to deceive the public into believing one of its favorite actresses would no longer be making films. Through this hoax, IMP achieved both its objectives: it cemented the association of Lawrence with her new employer, and it changed the terms of her recognition, transforming her from the Biograph Girl to Florence Lawrence.

Despite what some accounts have argued, the Trust companies were no more reticent about advertising their stars by name than their Independent counterparts. The MPPC's Kalem was the first firm to publicize its stars by making lobby cards of their images available to exhibitors; Edison provided full cast lists in its advertising before any other company; and Vitagraph promoted its premiere star, Florence Turner (the Vitagraph Girl), with personal appearances at the same time that IMP was capitalizing on the Lawrence rumors. Recognition of fan interest in stars fueled companies' efforts to promote them in whatever way possible. Just as film was a reproducible commodity that could be circulated easily, so too were star images, most obviously through photographs. Images of stars soon appeared in numerous different forms, on everything from postcards to pennants, from pillow tops to the handles of spoons. Every star image further spurred audience interest in the originating vehicles—the films in which they appeared. And, as audience investment in stars intensified, advertisers learned to employ stars to sell an array of consumer goods, connecting them to soap and perfume, among other health and beauty items. Such campaigns initiated a longstanding tradition of aligning stars with both consumerism and physical self-improvement.

With studios now employing the collective resources of publicity departments (Vitagraph's 1913 pamphlet claimed that to "popularize its players" was one of its promotion people's chief aims), an entire infrastructure developed to cultivate fan interest, including the emergence of publications designed to provide more information on the stars for a curious public. Several new publications emerged that devoted themselves to stories about stars, typically adorned with full-page photos. Journals such as *Motion Picture Story Magazine* and *Photoplay* existed chiefly to provide the public with a never-ending stream of copy about the stars whom filmgoers had come to adore. Popularity contests were held to determine which stars commanded the largest fan base, and as the industry structure shifted to privilege the presence of particular stars in feature films, the salaries of the most popular stars rocketed upward to reflect their market value.

The centrality of stars to the industry's publicity machine and to key industrial strategies such as block booking (in which theater managers had to accept numerous films packaged together) affirms the growing clout of actors, but also points to how quickly fan culture had developed around the figure of the star. Aiding in this process was the concentration of production activity on the West Coast, gravitating toward a cluster of communities near Los Angeles that would eventually come to be known as Hollywood. Although geographic and symbolic identification of the filmmaking community with this iconic name still lay in the future, the industry began to be associated more consistently with the West Coast from the mid-1910s onward. Filmmaking companies had been traveling west for the benefits of extended sunlight and varied terrain since the beginning of the decade, and by 1915 the Los Angeles Chamber of Commerce reported that "close to fifteen thousand residents earned their living in the film industry, drawing some five million in wages annually" (Stamp, "Filmland" 334). With numerous companies building extensive studios on the cheap land California provided, an image of exoticism and extravagance attached itself to motion picture production, especially when the studios promoted themselves as glamorous versions of municipalities, devising names like Inceville and Universal City. The latter studio actively courted visitors by offering tours that afforded firsthand views of the wonders of moviemaking. Fan magazines played their part in promoting the appeals of the so-called movie colony, featuring photo spreads of both the studios and the lavish lifestyles of select stars. Readers were encouraged to imagine the lives of those in "Filmland" as an enhanced version of reality, a parallel to the increased opulence on display in the films produced.

The film industry coveted the female audience in particular, in part because women aided its campaign for respectability, but equally because they were a prime consumer group. And with women (and children) a central target of motion picture promotion, through newspapers and mass-circulation magazines, in addition to theater advertising and fan magazines, custodians of public mores continued to pay attention to the content of motion pictures and the conduct of those making them. At the turn of the decade, exhibitors in New York convinced the People's Institute, a civic body, to establish what would become the National Board of Censorship. The Board viewed most of the films shown in the country, deciding whether they violated obscenity standards or condoned criminal acts. Despite this effort on the industry's part, state censorship boards emerged throughout the 1910s, arising in reaction to the perceived laxity of the Board (which was often seen as an arm of the industry it was supposed to oversee). Ohio, Pennsylvania, Kansas, and Maryland all set up censor boards during the decade, and a pivotal legal case emerged out of the industry's attempt to challenge the constitutionality of these state regulators. The Mutual Film Corporation sought to have the boards disbanded on the grounds that they thwarted free speech. In 1915 the Supreme Court heard the case and decided that movies were not worthy of the protection accorded the press and forms of artistic expression, opting instead to describe motion pictures as "a business pure and simple." For many years thereafter, this decision left cinema vulnerable to the prospect of increased external regulatory pressures; fearing the repercussions of oppressive state censorship, the film industry instead practiced various forms of self-regulation over the succeeding decades, steering clear of controversy and contentious subject matter in an effort to prove that it was nothing more than a purveyor of "harmless entertainment" (Grieveson, *Policing* 202).

The Feature Era Begins: Stars, Picture Palaces, and a New Business Model

The mid-1910s was a period of revolutionary transformation in the film industry, one in which virtually every practice of production, distribution, exploitation, and exhibition underwent profound reconfiguration. The upheaval recast not just the moviegoing experience but the entire business model upon which leading firms in the industry operated.

The years immediately preceding the advent of the feature had been a period of hyper-demand in which the industry's principal goal was to impose order and deliver a fixed commodity at a fixed price, and in which a well-defined oligopoly sought to stifle competition by controlling patents and exerting legal barriers to entry. The next phase involved a redefinition of both the industry's central commodity—from single-reeler to feature film—and its dominant exhibition venue—from small nickelodeon to grand picture palace. The focus shifted from simply coping with demand to doing everything possible to expand the market and maximize profit potential. The stupendous rise of the feature film and picture palace entailed a new commercial calculus: bigger, better films enjoyed in bigger, better theaters would generate greater public demand for cinema, and, in conjunction with considerably higher ticket prices and hugely increased seating capacities, would ultimately yield much larger profits. The costs would be much greater, but so would the returns. Bold entrepreneurs like Paramount's

Adolph Zukor proved the familiar economic dictum that you have to spend money to make money. Thinking big not only maximized profit, but also impeded competition. The more or less ineffectual legal constraints on competition employed by the MPPC gave way to brute economic constraints, as industry leaders turned moviemaking into a big money proposition demanding prohibitively huge capital and logistical resources.

The earliest experiments in the exhibition of feature films took place in 1912, when a handful of historical-biographical epics based on successful plays such as *Queen Elizabeth, Cleopatra,* and *Richard III* were screened in rented legitimate theaters. The publicity and commercial success they enjoyed led to a seven-fold increase the following year, when 56 features were made by American companies, and again in 1914, when almost 350 features were produced. Still, those numbers were insignificant next to the roughly 5,000 shorts that were released each year (Singer, "Feature"). Rank-and-file exhibitors were entirely satisfied with the daily-change variety format to which they were accustomed. Given the industry's well-established film-rental infrastructure and comparatively low rental prices, few saw any reason to rock the boat. Not only were feature films much more expensive to rent (around $600 or $700 per week for a large urban theater, compared with $100–$150 for a week of daily changed variety programs), they were also a hassle; since supply was erratic, there was no coherent distribution network, and contracts and prices had to be negotiated on a film-by-film basis with a scattering of different distributors. Moreover, mainstream movie theaters served an informal, come-and-go-as-you-please audience. Exhibitors understandably would have had concerns that long narratives demanding that the entire audience be in place from the start would curtail casual walk-ins. They also saw variety programs as inherently flop-proof, since, unlike features, a short film that failed to please would not spoil an entire showing. Consequently, feature films had virtually no impact on mainstream exhibition for several years after their introduction (contrary to accounts by many historians). Features belonged to an essentially different exhibition circuit comprised of playhouses, concert halls, and general-purpose auditoriums. In most cases, features were screened only irregularly, often just on Sundays, or during the summertime that was off-season in legitimate theaters.

This began to change at the end of 1914, however, when Paramount— by far the most active feature-film concern—introduced the first full-service standing-order rental program. Exhibitors contracted for a year's worth of films, two five-reelers a week. Booking features was now just as convenient as booking shorts. But the high cost was still a major problem for most theaters. Paramount established a zone-clearance system so that smaller theaters in smaller markets could pay considerably less than large urban first-run venues. Even so, Paramount's package was still well beyond the reach of a great many modest theaters. Features were predicated on a new calculus, designed for theaters that could sell tickets in high volume and at high prices. Big, well-appointed theaters profited very handsomely. Run-of-the-mill theaters—rural theaters, neighborhood theaters, vestigial downtown nickelodeons, dog-eared converted playhouses—were in a bind, not fancy enough to justify significant price hikes and, even with swanky remodeling, still less alluring than picture palaces offering newer films, grander amenities, and better music. More to the point, they still were simply too small to sell enough tickets to turn a profit after paying out the cost of feature programming. A great many theaters of fewer than 600 seats went out of business in the mid-1910s.

Feature films and picture palaces were mutually enabling and dependent, bound together like the two strands of a double helix. One could not exist without the other: high-volume, high-price exhibition norms gave producers the revenue necessary for making expensive, attractive features with major stars; expensive, attractive features with major stars were necessary to fill large theaters and merit higher ticket prices. The highest-profile early picture palace was the 3,500-seat Strand Theater in Times Square, which opened in mid-1914. It marked the inauguration of a theater building boom across the country. More than just an urban phenomenon, it reshaped the contours of film exhibition far and wide. As Zukor commented in 1918, "It is no longer surprising to find a $200,000 theater in a town of 25,000 people" (483).

Features surged in number after 1914 and by any measure constituted the film industry's dominant product by around 1916. Interestingly, more short films were produced in 1915 than in any previous year, but thereafter they declined sharply for several years, finally settling into a production level consistent with their new role as accompaniments to the main feature (Singer, "Feature"). The profit margin on shorts was slim, and studios that were behind the curve on the industry's transformation were never able to recover: Kalem and Lubin ceased production in 1916; Edison and Biograph called it quits in 1917; Essanay and Selig closed down in 1918. Vitagraph and Universal were able to survive the transition by focusing on serials (which, while shorts, resembled features in their reliance on high-profile star-centered promotion) and by ramping up feature production.

Although stars were a commercial factor in the industry from early in the decade onward, their importance in the film industry grew exponentially as

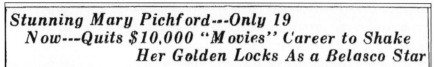

Stunning Mary Pichford---Only 19 Now---Quits $10,000 "Movies" Career to Shake Her Golden Locks As a Belasco Star

By Gertrude M. Price.

NEW YORK, Jan. 9. Mary Pickford of the "movies" has become a Belasco star!

A few months ago she was a $10,000 "movie" actress, the best paid girl in her profession.

The jump to the speaking stage was made over night. And now the little girl whose golden hair is a real "crown of glory" can smile down from her magnificent five feet and no inches upon hundreds of fame-fanned actresses.

Mary Pickford was the "Biograph" girl with probably the largest following among feminine moving picture players.

She is almost—not quite—19-years-old and is about as big as a good-sized minute. Even high heels and a suggestion of the pompadour in her wonderful curls won't make and perceptible difference to the "5" on the door where the family measurings are registered.

With his wonderful sixth sense for types, David Belasco "discovered" Mary Pickford and set her, with all her charming trimmings, into the center of the scenes of "The Good Little Devil," a fairy tale play after his own heart. Mary's role is the blind sweetheart, who finds happiness and sight through the good fairies.

"It's not the name part, my dear," said Belasco, as he patted her curls one day after a long, tiresome rehearsal, "but it's the beautiful, appealing part which you are to play in this production."

Trying to get five minutes chat with Mary Pickford is almost as difficult as trying to see the president. Not that she is "uppish" and "haughty," but simply because she is too busy to do anything but work. I managed to take Miss Pickford away from a party of girls she has promised to lunch with. I kept her for nearly twenty minutes.

"It's 1:40 now," said the stage manager. "Be at the 'Republic' at 2 o'clock for afternoon rehearsal." Mercy, how we rushed!

It took her fully five minutes to

Mary Pickford, from a photograph posed especially for this newspaper.

hat, get into her white coat and tuck her hands into an ermine muff.

By that time I had found out that Mary Pickford became the "daddy" of the family at the age of 5, when her own father died.

Her sister, Lottie Pickford, used to be in the "movies," but married and retired. She has a brother whom she put into the business, too.

The originator of "Goldy Locks" went into the moving pictures to make money, and she left them to make more money.

I ordered something I thought she might be persuaded to eat because

then spoiled the whole thing by pelting her with questions, after it was served.

"I'm so awfully, awfully tired and I'll tell you why," she said. "I worked two weeks longer in the pictures than I ought to have done after I had signed up with Mr Belasco."

"What for?" I asked.

"Well, the first week I worked because I wanted to give a party. I'll be 19 in April, but I've never had a real party.

"And the next week I worked be-

Only 19 — Salary $10,000 a Year

Mary Pickford's salary is already newsworthy in early 1913, detailed here in the *Des Moines News*. It would grow 200 times greater in the next five years.

the decade progressed. The amazing trajectory of Mary Pickford, the decade's leading star, drives this point home. When she joined the Biograph Studio in 1909 at the age of seventeen, Pickford's starting salary was $40 a week, a sizeable income for a young woman, equivalent to four or five times the earnings of an average public school teacher. Over the next eighteen months, her salary rose to $100 a week. In 1911, Carl Laemmle wooed her away to IMP with an offer of $175 a week. After another spell at Biograph, where she earned roughly $200 a week, and then some acting on Broadway, she signed with Adolph Zukor's Famous Players Company in 1914, starting at roughly $400 a week (a year-long contract of $20,000). Her box office appeal soon prompted Zukor to boost her salary to $1,000 a week. Within just a few months, Pickford's popularity (and her hardnosed business acumen) yielded another successful salary renegotiation: a January 1915 contract gave her $2,000 a week and half the profits of her productions (ten films a year). That deal would soon be dwarfed by another one signed in mid-1916: Pickford would earn a guaranteed *minimum* of nearly $16,200 a week (or, if more lucrative, about a third of a million dollars plus half the profits of her contracted six films per year). Additionally, she would be given her own studio, her own production and releasing company (Paramount Artcraft), total choice of cast and crew, top production budgets, and a host of other perks. Astonishingly, Pickford's star value would soon command even more. Two years later, Pickford signed with Zukor's key rival, First National, which offered her a package assuring earnings of at least $1 million a year—perhaps $2 million or more factoring in her 50 percent share of box office profit—for only three films a year. That translates into between $20,000 to $40,000 a week (or between $15 to $30 million a year in today's dollars) (Wing; U.S. Bureau of the Census, "Index" 91; Hampton 148–49; Balio 160–63).

Pickford's career is far from typical, needless to say. Nevertheless, the very fact that such a salary trajectory was even possible in the 1910s demands attention. It is important to stress that the story of Pickford's skyrocketing income is not just an early version of the kind of narrative we are familiar with today about, say, a waitress earning minimum wage in Los Angeles getting discovered and catapulting onto the Hollywood A-list. The Pickford phenomenon was utterly unheard of, with no precedent. Indeed, if it merited a newspaper article in 1913 when Pickford was making a jaw-dropping $200 a week, one can only imagine how mind-boggling it must have been just five years later when she was making 200 times that much.

What accounts for the increased centrality of stars to the commercial and competitive strategies of the film industry in the second half of the 1910s? To begin with, producers simply became ever more convinced that stars were the crucial magnet attracting ticket buyers. The industry took its cue from the empirical observation that fans fell in love with stars. The spectator's sense of personal affinity and connection to a star was, more often than not, what motivated moviegoers' film selections. Other factors, such as the production company or the story, while sometimes important, were secondary considerations. As Zukor noted, "A star is more important than the play [the narrative], for the people know the star and do not commonly know the play" (481).

Stars were particularly crucial, as already intimated, in the context of the industry's new higher-volume, higher-price business model based on bigger, better films shown in bigger, better venues. Stars were recognized as the most important signal of a film's presumed "bigness" and quality, and hence tied directly to the high-volume consumption. Leading producers were particularly keen to make films capable of capturing income from major first-class, first-run theaters. Since such theaters had the highest ticket prices, greatest box office volume, and an ability to assume the highest possible rental charge, the first run was by far the most lucrative (relative to number of screenings), accounting for one-quarter of a film's gross income. Access to first-class, first-run screens was limited, so failure to attain exhibition in a prime theater meant foregoing that income, losing out on ripple-effect income (first-run successes created publicity and boosted subsequent-run profits), and surrendering those benefits to a competitor (Seabury 50). Under such circumstances, the importance of star power was compounded. Paramount, in particular, aimed to monopolize first-runs by securing the services of the top-tier stars whose films invariably would be chosen by the owners of first-class first-run theaters.

Stars were also central to the drive for market expansion undertaken by Paramount and other industry leaders because growth required expansion into broader demographic sectors—winning over well-to-do audiences—and into all regional and international markets. The industry believed that stars were the key wedges into both. As Zukor noted with respect to the latter, "From [exhibitor feedback] reports, we have learned that a good play will go anywhere; that a star who is popular in Maine will be equally so not only in Arizona but also in England, China, and the Argentine. The whole world loves Mary Pickford" (481). Moreover, star magnetism became especially pertinent with the rise of the feature film, since longer narratives demanded greater characterological depth and psychological involvement on the part of spectators if these stories were to hold interest for five or six reels. The importance of star value grew in proportion to the reliance on longer, more sophisticated, narratives.

More concrete business practicalities were also a factor in the ascendancy of stars. Paramount and other distributors had established the practice of block booking, whereby an exhibitor was obliged to rent an entire year's worth of films altogether, sight unseen. This regularized producers' revenue by protecting them from the risk of losses that would be incurred when they made a film that, for whatever reason, fell far below the anticipated number of rentals. Producers tried to convince exhibitors that block booking was a win-win proposition, since overall rental costs could be reduced. As Hiram Abrams explained, "The exhibitor agreed to take the program of the producer over the contract period. The producer was thus insured against losses, while the exhibitor could have his films at a much lower price than if he had been compelled to pay for [a] producer's losses—for a good picture sold alone would otherwise have had to stand the money wasted on the bad ones" (Abrams 203). Whether or not this was true, exhibitors disliked block booking because it obliged them to buy blind and prevented them from tailoring film selections to suit audience preferences in their particular theaters. Throwing star vehicles into the mix made it much easier for producers to sell program blocks. Keen to secure probable hits, exhibitors were more willing to take a gamble on the unknown balance. In the late 1910s, Paramount switched to a modified version of block booking that they called the "star selective system." It involved contracting for star-centered blocks, composed of eight pictures a year all featuring the same star. The producer was again protected against unforeseeable losses, but probably the main virtue from the producer's perspective was that it was an efficient way of passing on the ever-increasing expense of star salaries. Abrams claimed that it was devised in part as a response to exhibitor preferences for smaller blocks, permitting at least some flexibility in program selection.

One final benefit producers accrued from stars should be mentioned. As the film industry became more and more rationalized, studios became increasingly concerned with commercial predictability. Success depended upon the accuracy of two calibrations. First, a film's production budget had to be aligned with its subsequent earnings. As Zukor put it, "Knowing the possible and probable revenue, then we can decide how much money can safely be spent upon production." Second, producers had to set a film's rental charge so that, relative to its subsequent box office performance, it was neither too high (creating angry exhibitors) nor too low (throwing away profit). Studios came to rely upon stars as the most reliable predictors of a film's possible and probable gross, based upon records of past performance. Expensive as they were, stars provided fiscal rationality. They were not actually expensive if they enabled outlay and income to be properly attuned. Losing money through inaccurate calibration was much more damaging to the bottom line. Given their utility along these lines, one can better understand why producers were willing to acquiesce to astronomical pay demands by the most consistent performers.

Some Reflections on Reflectionism

Scholars often take it for granted that films reflect the times in which they were made. Such reflection, however, can take any number of forms. A film might portray contemporaneous news events directly, effecting a kind of reportage about issues of public concern. Many films dealing with World War I would be examples in this decade. Or a film might engage with social issues and debates of the day, participating overtly in discourses already animating other channels of social commentary. Films advocating Progressive reforms (or, alternately, those highlighting the damage done by sanctimonious meddlers) might fall within this category. Typically, such social problem films forward some clearly communicated didactic position. Alternately, a film might tap into topical issues less for the sake of earnest message-mongering than for sensationalism and curiosity value. Many films, like those in the white slavery cycle of this decade, harbor some degree of ambiguity in this regard, accommodating opposing assessments of their motivations. Or, as it is commonly argued—probably correctly— films can (or cannot help but) reflect their cultural moment and influence spectators' conceptions of the world, in a more implicit, non-intentionalist way by displaying contemporary customs, norms, manners, lifestyles, trends, fashions, behaviors, tacit assumptions, material environments, consumer ideals, and so on. It is unlikely that a director shooting a thrilling race-to-the-rescue chase between a locomotive and a roadster, incorporating telegraphs, cut phone lines, and so on, proceeded with any consciously formulated objective of reflecting "modernity" or the spatio-temporal transformations brought about by new technologies. These elements of iconography are the raw materials for constructing stories and only inadvertently chronicle the cultural milieu. Finally, films often reflect their times in deliberate but indirect ways that normally fall even further below the threshold of spectator awareness. A case in point would be a kind of negative reflectionism underlying what kinds of films are *not* produced at a given historical juncture. One might assume that World War I primarily shaped American cinema through forces of propaganda (motivating depictions of Hun atrocities) or through moderately topical reportage (motivating representations of the experiences of doughboys or of the folks back home). But the war probably shaped American cinema more substantially through producers' sensitivity to escapist counter-impulses and situational biases. As Adolph Zukor observed in 1918,

> There are some styles that none of the people want right now. They do not want "costume" plays, fairy stories, or anything that is morbid or depressing.

La Tosca was exquisitely presented, but it did not take because it was in costume. In these war times, there is enough of the depressing in the air and people go to the movies to be amused. Therefore we have to cut out all costume play, "wig stuff," and "sob stuff." At the beginning of the war, war plays were fairly attended, but today the people find enough war in the newspapers. They do not care for war drama except in small doses and then only if the scenes are real and there is not too much featuring of some actor who they may think ought to be at the front and not merely playing at being a soldier. (481)

The chapters that follow aim to elaborate on various facets of cinema's relation to American social history. Throughout, it should be borne in mind that the two interacted in many different and complicated ways. This volume highlights some of the most illuminating examples of their crucial interrelationship.

1910

Movies, Reform, and New Women

SCOTT SIMMON

At the start of the decade, it was still possible to call "moving pictures" a "passing" fad that "have had their day" and to classify them alongside the roller skating craze, as did the feminist reformer Rheta Childe Dorr (228). But others saw the movies growing into the new century's defining mode of entertainment, and perhaps destined for something more. Typical, in both its awe over the phenomenon and its worry over unruly audiences and under-regulated films, was a magazine piece titled "A Theatre with a 5,000,000 Audience":

> Squads of police are necessary in many places to keep in line the expectant throngs awaiting their turn to enter the inner glories. . . . Five million people are thought to be in daily attendance at the picture shows. If it is a matter of public concern what sort of plays are run on the stage and what sort of articles are published in the newspapers and magazines, it is surely important that the subject-matter of the most popular medium of reaching the people be at least not degrading.

This chapter looks into a few of the more revealing movies of the year—a year without any agreed-upon canonical masterworks—and into some of the fears and dreams that movies inspired, but it helps first to remember what it was like to live then. Because it was a federal census year, it is possible to characterize life in the United States with a little more precision than usual. The population was less than a third of what it is today, some 92 million. The frontier lingered: the Pacific and Mountain West remained male-dominated (with 130 men per 100 women), while New England had more women than men. European immigration had declined from its peak of three years earlier in the face of nativist resentments and labor union pressures, although close to two million entered during the year, most settling in larger cities. Immigrants and children of immigrants made up roughly three-quarters of the population of most large eastern cities, including New York, Boston, Chicago, and

Detroit. For all the focus in the muckraking press on the problems of crowded cities, however, America was still predominantly a rural and small-town country: more than half the nation lived in communities of less than 2,500. Agriculture remained the largest occupation, accounting for some 12 million of the nation's 37 million workers, but if one includes manufacturing, construction, and mining in "industry," that adds up to another 11 million in occupations that were often dangerous: about 25,000 were killed in industrial accidents during the year (U.S. Bureau of the Census, "Thirteenth" 21, 54–55, 93–94, 98; Cashman, *Ascendant* 90, 67; Schlereth 55).

Rapid communication and transportation were still available only to a few. Eighty-five percent of homes lacked electricity; there was one telephone for every ninety people; less than 5 percent of eighteen- to twenty-one-year-olds went on to college (Schlereth 115; Cooper 136–37). The number of automobiles had grown to almost half a million (from fewer than ten thousand at the turn of the century), but that meant just one for every two hundred people (Cooper 133). Long-distance travel meant taking the railroads; travel within cities generally meant taking streetcars or trolleys. Rural travel meant walking or riding a horse, mule, or horse-drawn wagon. Even New York City had a horse population sufficient—as one of the era's intrepid statisticians calculated—to deposit three million pounds of manure and sixty thousand gallons of urine on its streets every day (Schlereth 20, 24).

With the year's first tests of electric "self-starters" in place of hand cranks on cars, driving was opening more widely to women (Cooper 134). Seven million of the nation's wage earners were women, who still had voting rights in only four sparsely populated western states. The November election added one more western state, Washington. More significant, however, was the increased shift toward a national suffrage campaign, including more activist tactics by the women's movement, such as the first large U.S. suffrage marches and a petition to Congress signed by 400,000 asking for an equal voting-rights amendment to the constitution (Flexner and Fitzpatrick 242–48).

Economically, it was a prosperous time, following the recession of 1907–08. American Federation of Labor unions had tripled in size since the turn of century, to 1.5 million members (Cooper 145). "Reform"—of cities, business practices, and the excesses of wealth—was in the air, even if few agreed on what it meant. President William Howard Taft, who had taken office the year previous, was more of an activist trustbuster than his predecessor, Theodore Roosevelt, but lacked the former president's charisma, notwithstanding his 350 pounds. ("When I hear someone say 'Mr. President,' Taft told an aide, "I look around expecting to see Roosevelt" [Cashman, *Age* 98].) The national midterm election ushered in a decade of Democratic control, with Taft's Republican Party ceding the House of Representatives for the first time in sixteen years and losing ten seats in the ninety-two-man Senate. Among Democrats swept into office were future presidents Woodrow Wilson (as New Jersey governor) and Franklin D. Roosevelt (as a New York state senator).

Audiences, Stars, and the Birth of Hollywood

Going to the movies at the start of the decade most often meant going to nickelodeons, an accurate enough name in terms of ticket prices, although ten cents was becoming common in larger cities. The year saw many reports about the demise of live popular theater, and with surprisingly little lament. A *New York Times* article, "Moving Pictures Sound Melodrama's Knell," asked, "Why pay 30 cents to see a rehash of an ancient theme by an obsolete troupe of archaic players when for 10 cents the village critic can see . . . a play by Shakespeare with all the appearances and vanishings of Banquo's ghost or Puck effectively wrought by the film art?" Both entertainment options sound inexpensive, but one must take into account that average percapita income was $517.

Reformers were not amused. Dour accounts of the typical moviegoing experience regularly appeared in muckraking periodicals like *McClure's Magazine*, which reported that "the moving-picture show has become a problem in all large cities," especially because "the managers paid no attention to ventilation" (Hendrick 383). *Health* magazine fretted over "eye strain," "unsanitary conditions," "foul air," as well as "another aspect . . . which we hesitate to discuss. . . . The performances being of necessity given in a darkened house, opportunity for undue familiarity between the sexes is afforded" ("Moving Pictures"). Few others hesitated to dwell on the opportunities dark theaters afforded for fraternizing between the sexes.

The key technical fact about American movies in the immediate pre-feature era—central to both moviegoing this year and to the sense one can feel today of these films' desperate narrative compression—is that virtually all films were standardized at "one reel" in length (that is, from about 700 feet to a maximum of 1,050 feet of 35 mm film). This meant that the longest films, seen at the slowest of the variable projection speeds, would run about seventeen minutes. Most films were shorter, and from these building blocks theater managers constructed their shows, sometimes by mixing in vaudeville acts but usually by interspersing films with songs—typically this year three reels of film divided by two songs (Altman 182–93; Abel 127–33; Bowser 191).

Films were virtually everywhere, not only in schools, YMCAs, and department stores. On Sundays in Manhattan's 1,600-seat Grace Methodist Episcopal Church, life-of-Jesus "Passion Play" films were "thrown on the screen just back of the pulpit." On other days the church showed more secular movies on the theory "that if the people fill the building throughout the week they will be more likely to fill it on Sundays" ("Pictures in Church"). Contrary to the nervous troubles predicted for viewers by *Health*, the Nebraska state asylum for the insane installed a projector because "these pictures appear to soothe patients and . . . they can watch them without the exciting effects of other forms of diversion" ("Pictures to Soothe Insane"). A screen was installed for bored commuters in Pittsburgh's central railroad station, with films changed daily, if subjected to one bit of censorship: "'There will be no pictures of train robberies,' said Albert Swinehart, who is in charge of the Pennsylvania Railroad detectives, 'nor of train wrecks. It would leave a bad impression on the minds of the travelers'" ("Films for Commuters").

At nickelodeons, moviegoers came to know on which days of the week new films from their favorite companies were shown; the most popular were from Vitagraph and Biograph. Sadly for today's viewers, a huge fire in July at Vitagraph's Manhattan studio ignited the company's entire twelve-year library—one factor in the poor survival rate now of Vitagraph films ("150 Trapped"). This was also the year when the monopolistic Motion Picture Patents Company—known to most simply as "the Trust"—was at its most powerful, but behind the scenes came the first hints that the industry was already growing out of its control.

An early indication of the emerging star system came when Carl Laemmle's aggressive Independent Moving Picture Company (known by its IMP or "Imp" acronym) tempted away the most recognizable actresses—Florence Lawrence and then eighteen-year-old Mary Pickford—from the Biograph Company, which was holding out against mention of its actors' names. Lawrence, the "Biograph Girl," had jumped to IMP near the end of the previous year, and it was in March that the company sprang the era's best-remembered publicity stunt, planting news stories of her death and then piously refuting them in "We Nail a Lie" advertisements (Bowser 112; Abel 232–33). The term "star" seems to have first been applied to film actors early this year, and a February *Los Angeles Times* article described how fans recognized favorite players even when films and promotional posters lacked credits: "Regular patrons of the many moving picture theaters of the city—and most of the patrons are regulars—have learned to know the different characters of the pictures, and no matter what character is assumed by the actors, their mannerisms are easily detected. . . . To see those whom they have learned to know, large numbers of them flock to the motion picture theaters." The headline added that "Real Stars May Be Seen in Los Angeles, Too." That is, movie patrons—"these same young persons"—could "stroll through the lobbies of half a dozen Los Angeles hotels" and "encounter the majority of the characters they have admired upon the screen" ("New Hero"). As another February *Los Angeles Times* article noted about location shooting, "The participants have been handicapped by the number of spectators. That is one of the things most dreaded by the picture actors" ("In the Motion"). Movie fan culture had evidently arrived.

The L.A. dateline of such news items seems unremarkable now, but that winter of 1909–10 was the first time major filmmaking companies put down roots on the West Coast. With the Trust companies and Independents together supplying about fifty films a week, studios couldn't dream of slowing for the winter. The *Los Angeles Times* already trumpeted that the "Climate and Scenic Settings Here are Ideal" for motion pictures in February, when it counted "upward of 200" production personnel in the city. With the many new warm-weather studio locations—including IMP in Cuba, Méliès in San Antonio, Vitagraph in San Diego, and Essanay in northern California—few would yet have guessed that "Hollywood" alone would win out and become synonymous with American studio filmmaking, but the *Times* exhibited a prescient boosterism in talking about the touring companies: "At first they came here to escape the snow and ice, but the bright quality of the sunshine and the number of clear days in which they may work, together with the variety of scenery, has all been found ideal, and their making here is now permanent" ("In the Motion").

Those first fan-culture articles also give hints about who was going to the movies this year. To judge from commentaries and a precious few surveys, what was new about the audiences, especially in comparison with those who attended live melodrama and vaudeville, was the increased proportion of children and young women, and notably from the working classes. It's anecdotally evident too that most polite society did not deign to go to nickelodeons—although they would willingly see movies in lecture halls and the other socially acceptable venues. Even the industry paper *Moving Picture World* admitted in April, "It cannot be pretended that as yet the moving picture in any of its phases has attracted the sympathetic notice and patronage of the educated classes" ("Educated"). The relatively short duration of nickelodeon programs—typically about an hour this year—also meant that workers were able to squeeze in time for movies, even when only 8 percent of them had a regular schedule of forty-eight hours a week or less (Cashman, *Ascendant* 96). A survey by the reformist Russell Sage Foundation about the mill town of Homestead, Pennsylvania, discovered that "many people . . . find in the nickelodeon their only relaxation. . . . On a Saturday afternoon visit to a nickelodeon, which advertised that it admitted two children on one ticket, I was surprised to find a large proportion of men in the audience" (Byington 111).

Though this report's author was taken aback by the number of men in the audience, worried reformers focused much more on children and female viewers. A survey of a Connecticut town at the end of the year found 90 percent of children ten to fourteen going to the movies, more than half attending once a week or more, and over a third going without a parent or guardian (Jump). Percentages in a survey by New York City's reformist People's Institute were higher, with "fully three-quarters of the children" attending at least once a week (Inglis).

Concerns about children centered on their exposure to films about crime, and a seemingly endless series of news stories bemoaned how previously angelic kids spiraled downward toward their destruction because of the movies. "Turned to Arson by Moving Pictures" told of a twelve-year-old girl who twice set fire to her Bronx apartment house after her father failed to pay the $50 demanded by an extortion note she left for him signed by "the Black Hand" (the popular name for the Italian mafia, especially in movies). She told the judge she had devised the scheme by combining plots from two films. Her hapless father, who had taken her to those movies himself, received a stern lecture from the judge: "Fathers should be very careful about such things and see to it that pictures that exert evil influence are not seen by their children." Pittsburgh officials blamed a rash of streetcar crimes on popular western movies that depicted daring stagecoach robberies. The *New York Times* concluded in August that the growth in such crimes could only be explained by the hypnotic power of film on the susceptible young ("Moving Picture Hypnosis").

Recurring worries about the morals of teenaged girls and young women permeated such accounts, prompting claims that their repeated attendance at movies would lead to the compromising of those morals. Because they could be paid less, women had for some time been replacing male workers in increasingly mechanized factories, and for more than a decade women had dominated the sales force in department stores (Schlereth 57, 151). The special problem for reformers was that long working hours meant that young women were now going to the movies unchaperoned in the late evenings, too. A survey taken this year of Chicago shopgirl life found a typical working day of nine or ten hours for salaries ranging from $2.50 to $11 a week (with much of that given to parents), leaving the inexpensive movies one of the few entertainment options and the evenings almost the only time to go. The president of Chicago's Juvenile Protective Association in reporting on this survey warned that in nickelodeons "the darkness afforded a cover for familiarity and sometimes even for immorality" (de Koven Bowen 56, 14).

One of the year's best-selling novels, Reginald Wright Kauffman's *The House of Bondage*, fleshed out this narrative. Its heroine, Mary, a high school senior in a small Pennsylvania town, allows herself to be taken to a nickelodeon by a handsome Hungarian immigrant. The chase comedy they watch seems unobjectionable, but it is shot in New York City and the chase goes past the Waldorf and Park Avenue hotels, plunging Mary into a "fairyland" of riches. Twenty pages later, she's in Lower Manhattan, her drink drugged, and the next morning she wakes up naked in a strange brass bed, her face in the mirror "alien, a ruin, an accusation." Her life as a prostitute spirals downward for the next four hundred pages (Kauffman 27, 53). Lest anyone think the novel exaggerated, later editions reprinted as an appendix the June findings of a New York grand jury—known as the Rockefeller Report—on the "white slave traffic." "Mention should be made," the report said, "of the moving picture shows as furnishing to this class of persons [the 'so-called pimp'] an opportunity for leading girls into a life of shame. . . . In spite of the activities of the authorities in watching these places, many girls owe their ruin to frequenting them" (Kauffman 475–76). The same month, Judge Frederick B. House made a sweeping indictment: "Ninety-five percent of the moving picture houses in New York are dens of iniquity. More young women and girls are led astray in these places than in any other way" ("Unwarranted").

While commentators feared the influence of moviegoing on young women, a few pointed out how women might be influencing motion pictures. As Bertha Richardson suggested in her revision of *The Woman Who Spends: A Study of Her Economic Function*, women were a growing force in "the economics of consumption, otherwise known as the spending of their money" (21). The nickels from new audiences added up, and the year saw active, heroic female leads take the screen.

New Heroines

By this time, film audiences had already grown accustomed to genres—relatively formulized plot patterns. As Eileen Bowser points out, in this era when nickelodeon programs always were built from several short films, exhibitors expected to receive new films in three large genre categories—comedies, dramas, and westerns. A "balanced program" of genres was the ideal (Bowser 167–68). Below we look into a few genre films as well as a couple of less easily classifiable titles, and take as our guides the year's many female heroines: in the social drama *A Child of the Ghetto*, the westerns *Ramona* and *The Red Girl and the Child*, the Civil War film *The House with Closed Shutters*, the Shakespeare adaptation *Twelfth Night*, and the advertising film *The Stenographer's Friend*.

One fact needs noting about the films of this year: more than in any other except 1909, film survival distorts film history. It is not possible to say with any precision how many films in total were made in the United States this year—there are no surviving production records for most companies and most nonfiction film types—but it would be a reasonable guess that at least 3,000 films were released. (This impressive number is less surprising when one remembers that most theaters changed programs daily and that the Trust and Independent distribution "exchanges" competed, each with a full slate of releases.) Another fair guess would be that at least 90 percent of these titles are now "lost"—that is, all copies were thrown away, allowed to deteriorate, or burned in such fires as the one at Vitagraph. This has been the common fate of the first thirty-five years of filmmaking worldwide, but the particular distortions this year come from an unusual imbalance. Films directed by D. W. Griffith for the Biograph Company represent more than one-quarter of the surviving U.S. fiction films of 1910, well over half the year's U.S. films of all types currently viewable in archives, and more than three-quarters of the year's U.S. titles currently viewable outside of archives. A full history would want to correct this imbalance, but one-reel films from the pre-feature era remain difficult enough to see under any circumstances, and so I have chosen titles to discuss below mainly from among those available on video. It is compensation that, this year at least, Griffith's films *are* unrivaled in stylistic sophistication, if not in their range of subjects.

Some of the year's most fascinating films are in a genre that doesn't have a precise name: docudramas of social reform, melodramatic reflections of the concerns of the Progressive Era, such as Griffith's *Simple Charity*, which contrasts "the red tape" of reform societies with an impoverished

Dorothy West (in shawl, foreground) on Rivington Street, Manhattan, in *A Child of the Ghetto.*

woman's selflessness. Griffith's *A Child of the Ghetto* manages to be both a documentary-inflected look at social problems and a timeless fable. It opens in a dingy tenement room in Manhattan's Jewish ghetto, as a girl in her late teens (Dorothy West) watches her mother die. "SHE MUST FIGHT LIFE'S BATTLE ALONE," an intertitle tells us as the girl ventures among "THE STRUGGLERS" of Rivington Street.[1] The documentary exterior shot, like several in the film, is evidently taken with a hidden camera in a street crowded with pushcart peddlers and shoppers, and it takes a moment to spot the actress among them. In a ghetto garment shop, she picks up home-assembly work, but when she brings back the finished goods, the owner's son plants on her money stolen from his father's wallet—leading to the presumption of her guilt and pursuit by a policeman, Officer Quinn. She loses him on the Lower East Side and hops a trolley into the country, where she flees along a dirt road until collapsing outside the gate of a rural home. Rescued by a farmer and his mother, she "LEARNS TO SMILE" and to find love. Some time later, Officer Quinn heads out for "A DAY'S FISHING" and stops for water at that very farm. (Such coincidence is at the core of melodrama.) The film toys with suspense—through staging and cutting—first over whether

Quinn will see the young woman and, after he does, whether he will remember who she is. Quinn finally does puzzle out the mystery and runs back to make the arrest. But her pleas, or perhaps just the country atmosphere, make him hesitate, and when the farmer walks up, Quinn pretends to search for something lost in the grass to explain his return. He strolls back to the river with a smile.

The film, like so many this year, draws from America's long cultural clash between urban modernity and rural traditionalism. The speed with which films were made and released meant that it was easy for them to react to contemporary events. *A Child of the Ghetto* may have drawn one inspiration from the New York City garment workers strike known in labor history as the "Uprising of the Twenty Thousand," which was settled in February. Especially newsworthy—thanks to the backing from Manhattan socialites—was the strike's leadership by the teenaged Clara Lemlich, who used Yiddish to rally the strikers, young women earning about six dollars a week (Howe 295–300). Filmed two months after the conclusion of the strike and released to theaters in June, *A Child of the Ghetto* feels like a nostalgic recuperation of the sympathy shown by the public—and no doubt especially by nickelodeon audiences—to the plight of young garment workers. A slatternly landlady shoos the girl into the streets after her mother's death, a melodramatic enactment of the fact that housing for "fighting life's battle alone" was simply not affordable on one garment worker's salary. (About 90 percent of female factory workers and clerks lived with other family members [Peiss 52, 204].) "Child" is not the name one would apply now to the film's teenaged heroine, but it ties into questions of child labor being debated in this year's midterm elections (Cooper 159).

Unlike the film's documentary snapshot of the city, the rural world—with its lazy river, broad shade trees, and grazing cows—comes across as a timeless "pastoral" (a genre category in Biograph's advertisements this year for *In the Season of Buds* and *A Summer Idyl*). Three dancing girls, dressed in white, laughing, waving blossoming branches, are presumably younger sisters of the farmer but also symbols of the bucolic freedom thus far denied the immigrant city girl. The film's solution will be to integrate the Jewish girl into a country home (just as the Irish cop Quinn represents an earlier wave of assimilated immigrants) and to protest the masculine bustle of commerce via female images. (Biograph films this year are less sympathetic to men who complain of the urban system, as in *The Iconoclast*, where a printing plant worker's sarcastic gestural style illustrates—in the words of the company's publicity—how "selfishness is the seed of irrational socialism, nurtured mainly by laziness and, very often, drink.") Social reformers also drew on the traditions of women's place on the farm to protest city problems. Jane Addams asked, "Is that dreariness in city life, that lack of domesticity which the humblest farm dwelling presents, due to a withdrawal of one of the naturally cooperating forces? If women have in any sense been responsible for the gentler side of life which softens and blurs some of its harsher conditions, may they not have a duty to perform in our American cities?" (Addams). *A Child of the Ghetto* critiques urban problems via longstanding romantic ideals, both of pastoralism and the woman-centered home.

The film has the year's typical style. Compared to 1909, editing tempos are slightly faster, cameras move slightly closer to the actors, who are more restrained, and intertitles are slightly more frequent (Keil, *Early* 62, 145). George O. Nichols as "Officer Quinn" manages to convey a complex series of emotions primarily through facial expression—when he puzzles out just where he might have previously seen the girl. Previously the camera was seldom close enough to the actors to allow for such subtlety. To our eyes, the typical framing of actors this year—with two-thirds of their bodies usually in view—still seems distant, but the camera was now close enough for audiences to read actors' lips, as is indirectly evident from a December front-page story in the *New York Times* headlined "Object to Film Profanity": "Deaf mutes are complaining against the use of profane and indecent expressions by players in moving picture films . . . these shows are the chief source of amusement for the deaf, and they are prevented from enjoying them because they are able to understand what is being said by the characters on the screen."

The West and the War

Of the three large categories of films that made up a "balanced" program—comedies, dramas, and westerns—the prominence of the last seems most surprising today. From a survey of trade-paper reviews, Robert Anderson calculated that one out of every five films released this year was a western (Anderson 25). But the genre was then wider and more fluid than in Hollywood's "classic" era. Westerns encompassed not merely tales of early frontiers but contemporary stories as well. After all, the last Indian Wars conflict (at Wounded Knee, South Dakota) was only twenty years past, horses were still everywhere, and the distinction between films of the "Old West" and those set in the present was often hazy. A partially surviving Selig cavalry western (whose title is lost) seems surely to be taking place in the nineteenth century—until one spots the 1910 calendar on the commandant's

Alessandro (Henry B. Walthall) and Ramona (Mary Pickford) at the Rancho Camulos, California, location for *Ramona*.

wall. Westerns were also not nearly so centered on male heroics as they would come to be, and the popularity of plucky cowgirls grew over the next two years. What were revelatory to audiences this year were westerns that began to exploit the actual landscape of the far West. Among films available today, most spectacular in its use of this landscape is Biograph's *Ramona: A Story of the White Man's Injustice to the Indian*, again directed by D. W. Griffith.

This is the first of the four American film adaptations of Helen Hunt Jackson's 1884 best seller, written to protest the near-genocidal wrongs against California's Native Americans. As an unusual credit title suggests, the film was also among the first authorized book adaptations, apparently costing the Biograph Company $100 for the rights and helping to make it "the most expensive picture put out by any manufacturer up to that time," at least according to Griffith's wife (Arvidson 169). Set mainly in the late 1840s, just after Mexico's defeat by the United States but before California statehood, Jackson's story—which the film follows closely in outline—centers on the star-crossed love of Alessandro, a mission Indian, and Ramona, from an aristocratic Mexican family. For the four-day shoot, from 30 March through 2 April, Biograph made a further location trip fifty miles north from Los Angeles. The company's ads promoted the "absolute authenticity" of filming in "the identical locations and buildings wherein Mrs. Jackson placed her characters." In the years since the novel's publication, a flourishing tourist industry had grown around these "real" locations— the settings Jackson had used—and most editions by this time came illustrated with photos of Rancho Camulos, which the film uses as its hacienda. Unusually for this year, even the film's one interior space—the room where Ramona is told by her stepmother "THAT SHE HERSELF HAS INDIAN BLOOD"— is shot on location. That revelation of Ramona's racial heritage is surprising without the novel's back story of her adoption, and many of the film's other intertitles (such as "THE MEETING IN THE CHAPEL" and "THE INTUITION") suggest illustrations of famous moments that audiences might have been expected to remember from the novel or its forty-some previous stage adaptations (including one in 1905 in which Griffith had played Alessandro). Ramona, age nineteen at the start of the novel, is played in the film by Mary Pickford, then a week shy of her eighteenth birthday and not yet the "Picture Personality" that *Moving Picture World* would profile in December, in another hint of the growing star system ("Miss Mary"). In less than a year, she had made sixty films.

Ramona is a tragedy, compressing several years into its quarter-hour running time, as Ramona and Alessandro (played by Henry B. Walthall) are pushed ever higher into the wilderness by white men who claim their land. The burial of their infant receives a spectacular mountain backdrop unlike anything in previous westerns, but the shots that prompted most praise occur earlier, when Alessandro watches his tribal village burn, filmed with extreme depth of field. "Attention should be called," wrote the *New York Dramatic Mirror*, "to a few remarkable scenes—one of them the destruction of Alessandro's village, which we see with the poor Indian from a mountain top looking down into a valley a mile or more away. The burning huts, the hurrying people and the wagons of the whites are clearly visible, though they appear but as mere specks in the distance" (Pratt 84).

As is not unusual among the year's films, the female lead is the emotional pillar, and Ramona survives after her husband is driven mad and murdered. The film's final shot, in which Ramona is comforted at Alessandro's gravesite by her stepbrother Felipe (Francis J. Grandon), only hints at the mitigation of the tragedy—and the political critique—in the conclusion of the novel, where Ramona and Felipe marry and abandon the United States to move to Mexico. In the transition from novel to film, most of Jackson's social protest was lost, and movie reviewers went out of their way to deny that any lingering protest might hit home. Louis Reeves Harrison, reporting on a packed screening in June, found *Ramona* "a veritable poem" and suggested that "the producers have advanced a step in the evolution of a new art," but stressed that "the idea of the white man's injustice to the Indian did not reach out into the sympathies of the audience at all."

Easily the most prominent subgenre of westerns this year, however, remained films about Indians, as it had been for the past two years. At least ten Indian westerns were released each month. For several reasons, especially the landscape of the East Coast where most Indian films were shot, they drew more from James Fenimore Cooper's novels of sociable natives than from the post–Civil War plains battles that became the model for a half-century from 1911 onward (Simmon, *Invention* 12–54). Several companies had a sideline in Indian westerns, including Selig, Lubin, and Biograph, and among the most fascinating are those directed for Pathé by James Young Deer, of Winnebago ancestry. Although not currently available outside of archives, Young Deer's *The Red Girl and the Child* is his most engaging surviving film. It stars his wife, Lillian St. Cyr—also a Winnebago, who acted under the name Redwing—as an Indian maiden who starts in a traditionally passive characterization. Her attempts to sell beadwork elicit only taunts from some loutish cowboys, who have ridden their horses into the saloon. By the end of the film, however, she displays heroic mastery, leading a horseback chase for the kidnappers of the son of the one cowboy—seen earlier as a solid family rancher—who had attempted to defend her. Disguised in men's clothes, she tempts the kidnappers to chase her and the child over a rope she has strung across a sheer-walled canyon, alongside a spectacular waterfall. Audiences are entirely on her side when, with savage pitilessness, she cuts the rope, sends the pursuers plummeting to their deaths, and rides back to reunite the family. James Young Deer, who came to scenario writing and directing from Wild West shows and small parts in films, was never a subtle director of actors, but his staging of the action sequences and use of landscape here show great flair. (Although it's less compelling, *White Fawn's Devotion*, Young Deer's only other identified surviving film from this year, can be more easily seen. It too is racially iconoclastic, ending with a white pioneer happily reunited with his Indian wife and their child.) Young Deer's first westerns were all shot in New Jersey, and *The Red Girl and the Child* in particular finds open plains that nicely impersonate the West. Later in the year he was appointed "Director and General Manager" of the Los Angeles unit of Pathé, for whom he directed about 120 films (of which about a half dozen survive).

Westerns this year were not particularly violent. Deaths often occur off-screen, and many Indian westerns are close in storyline to family melodrama. More than Hollywood sound-era westerns, these earlier ones faced censorship pressures, as is evident from those news stories about the movies' influence on children. The National Board of Censorship, the film industry's new self-censorship group based in New York, claimed to inspect "at least 90 per cent of the total output of motion pictures placed on the American market" (Storey). The board's goal, as with later production codes, was to preempt local censorship. In that it was only partially successful this year. A Cleveland reformist group, surveying 290 films shown in May, found that 13.4 percent showed robbery, 13.1 percent showed murder, 8.2 percent had "indecent suggestions," 5.8 percent represented "domestic infidelity," with 40 percent overall "unfit for children" ("Moving Picture Shows").

There was some question whether westerns remained truly popular. In a December article titled "The Indian and the Cowboy (By One Who Does Not Like Them)," *Moving Picture World* declared "the public . . . [is] tired of this plethora of Indian and Cowboy subjects." The same month, the *Los Angeles Times*, witnessing the arrival of so many film companies, came to the opposite conclusion in "Western Types Are in Vogue: Eastern Audiences Clamor for Cowboy Scenes." In hindsight, both sides were right. The western genre was changing rapidly thanks to the new locations, and what may have wearied the public were westerns filmed in "the peaceful wilds of New Jersey" (as *Moving Picture World* mocked), with their pastoral landscapes and relatively nonviolent stories.

An action genre growing in popularity was the Civil War film. Again, almost all of the year's surviving examples are Biograph films directed by D. W. Griffith, and in this case the genre brought out his ambitious best: *The Honor of His Family, The Fugitive, In the Border States*, and *The House with Closed Shutters* (and the two linked reels *His Trust* and *His Trust Fulfilled,* shot in November for release in 1911). All of them hold up remarkably well by mixing war stories with family psychodrama, and the battles are almost invariably fought within earshot of the soldiers' homes. One only needs to compare Griffith's Civil War films to Vitagraph's *Ransomed; or, A Prisoner of War* to see how relatively primitive in editing, camera style, and even story complexity may have been his competition. Among Griffith's entries in the genre this year, *The House with Closed Shutters* is the most remarkable. Released in August, it is an elaboration on *The Honor of His Family*, which had been released in January, in which a loving southern father must murder his cowardly son and return the body to the battlefield to uphold the family name. For all his Civil War films, Griffith infused unexpected elements from the woman's melodrama—with its conventions of suffering and private triumphs—as a metaphor for the South's experience.

The House with Closed Shutters begins with a young Southerner, Charles (Henry B. Walthall), cheered off to the war by townsfolk and his proud mother and sister Agnes (Dorothy West), who literally wraps herself in the flag. Trusted with a dispatch by Robert E. Lee, he proves himself only a "DRINK-MAD COWARD," in an intertitle's words. He flees from sight of the wounded back to the sanctuary of the family mansion, where even the (blackface) slave shakes his head in shame. After his mother and sister are unable to break through his drunken panic, Agnes dons her brother's uniform, cuts off her hair, and displays a hell-bent valor, delivering the dispatch through enemy lines and then dying heroically while retrieving the Confederate flag. The large-scale, smoke-filled battle—the most riveting that reviewers had ever seen—contrasts with the confined interiors of the home, as Charles sobers into some sense of his failure.

But this is only the first two-thirds of the film: the narrative has more than twenty-five years to compress into its final six minutes. The suffering mother (Grace Henderson) must now invent a gender-shift fiction to account for the shadowy figure hidden behind closed shutters, and so she deceives Agnes's two suitors into thinking that the brother's battlefield death has driven Agnes insane. A revelation scene, when the white-haired Charles finally flings open the shutters at the moment of his death, closes out the film.

The House with Closed Shutters transforms the southern belle into another impressive action heroine. In many films this year, women regularly have capacities beyond men to remedy misfortune, especially if they can cross-dress, as in *The Red Girl and the Child* and several other of Griffith's Biographs, including *Taming a Husband* and *Wilful Peggy*. There may be some historical justification for the heroism, if not the gender transformation, in *The House with Closed Shutters*, because antebellum upper-class southern girls were trained to ride and shoot alongside their brothers. As Richard Abel has traced, later films in the silent Civil War cycle made a point of reinforcing male heroism (Abel 143–60), but the films this year are more adventurous with gender. The elements in *The House with Closed Shutters*—the dark family secret, the mysterious gothic mansion, the emotional extremes, the force of honor, the burden of history—are traits of "the southern," if one thinks of it as a regional genre like the western. For Griffith the dark mansion in *The House with Closed Shutters* embodies the years of Reconstruction as something to which male failure in the war can't help but cling. As Tom Gunning has argued in a penetrating essay on the film, "*The House with Closed Shutters* is precisely the sort of Biograph ripe for rediscovery and deserves an acknowledged place in film history" (Cherchi Usai 4: 146).

▰▰▰▰▰▰ Uplift: Art, Education, and Nonfiction

The highest praise from film reviewers at this time came for literary adaptations. "A most encouraging tendency of the picture play business is that of 'picturizing' well-known plays and books," noted the *Los Angeles Times* ("Films Thrive"). Among the year's most entertaining adaptations are the first full-reel versions of Mary Shelley's *Frankenstein*, produced by the Edison Company, and of L. Frank Baum's *Wonderful Wizard of Oz*, from Selig Polyscope. Although both are stylistically simple and slowly cut, they include wonderfully imaginative moments: Frankenstein's monster forged in an industrial furnace; Dorothy, Toto, and the Scarecrow blown into Oz on a whirling haystack.

Vitagraph's *Twelfth Night*, which closely follows the contours of Shakespeare's play, was perhaps the most sophisticated adaptation this year. Certainly the company thought so, calling it "the best of all" its Shakespeare films and claiming that a "Shakespearean player of country-wide fame" was one of its producers (Uricchio and Pearson 58). Adaptations from Shakespeare were one way the film industry could promote itself as an ennobling enterprise—not just a low business tempting children to crime and women to ruin—but one must remember too that Shakespeare's plays were closer to popular entertainment than they have become (an evolution traced by historian Lawrence W. Levine [14–81]).

At the usual fifteen minutes for a full one-reeler, *Twelfth Night* emerges as compressed without seeming unduly rushed. Its intertitles clarify the complicated plot for those with no knowledge of the play, and squeeze as much as they can into relatively few words (e.g., "One Week Later. Viola, believed to be a boy, is admired by the Duke, becomes his page and is sent by him with a message to his sweetheart Olivia"). The film finds space for both the main romantic drama and the comic subplot in which the aristocratic Lady Olivia's maid and houseguests torment her pompous steward Malvolio (played by Charles Kent, who may also have been the film's director). Shakespeare's story made for yet another of the year's cross-dressing films. (And, in Vitagraph's amusing inversion of Renaissance convention, Olivia's twin brother is played by an actress, Edith Storey.) The young leading character, Viola, played by Florence Turner (another early star, known as the "Vitagraph Girl"), survives a shipwreck on a foreign coast, as does (to her later surprise) her twin brother, whose rescue is nicely staged in the surf near a real shipwreck, if clearly a long-weathered one. Viola's disguise as a male page who calls herself "Cesario" leads to the round-robin of mistaken romantic yearnings. For those in the audience familiar with the play, the film is packed with details that flesh out the drama without being essential for the plot (such as Malvolio's insistence that "Cesario" take his mistress's Olivia's ring as a token of her growing infatuation with the handsome page).

The film's acting style is complex even while adhering to theatrical traditions. The presentational acting communicates through a distinct series of codified gestures, as in the exterior shot when Viola first sees Olivia with her courtiers. Initially alone in the garden, Florence Turner runs through codified representations of despair (staggering over to a column, her hands up to heaven, then back of hand to brow), surprise (hands to cheeks), recognition of Olivia's beauty (fingertips to lips, hands over heart), and then a comic recognition of ironies to come (pointing to her male costume). Although the camera never moves throughout the film, until the end *Twelfth Night* deftly handles foreground-and-background spaces, as when Duke Orsino, in his introductory scene, rouses himself from romantic despair to step toward the camera to be struck by the beauty of his ostensibly male page. The limitations of Vitagraph's staging become evident, however, when most of act 5—the complicated sorting out of mistaken identities, the formations of new couples, and the exile of Malvolio—is represented in a single two-minute shot, with the eight major characters lined up across the frame, as three others look on. At the time, however, such theatricality was the hallmark of "quality" films such as those adapted from Shakespeare (Keil, *Early* 136–37).

There were other Shakespeare adaptations as well: Selig's *Merry Wives of Windsor* and the new Thanhouser Company's *Winter's Tale*. Adaptations were also imported from Europe: a French *Hamlet* and *Macbeth* and an Italian *Othello*, *King Lear*, and *Merchant of Venice*. It was hard to compete with the real Venetian canals in the last of these. Silent Shakespeare, of course, omits an essential thing, and the one-reel versions faced mockery even this year. One writer imagined a monologue by a "MOVING-PICTURE-SHOW MANAGER (to WILLIAM, *the Playwright*)": "Let's take up this here Lear thing. I think there's pretty good stuff in that, but there's got to be more action than you've laid out. Now how would it be to have the two bad daughters chase the old man with a broom down the main street. . . ? Perhaps we can run the film backward and have Lear chase himself. What do you think of that? . . . Take that Othello sketch and bury it, Shakes. You know what they did to the Johnson fight pictures. No colored stuff goes" (Tilden).

This last allusion is to the year's film that provoked by far the most controversy: the record of the fourth of July heavyweight championship prizefight in which African American Jack Johnson easily knocked out former champion Jim Jeffries, who had said he was fighting "for the sole purpose of proving that a white man is better than a Negro" (Grieveson, *Policing* 126). Reformers' cries to ban brutal fight films were an unconvincing cover for the desire to prohibit this particular film and its display of black power (Bernardi 170–200; Grieveson, *Policing* 121–50). Ex-president Theodore Roosevelt returned from his African safari—subject of another of the year's notable nonfiction films—to pontificate that, although boxing itself was "a vigorous, manly pastime . . . the moving-picture part of the proceedings has introduced a new method of money-getting and of demoralization." *The Johnson-Jeffries Fight* and the two-reel *Roosevelt in Africa* were among the special event films that broke from the one-reel limitation. Fictional dramas presented a trickier proposition, but Vitagraph had led the way in 1909 with longer episodic narratives that stood on their own as one-reel pieces. The company released the five reels of *The Life of Moses* over three months beginning in December 1909, and by the following April a few special screenings collected the reels to show together—thus arguably making for the first American feature film (Uricchio and Pearson 160–94).

Travel and sponsored films were seen widely in nontheatrical venues but had a place in nickelodeons, too. A survey by the *New York Dramatic Mirror* in the middle of the year classified 9 percent of theatrical releases "educational" (Bowser 168). In March, *Moving Picture World* began a column, "Education, Science and Art and the Moving Picture," with a discussion of *The Housewife and the Fly*, a British film about contagion carried by flies, which civic groups screened widely across America ("House Fly Actors"; "Fearful Fly"). The film's distributor was George Kleine, who in April published his 336-page *Catalogue of Educational Motion Pictures*, detailing 3,000 films available for rent to "universities, colleges, scientific and library institutions as well as to traveling lecturers" (Abel 172).

The Stenographer's Friend; or, What Was Accomplished by an Edison Business Phonograph is the only sponsored film of the year that is easily viewable; for an infomercial, it emerges as charming. In an example of early corporate synergy, it was produced by the Edison Manufacturing Company for the Edison Business Phonograph Company. At the center of its light comedy is a "working girl" (women now made up almost half of clerical workers [Schlereth 67]), and the film seeks to demonstrate how productivity and gendered office politics improve after the introduction of Edison's wax-cylinder dictating machine. (Right from its invention in the 1870s, Thomas Edison had assumed that the main use for the phonograph would be in offices.) The opening intertitle announces "Shorthand Troubles," which introduces the small business office in the film—all male save for the one female secretary—and its prominent wall clock. It is close to 6 P.M. and the

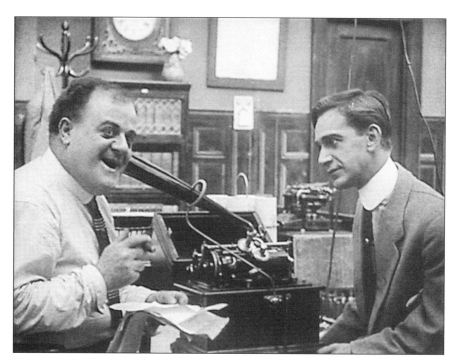

An office worker (John Cumpson) hears his dictation played back to him in *The Stenographer's Friend; or, What Was Accomplished by an Edison Business Phonograph.*

increasingly frenzied office manager, his desk a mass of disorganized papers, is shouting half-understood dictation to a young female stenographer. He is further distracted when another man seen through a door to a back office comes forward to also demand her attention. The two veteran comic actors (Marc McDermott interrupted by John Cumpson) play the scene with just enough exaggeration to make the scene believable and amusing, in proto-sitcom style, with a fixed camera set-up through the first third of the eight-minute short film. At the end of a subsequent day, our pretty stenographer has already put on her hat when her bosses' demands for more working hours cause her to break down into (comically exaggerated) tears. Luckily for everyone, at this point a dialogue intertitle announces, "Let Edison help you," which turn out to be words of an Edison salesman. He steps into the office to promote the wonders of the company's dictating machine, through a little industrial demonstration dropped into the center of the narrative. The film cuts to its first close-up to observe how the machine records speech, allows for corrections of mistakes, and plays back—much to the amazement of John Cumpson's character—and then we see how the wax cylinders can be shaved by an office boy for multiple reuse. Although this technical demonstration appears directed at men in the film audience, the office drama that surrounds it seems directed at young women in nickelodeons: the story reassures female office workers that the introduction of such a machine creates only harmony and makes the workload less unpredictable and more "pleasant." The film is thus responding to opposition that had already arisen to the dictating machine from stenographers who feared unemployment, and, in truth, the introduction of such machines allowed the replacement of skilled shorthand stenographers by lower-paid employees known as "typewriters," who needed only to know how to type from the recordings. In the film version, however, with the arrival of her "friend" the phonograph and its miraculous "doubled results" and time-saving improvements, "everybody" in the office is "happy" and all bow down in the final shot to Edison's jaunty, straw-hatted salesman.

▬▬▬▬ The Start of Something . . .

Many of the claims for the "educational" value of movies were self-serving, a cover for corporate pitches like *The Stenographer's Friend* and for wider film industry promotions. The impressively large number of films in Kleine's educational catalog reminds us, however, of the rapidly expanding uses for films. Edwin Slossin's classic and witty study of the state of higher education this year, *Great American Universities*, indirectly documents that movies were already part of teaching, especially in classes focusing on social reform:

> A professor of sociology . . . had discarded the antiquated lantern-slide system and introduced a moving picture apparatus, which showed slum life and settlement work with great vividness. At the close of the lecture he asked a favorite student loitering by his desk what he thought of the innovation. The student commended it with the moderation of manner and falling inflection characteristic of Seniors, but added: "Say, Professor, couldn't you run in some illustrated songs to relieve the monotony?"   (Slossin 498)

In contrast to the pervasive fear-mongering about nickelodeons, several defenses of the movies sensed that the medium was offering something exhilaratingly populist. An unsigned article in *The Independent* argued with sophistication that film, with its "alternating scenes" of editing and its shifting points of view, was opening up entirely new ways of understanding the world: "The cinematograph is doing for the drama what the printing press did for literature, bringing another form of art into the daily life of the people. . . . The moving picture shows are in general superior, both artistically and morally, to the vaudeville and melodrama that they have driven out of business. It is a mistake to suppose that their amazing popularity is due altogether to their low price of admission" ("Drama"). A commentator in *Life* magazine foresaw the dawning of our "wired" global village: "Moving pictures . . . have about them a news-imparting quality which may make them a permanent part of the apparatus of modern civilization. For ten cents a lick, more or less, we have seen King Edward's funeral [on 20 May] and Colonel Roosevelt's reception [in Africa]. . . . Most of the great recent inventions work to overcome space and make the people of the earth better acquainted . . . to make this wired-up planet a neighborhood" ("How Fast").

Filmmakers this year knew they were entrepreneurs in an exciting new business, and many also suspected that they were just at the start of something unimaginably larger. The *Los Angeles Times* put it this way: "The moving picture men do not know where they are going but they're on their way. The picture drama is still in a raw, crude state. . . . The fact is the moving picture show of today consists only of the tools to carve out an artistic future" ("Films Thrive").

NOTE

1. Intertitles are quoted throughout this essay with the capitalization styles used in the original films.

1911

Movies and the Stability
of the Institution

EILEEN BOWSER

Fifty years after the Civil War, popular culture explored the deep scars in
the national body from that divisive conflict that left a nation still in a
search for reconciliation. Monuments to war heroes were dedicated, commemorations were held on the old battlefields, and historic battles were
reenacted on the original sites. Such memorializing events established cultural traditions and enshrined tourist attractions that continue to flourish
up to present times. Perhaps most impressive of all these endeavors was
Francis Trevelyan Miller's ten-volume *Photographic History of the Civil War*,
an epic work replete with over one thousand Mathew Brady photographs.
While endeavoring to heal the wounds of its own Civil War, the United
States watched over its southern borders, monitoring the progress of the
conflict in Mexico. The Mexican Revolution that began in November of the
previous year led to the resignation of Porfirio Diaz in May and the short-
lived presidency of the revolution's leader, Francisco I. Madero, who was
thrown out in December by the folk hero Emiliano Zapata, and eventually
murdered by his replacement, Victoriano Huerta. American motion picture
companies hurried to the border to film as much of the battles as they
could to capitalize on the American public's fascination with the turbulent
events in Mexico. Kalem announced a series of Mexican war films, beginning with *The Mexican Filibusterers*. Images of Mexicans as "greasers" and
stereotypical villains infiltrated popular culture. However concerned
Americans were with Mexico, the efforts to assimilate the waves of immigrants from southern and eastern Europe loomed as the larger issue for the
nation. As the old divisions of the Civil War seemed to be healing, the
country had to deal with the absorption of great waves of newcomers: poor
and unskilled, often non-English speaking, and Catholic or Jewish. The
reformers of the Progressive Era sought new solutions to the problems created by the arrival of the immigrants. Because a paternalistic society under
control and in good order was considered both desirable and possible in

this optimistic era, and good for business as well, some of the most successful businessmen and respectable members of society supported the
growing number of institutions and programs dedicated to improving the
lot of the poor and uneducated.

Tragic events in the workplace heightened the need for greater oversight
of labor practices. The most infamous of these was New York's Triangle Waist
Factory fire on 25 March that resulted in the shocking death of over a hundred young women. The executives of the company above the factory floor
fled to the roof, ignoring the workers stuck below them behind locked or
blocked doors. Spectators could never forget the heartrending sight of young
women in billowing skirts leaping from ninth floor windows to certain death
on the sidewalk below. The Triangle disaster gave strength to the labor union
movement and immediately made unsafe working conditions a vital topic
of concern. The working woman was a growing force in national life. In
California, women won the right to vote, the sixth state to grant this right.
Although the majority of accounts of the suffragette movement that appear
in popular culture were comedies that mocked the movement, the heroine
in a melodrama often was a strong woman taking her place in the world of
labor beside men, driving cars, managing a lonely telegraph outpost, or
working in the factory line. The labor movement, usually portrayed in the
motion pictures from the viewpoint of management (film producers were
management, after all), was nevertheless depicted in several movies from
labor's point of view: in one of the more sensational films, Reliance's *Locked
Out* (a lost film), the ghosts of strikers shot down by police confront the
owner of the factory, who dies from the shock.

The business world found supportive inspiration in efficiency expert
Frederick Taylor's seminal book on the influence of industry upon American life, *The Principles of Scientific Management*. Taylor's time-and-motion
studies were the foundation of the assembly lines in modern factories and
reinforced capitalism's need to hold control of social forces. The scientific
management principles introduced by Taylorism also infected the motion
picture industry. David Hulfish published his manual *Motion Picture Theater
Management* in an effort to bring scientific management to motion picture
exhibition. The practices of the Motion Picture Trust Companies, soon copied
by the Independents, led to standardization in all parts of the industry, from
production to distribution. The one-reel film and the daily release system,
the star system, genre films, film promotion, and even the very systems
used in the creation of films were internalized in the institution of the cinema. At the same time that these fixed systems provided stability, they limited experiment and change.

Yet Taylor's principles did not go unchallenged. As might be expected, the unions consistently protested their implementation into the workplace. When, for example, Taylor won a contract to introduce scientific management to the federal arsenals, the workers at the Watertown Federal Arsenal went on strike, and the federal courts ultimately ruled that Taylorism was biased, inaccurate, and unscientific. Such objections did not prevent Henry Ford from adopting the assembly line to the production of the Model T Ford. In October, after a long-running legal battle, Ford defeated the inventor/patent attorney Henry Seiden and brought an end to Seiden's collecting license fees from manufacturers. That opened the way for Ford to expand his production line and produce his Model T at a cheaper price. He made the automobile affordable to the workingman and forever changed modern America's mobility. Two other legal decisions were of importance in American life. In one, Kalem lost its appeal in the suit initiated by Harpers in 1907 for the film company's use of *Ben Hur*, a legal decision that ordered motion picture producers to recognize the copyright of authors instead of making free use of books and plays. It was a decision that testified to the growing status of the motion picture. In the second, the U.S. Supreme Court split up two mighty companies, Standard Oil and American Tobacco, charging restraint of trade in contravention of the Sherman Anti-Trust Act, which was designed to prevent trusts from conspiring to reduce competition.

The Motion Picture Trust and Industry Expansion

The motion picture industry did not heed the lessons of the Standard Oil and American Tobacco breakups. The Motion Picture Patents Company, in the service of its goal to bring control and stability to the business, completed the actions that would lead to its own breakup by the court a few years later. General Film, the new distribution arm of the Motion Picture Patents Company, succeeded in buying up all the licensed exchanges in the country except one, the Greater New York Trading Company owned by William Fox. He held out and went to court to charge restraint of trade. For the moment, however, the Trust was as much in control as it would ever be and the stability of the new business was assured. Investors now had more faith in the future of motion pictures, and that led to rapid expansion of production. On 14 February, Eastman Kodak obtained an amendment to the agreement with the MPPC to permit the manufacturer of film stock to sell to unlicensed production firms, a swiftly expanding market that could no longer be ignored. Independent production was growing in strength, big enough that by the end of the year, Independent production and distribution systems began to threaten the Trust's hegemony.

The new stability of the industry led to the investment in studios, laboratories, and attendant industries, and also encouraged production companies to travel more widely, searching for variety of locations, climates that permitted filming outdoors in winter, and, for some Independents, escape from the spies that Edison employed to catch unlicensed use of its cameras. The large companies set up more than one production unit working in different parts of the country. Some followed Kalem to Florida, and Kalem sent a unit to Ireland. Others went to Colorado, Texas, and Cuba. For the most part, however, California was the destination of choice. California had the desired moderate climate and a wide variety of striking landscapes, including sea, mountains, and desert, all within easy reach. After seeing the wonderful results of the winter trips to California, most companies decided to establish a permanent studio there. By April, a journalist claimed that Los Angeles had reached a position in the motion picture manufacturing business second only to New York.

Several steps were taken toward the incorporation of stars into industry practices. At the beginning of the year, J. Stuart Blackton of Vitagraph began *Motion Picture Story Magazine*, with the cooperation of the other Trust companies, to promote their product: stories of new films were published together with photographs. Responding to demands from the public for information about the actors, the periodical soon took on the look of a fan magazine. Trade periodicals began to publish star photos and answer inquiries. Star photo postcards were offered for sale in bulk by exhibitors to resell to their patrons. By the end of July, answering demands from exhibitors, five licensed production companies and two Independents were introducing the lead cast members at the beginning of the more "important" films, but still, most films did not carry any cast credits. The advertising value of the stars was clear to the exhibitors because, as they had discovered, stars were a great draw for the public. It was less obvious to the producers, limited by their own system in the price they could ask for any one film and concerned that an actor who became famous would demand more money.

In the process of stabilizing the film industry, the kinds of films produced were also standardized to fit into the system of distribution. With only a few exceptions, films were no more than one reel in length. When filmmakers wanted more time to relate more complex stories, they were frustrated. The rare two-reel films, such as Biograph's *His Trust* and *His Trust*

Fulfilled or *Enoch Arden*, or the three-reel films, including Thanhouser's *David Copperfield*, Vitagraph's *A Tale of Two Cities*, or Selig's *Cinderella*, had to be released as separate reels, a few days apart, or shown outside the normal distribution system, as foreign features often were, as special events in legitimate theaters and opera houses. Producers in other countries, without a similarly restrictive release system, found it easier to expand the length of films into features.

Even as other nations expanded into feature production, domestic companies concentrated on particular genres suited to the single-reel format. Genres were easy to publicize and fit exhibitors' need for a balanced program of dramas, comedies, and westerns. By mid-year, the combined MPPC firms were able to offer such a balanced program to their subscribers. What the industry called "drama" can be divided into two chief categories: the action suspense thriller and the moral melodrama. The latter category was driven by the forces of reform and uplift and also, on the part of the industry, motivated by a wish to attract the middle class to the movies. "This is culture, this is refining, this is educational," said Epes Winthrop Sargent of *A Wreath of Orange Blossoms*, one of many Griffith Biographs made in this mode.

Bobby, the Coward: A Story of the Streets of New York

It is in the moral melodrama that we can most clearly see the shift in film-making that began to build on the methods developed to relate the events of a story clearly. Now the aim was to involve the spectator in the thoughts, feelings, and motivations of the characters, to depict psychological intensity, to draw on the emotions of the audiences, to educate them, even, perhaps, to change them. Among all the genre films of this year, the best of the moral melodramas of the Biograph Company stand out. There is much evidence that they had a strong appeal for the public. Critics and social progressives praised them, exhibitors were eager to get them and proudly announced them in front of the theaters, and people responded by attending in great numbers. They were films that drew on the spectator's emotions and raised consciousness and understanding of human behavior and ideals. If Biograph's films appear overrepresented in this essay, however, it is rather due to the accidents of history. Biograph produced about the same number of films produced by the other members of the MPPC at this time of the organized production and release systems, but almost all the Biograph original nitrate negatives survived: they were kept by the Empire

Trust Company that ended up owning and storing them, surprisingly not destroying them even after sound movies were born, and subsequently they were acquired and preserved by the Museum of Modern Art. The inventory of other companies suffered enormous losses, often surviving in only a few incomplete worn projection prints. Edison's backlog also survived in the Museum of Modern Art, but somehow with many more gaps. The paper prints submitted for copyright with the Library of Congress, the source for a vast part of our early film heritage, dwindled to almost nothing in this year, for reasons as yet unknown. Perhaps this was because, though not yet formalized, the move was already under way to revise the rules to recognize motion pictures as a unique new form instead of as photographs, and subsequently the unfortunate decision was made not to retain the nitrate film copies that were submitted for copyright instead. We thus have a very unbalanced view of film production in this year if we base it only on the films we can examine.

The characters of these Biograph short stories are drawn from contemporary life, and many from urban life, as we find in *Bobby, the Coward*. This is life in the tenements of New York's Lower East Side, not far from the Biograph studio on Fourteenth Street. And this is a character study of an adolescent boy who lives there and struggles to find a way to help his family survive. The slums were a new phenomenon of the early twentieth century, due to the rapid growth of big cities and mass immigration, and the well-to-do visited them as curious tourists and as benevolent reformers. The prosperous-looking people to whom Bobby returns the dropped purse are an example of such slum tourists. Robert Harron plays the leading role and lends his own name to the film's title. Harron began at Biograph as an office boy, errand runner, and occasional extra. He helped support a very large family from a young age, and thus in some ways resembled the boy he plays in *Bobby, the Coward*. At Biograph, notorious for refusing to name their actors, D. W. Griffith proved his ability to create new stars as needed after Mary Pickford, Marion Leonard, Arthur Johnson, and Henry Walthall left to join other companies, by bringing forward Blanche Sweet (see *The Lonedale Operator*) and Bobby Harron.

The family in the film consists of three people: the old grandfather is an invalid, the sister is younger than Bobby, and Bobby is their sole support. Bobby goes out in the streets to look for work and, discouraged, is intimidated by a gang of street toughs in front of his sweetheart, who lives in the same building. She scorns Bobby as a coward. A man and woman touring the slums pass by Bobby in the street, and the woman unknowingly drops her purse. Bobby finds it, takes it inside the building, and is overjoyed to find that it contains a lot of money. Then his conscience struggles with his needs. He goes out to look for the couple and returns the purse to its rightful owner. He earns a substantial reward for his honesty. Unfortunately, members of the gang are watching and they follow him home. Two of them decide to return after dark and rob him of his prize. When they do, Bobby's real courage asserts itself in the need to protect his family. He fights them off single-handedly and turns them over to the police, who have been summoned by his little sister. The neighbors are watching the scene with admiration for Bobby, and his sweetheart changes her mind about his bravery.

The Biograph production records (preserved at the Museum of Modern Art/Film Study Center) list locations for this film as the New York studio and Fort Lee, New Jersey, but I think this must be a recording error, as I find it impossible to identify a single shot that looks like the small rural town with unpaved streets that Fort Lee was at that time. The camera register that logs in the daily locations contains a few obvious errors of this type that might stem from "filling in" the record at a later date, the more likely in the confusion of the company's cumbersome move by train from one coast to the other. *Bobby, the Coward* is the first production after the return from California the last week in May. Biograph often did send its company across the Hudson River to film there, but it does not make sense that they would do so for a film that consists of scenes made in the studio and the teeming streets of the Lower East Side, a very short distance from the studio. It is these crowded street scenes that are the most memorable for a modern audience, and probably were fascinating for viewers at the time. The street scenes seem to be documentary, as though filmed by a hidden camera, and yet careful analysis shows that Biograph actors are in the midst of the crowd of extras, undoubtedly guiding the action to get the results the director wanted, while blending in seamlessly. While some stray participants do look at the camera, they are not noticeable in the general chaos. In fact, our view of the city scenes is quite restricted. As Tom Gunning (*Cherchi Usai* 5: 85–91) and Jean Mottet have pointed out, these scenes are very tightly framed by the camera, showing nothing beyond a sidewalk full of people, a doorway, a shop window, a few people crowded together, and nothing above the ground floor. There are no shots of the skyscrapers then in existence in New York, no streetcars and vehicles, none of the grand vistas of the larger city typically seen in films exploiting the New York setting. Shots showing the slum dwellers at the entrance to their tenement feature them hemmed in by their poverty and nearly as restricted in the streets as they are in their overcrowded tenement homes. These images have been related to other pictorial sources of the time: the photographs of Jacob Riis and the painters of the Ash Can school (such as William Glackens and John Sloan), yet it is in movement that Griffith captures a "sense of a space boiling over with human activity" (Cherchi Usai 5: 89). It was the energy in the city streets that inspired these memorable compositions, which will be even more strongly felt (and more strongly controlled by the director) in a number of Griffith's urban films in the next few years.

The Lonedale Operator and the Modern Film Heroine

The Lonedale Operator is the classic D. W. Griffith thriller, the kind of film that kept Biograph films in demand all over the country. It illustrates Griffith's mastery of the skill of parallel editing for suspense, now fully developed and allowing for added complexity. The daughter of the telegraph operator at an isolated railway station takes her father's place when he becomes ill and bravely defends the station against thieves until her sweetheart can come to the rescue in the train's engine. Within the ninety-eight shots, more than he had ever used before, and probably more than any other filmmaker of that time, Griffith builds the suspense through his powerful use of cross-cutting, the propulsive alternation of shots set in distinct spaces, typically tied together by a strong, controlling timeframe. In the interest of sustaining excitement and, let us add, to efficiently use the limits of the one-reel film, shots are short and begin in mid-action. Suspense is increased by means of the tactics of delay. When the heroine telegraphs for help, the operator at the other end is dozing and does not immediately respond. The tension shows in her posture and gestures when she fails to get a response, and then relaxes as the other operator wakes up and responds: the tension passes between the shots to inflect his posture as he urgently records her message. The camera is placed closer to the heroine to show her expressive face as the suspense grows, and in an extreme close-up exposes her ruse of pretending that a monkey wrench is a gun with which she holds the thieves at bay.

The *Lonedale Operator* has drawn the attention of several influential scholars. Kristin Thompson, in a formal analysis of the film, shows that the three threads of the action—the heroine at the station, the robbers trying to break in, and the engineer and fireman racing to the rescue on the engine—are symmetrically balanced (Cherchi Usai 5: 18–22). The shots do not simply get shorter to increase the excitement. The train racing to the rescue consists of a two-shot sequence each time we return to it, showing the scene in the cab and a long shot of the speeding train, and each sequence is about the same length. In contrast, the scene at the station, with its alternation of the robbers trying to break in and the telegraph operator frantically trying to get help, varies in length according to the speeding up or slowing down of the suspense; again, the sequence repeats the pattern of shots each time the action returns to the station from the train. Thompson also shows how the use of props in the hands of the actors in the opening scenes is expressive of their feelings: Blanche Sweet is flirtatious with the help of a magazine and Wilfred Lucas masterful with a glove he carries, a prop he will use again later. Another privileged object, the monkey wrench, is quietly present in the station but not emphasized with an extreme close-up until the moment when it is revealed that the tool has masqueraded as a pistol while Sweet held the robbers at bay.

The Lonedale Operator is an example of efficiency in motion picture production. Sections of Tom Gunning's essay on the film, "Systematizing the Electric Message," are especially relevant for this chapter, where we have described the film industry's establishment of systems for production, distribution, and exhibition in the interests of greater efficiency and control. Limited to the one-reel format and the need for producing that reel every few days, producers also had to find ways to systematize the making of the product. Since the same price would normally be paid for each film, any economies in production would serve the profit margin. Take, for example, the use of repeated set-ups and parallel editing: it is practical and time-saving to film all scenes in one location, retaining the same set-ups, and then move on to film all scenes in the other locations. To end up with the right shots to interweave in parallel editing there must be careful pre-planning and a systematic filming of scenes. This concept is key to understanding the underlying theme of this chapter. As Gunning notes: "The brevity of the one-reel films dictated a limited number of elements, allowing spectators to notice repetitions that might be missed in a longer film. . . . Production efficiency and economy led to formal economy, a systematic use of elements" ("Electric Message" 22). Gunning goes on to remark that the few shots in *The Lonedale Operator* that escape the repetition scheme and/or involve a change in set-up are awarded importance by this positioning and are reserved for scenes of special emphasis.

The telegraph played an important role in American life, providing instant communication in a day when the telephone did not yet reach over very great distances and was not yet ubiquitous, and when mail had to travel for days or weeks across the country by train. As it happens, the very first airmail delivery service was inaugurated in October, an event captured on film at the airfield on Long Island, New York (*First Mail Delivery by Air-*

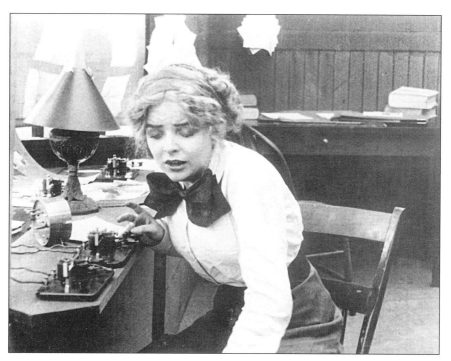

Blanche Sweet, as the train station telegrapher in *The Lonedale Operator*, typifies the New Woman's engagement with communication technologies.

plane, preserved at the Library of Congress). Business correspondence routinely used telegrams for faster communication and for emergencies. For such tasks as routing the vast network of speeding trains from one track to another, avoiding collisions, or preparing freight for fast pickup, the station telegraphers formed an essential function, bringing these two modern technologies into a close and dependent relationship. In this period in American life, railroads were dominant in long-distance transport of people, goods, and supplies. Motor transport and the highways that it demanded were as yet extremely limited.

As for our heroine who steps in to fill this important task of guiding transport, she is the New Woman of the modern age, capable of man's work. Blanche Sweet, playing the role of this modern competent young woman, was just being tried out in leading roles, a substitute for the recently departed Pickford et al. Sweet proved to have the desired magical screen appeal, and this film established her as a new star. She undertook the majority of the important female leading roles from then on through the end of the year. *The Lonedale Operator* shows the dangers of the workplace for a woman and at the same time demonstrates her ability to handle them. Female telegraph operators were common as replacements for male operators after the industry experienced a major nineteenth-century strike, because women would work for less money and accept more tedious and exacting work. (For the same reasons, women took over the operation of telephone switchboards.) The job held its dangers, particularly out on the western plains, where many a pioneer woman held all the responsibilities for a lonely station, armed with a gun. Women escaped the arduous jobs in the factories and the mills by becoming telephone switchboard operators and typists in offices, but to be a telegraph operator meant entering a more public sphere. Despite the prevalence of women holding the position in real life, in early cinema, most (although not all) heroic girl telegraphers swing into action only when a father or other male figure is kept by circumstances from doing his job, which may reflect lingering unease on the part of male filmmakers about this advance of women on the workplace. Like the young women in other Griffith films, Blanche Sweet presents a mixed picture of appealing and helpless femininity who is nonetheless heroic and quite capable of action in the crucial moments: she is breaking out of the Victorian stereotype.

The Ranchman's Nerve: Westerns on Location

As demonstrated by the demands of exhibitors, the popularity of westerns was at a peak, and the daily program that did not include one was incomplete. The western is a uniquely American genre that other countries could not match, although that did not stop them from trying. The western's popularity was deplored by upper-class reformers, who thought the violence and shooting to be bad influences on the small boys who loved them. Despite the reformers, so popular was the western that Independent production companies such as American Film Manufacturing specialized in just this genre.

The American Film Manufacturing Company was an independent firm founded late in the previous year by two exchange men in Chicago, John Freuler and Samuel Hutchinson. They jump-started their company by raiding the licensed company, Essanay, of almost its entire production staff: they lured away three directors and seven actors, including Essanay's biggest star, J. Warren Kerrigan, along with numerous technical people, leaving the company with little more than the personnel connected with Broncho Billy Anderson westerns. Allan Dwan, Essanay's scenario editor, was drafted for the same role at American, but he soon moved on to become American's chief director. Dwan proved to be a competent and forward-looking director, with a very long and active career ahead of him.

In April, American announced a new policy of specializing in westerns. The Selig Company of Chicago, among others, was already concentrating on westerns, boasting of the advantages of having the western landscape near at hand. The American branch of Pathé, criticized for its inauthentic western films made in New Jersey, sent a company out west under the leadership of the director, James Young Deer, the same Winnebago Indian from Nebraska who also appeared in films for Kalem, Biograph, Lubin, Vitagraph, and The New York Motion Picture Company. With the trade periodicals promoting the uniqueness of this American genre, as part of the goal to reduce foreign competition, Pathé was merely trying to beat Americans on their own territory at their own game. The American Film Manufacturing Company worked briefly in Arizona and then moved on to California in the summer. A new distinctive trademark was designed for American's westerns: a cowboy on horseback throwing a lariat.

The Ranchman's Nerve is a typical western adventure thriller, a mythic tale of good versus bad men, showing courage, generosity, honor, and the ancient code of chivalry, with a bit of dime-novel theatrics thrown into the mix. A notorious outlaw who is considered the terror of the mountains holds up an express rider. The sheriff organizes a posse of ranchers to go after the bad man. The sheriff is seriously wounded by the outlaw before they can capture him and looks for "a man of nerve" who has the courage to lead the posse in his place. Today, we would probably say "guts" instead of "nerve," now a little old-fashioned when used in this sense. As a curious test of "nerve," the ranchers in the posse pair up, with each of two men holding a corner of the same neckerchief in his teeth so that the distance between them cannot be lengthened, at which time the men draw a knife for a fight. J. Warren Kerrigan wins this rather bizarre contest, and under his leadership the posse renews its pursuit. In the rugged mountain landscape, one member of the posse is shot off his horse by the hidden outlaw, and again the posse is prepared to admit defeat. To set an example of bravery to the increasingly reluctant posse, a cool Kerrigan announces that he will bring the outlaw in single-handedly without a gun. Kerrigan climbs rocks to the outlaw's hiding place high in the mountains, outfaces him, and captures his gun. The outlaw's sister is with him in the hideout, and Kerrigan tells the bad man: "For the sake of the woman, I'll give you one hour to get across the border." But later, when the outlaw returns from Mexico, prepared to get his revenge, his sister, now in love with the courageous man who defeated her brother and let him go, shoots her own brother to save Kerrigan's life.

The Ranchman's Nerve displays all the qualities that made westerns so appealing to broad audiences: great western landscapes, exposed in wide panorama shots; a moving camera that followed the swift-moving action; plenty of thrills involving a hero and a bad guy; a background drawn from the recent past of westward expansion in America; and authenticity, a quality much praised by film critics, especially for westerns and Indian films. The actors ride their horses as though they have lived a lifetime on horseback, and wear well-worn clothes. Though three of them wear the shaggy sheepskin chaps that will later become a fancy-dress cliché of singing cowboys, here the same outfits seem weathered and sufficiently authentic. *The Ranchman's Nerve* is filmed close enough that figures often fill the frame, from the knees to the heads. The western genre, when shot in western locations, the camera panning and tilting to follow groups of men on horseback over rough terrain, took on a life of action and adventure that seemed uniquely cinematic, even while forces of uplift sometimes denigrated it as low-class entertainment, lacking in cultural or educational values. Nevertheless, reformers could not defeat the westerns' great popularity, as companies learned that action sold better than uplift. When Kalem tried to introduce a series of films made for children, they gave up after a few weeks because the exchanges said they were not as desired as westerns.

Swords and Hearts: Action in the Civil War Film

The film producers participated enthusiastically in the Civil War commemorative projects. Amid the swell of Civil War motion pictures (at least seventy-four of them were made this year) and the plays, the dedication of monuments, and the battlefield reenactments, Griffith produced his ninth film for Biograph with a Civil War setting.[1] Many of the earliest Civil War films, made by Northerners because that is where most producers were to be found, tended to express the viewpoint of the Union side in the war. By this time, however, the romantic and chivalric ideals of the defeated Confederacy were more commonly seen in the Civil War movies, even those produced in the northern states. In the interests of reconciliation, however, a goal that underlines all of the fiftieth anniversary commemorations, Civil War films frequently were politically neutral at their base, dwelling instead on the tragedies of families split between the two sides.

David Mayer has described the kind of theatrical and literary antecedents that provide the elements in this melodrama of the Confederate side of the war and Reconstruction (*Cherchi Usai* 5: 110–14). There was nothing particularly original in the well-worn conventions of *Swords and*

Dorothy West attempts to comfort Wilfred Lucas, whose devastation at the destruction of his home is expressed by keeping the actor's back to the camera in *Swords and Hearts*.

Hearts: the son of an aristocratic southern family whose wealth comes from tobacco becomes engaged to a young woman of his class before setting out to join his company in the Confederate army. The farewell scene is witnessed by a poor girl and her father, who scrabbles a living from selling the produce he has raised. The father is filled with resentment for the rich planter class, while the poor girl looks on and secretly falls in love with the aristocratic son. When the son comes home to visit his fiancée, it is the lower-class young woman who helps him escape the Union soldiers. She is the strong and independent woman portrayed in many films of this period. In a dramatic chase sequence, she dons the rebel's uniform, tucks her hair up in his hat, and bravely rides away on his horse, drawing the Union horsemen in pursuit. Meanwhile, her father leads a band of lawless "bushwhackers" in an attack on the planter's house and is killed, while the house is burned and the old planter dies in the fire. The faithful black slave has saved the strongbox containing the family wealth by burying it, and he is the one to tell the hero what the brave lower-class girl has done for him. When the rebel soldier returns after the war, he sits defeated before the ruins of the family mansion, his back to the camera. An effective Griffith trope, a back view of an actor subtly expresses a strong emotion by contrarily hiding it from the camera's gaze. The angle of the shot had its origins in the current vogue for actors on stage to turn their backs to the audience for intense scenes. The returned soldier's fiancée has turned her attention to a Union officer. The rebel scion of the ruined family turns for solace to the young girl who secretly loved him and saved him from capture, while the old servant brings forth the box containing the family valuables and restores them to the owner.

Swords and Hearts tells of the suffering of the South, from a southern viewpoint: however, the evil attack on a southern plantation owner's mansion is not blamed on the terrorizing Union army unit, but on a band of lawless poor white men, known as bushwhackers, who are taking advantage of chaotic wartime conditions. The historical record shows various types of roving lawless bands in existence during the war and in the Reconstruction era, on both sides or on no side, some of them ordinary citizens banded together to try to protect their property. By thus placing the blame in *Swords and Hearts*, the scene serves the purposes of reconciliation more than those of history. The bushwhackers provide a convenient scapegoat for an era of reconciliation. *Swords and Hearts* does not dwell on the tragedies, however. It is most of all a thrilling action melodrama with an active modern woman as its heroine. The disguised heroine's frantic horseback ride is an example of crosscutting among streams of action for the utmost in suspense, a technique that Griffith built on for his thrillers. Meanwhile, the former slave who remains loyal to the family is a cliché of the Civil War films, as in Griffith's *His Trust* and *His Trust Fulfilled*, in which the loyal slave is the chief character of the two-part film.

The Railroad Raiders of '62: Movies and Trains

The Railroad Raiders of '62 is based on a real event from the Civil War that took place in Georgia on 12 April 1862, when Andrew's Raiders attempted to steal a Confederate train behind enemy lines and take it across the union line to Tennessee. The film is a historical documentary, although the term did not yet exist. It does not attempt to fictionalize history even if it is not accurate in every particular. The film participates in the Civil War fervor of this anniversary year, although its factual nature is atypical. We cannot look to it as an example of the genre. It does fall in line, however, with the current fad for live battlefield reenactments and the public interest in Civil War history, or a romantic version of that history.

Although Kalem producers and the film's director, Sidney Olcott, surely did not think of it that way when the film was made, *Railroad Raiders of '62* is also the first of a series of highly popular railroad films in which Kalem specialized, and therefore it came to constitute yet another genre. (The film even made a reappearance as chapter 19 in Kalem's serial *The Hazards of Helen*.) The steam engines used in making the film are from the Civil War era, the same type as the famous engine *The General* that was stolen by Andrew's Raiders in 1862.

The action begins with a group of federal soldiers who step forward when asked to volunteer for a special mission behind enemy lines. The camera is rather close to the actors in this scene, their figures filling the frame, photographed from their knees upward. Most of *The Railroad Raiders of '62* is shot at a greater distance, and much of it head-on to the action or the reverse, directly away from the camera, with the camera mounted on a moving train for much of the film. A Union soldier wearing women's clothing as a ruse manages to flag down the rebels' steam engine, which is pulling a single flat car. "She" pretends to faint beside the tracks as the engine slows. The train stops, and the engineer and stoker jump down to help her. Andrew's Raiders emerge from the bushes and capture the train at gunpoint. As they speed away, the "woman" jumps on board and sheds the female disguise amid a gun battle. The aim of the raiders is to take the engine north to Tennessee behind federal lines. The train's crew chase after the stolen engine in a handcar, with this chase taking up the whole film. When the pursuers come close enough, a gun battle breaks out. At last, the stolen train runs out of wood and water and is abandoned. The end of the film is missing in surviving materials, but the film is nearly complete. The missing ending may have included the capture of the fugitives and the return of the locomotive to its home. It is unusual for the time that such a film has no single hero and no heroine and that there is little individual characterization to enlist spectator sympathies. The attraction for the audience lies solely in the excitement of the chase, constant action, and the novel sight of vintage steam engines in operation. This film does not build in intensity with the hail of short shots and crosscutting between the pursuer and the pursued as we find in Griffith's films of this year, yet it does build suspense. The suspense is created in part from the race between steam engines portrayed in mounted moving camera shots and in part from the device of interruption: these breaks in the forward movement are created by such devices as the need for the rebels to stop and get up steam and to collect soldiers, the tearing up and repair of the tracks, and the need to replenish fuel for the stolen steam engine.

The railroad and cinema were closely linked from the beginning. We need only mention Lumière's and Edison's arrivals of trains, the travel films with mounted moving cameras, and Hale's Tours, among others. Scholars

have worked out theories of how the experience of riding on trains corre-
lates to the way in which we see moving images in other contexts. Gender
studies has argued for the masculine symbolism of the train, a powerful
intruder in a feminine landscape, while feminism has discovered the rise of
women in the work world of men during the era of rail expansion; in this
chapter I have singled out the independent women train station agents and
telegraphers. Beyond this, trains were an obvious site of fast movement and
involving action; with *The Railroad Raiders of '62*, producers discovered a
new genre to meet the needs of the established systems of distribution and
exhibition, and Kalem followed up with a long series of railroad thrillers.

Little Nemo in Slumberland: The Comics Meet Live Action

Little Nemo in Slumberland, although made by Vitagraph, a major production
company and an important member of the Trust, was produced outside the
rigid system that provided daily releases for the avaricious exhibition venues. It was a special production, an exception to prove the rule. Other companies also made distinctive films outside the system from time to time, but
they were rare enough to earn their name as "specials." The special status
of *Little Nemo* (as it was often called) derives in part from the way that it
adapts its subject matter, drawn from a comic strip by Winsor McCay.

McCay was a graphic artist famed for his daily cartoon strips in the *New
York Herald*, but also known for his performances in vaudeville as a lightning sketch artist. The film trades on McCay's status as a showman at the
same time that it invites its audience to contemplate the process of creating
animation in the cinema. Fittingly, J. Stuart Blackton, director of the live
action sequences in *Little Nemo*, had produced several animation films for
Vitagraph prior to this release and shared McCay's talent for lightning
sketches. In the film's early stages, McCay demonstrates to a group of
friends, including Blackton, how the film we are about to see is made.
Unlike professional illusionists, he wants the audience to understand how
the trick is done. In its blending of performance and process, *Little Nemo*
becomes a key work in the history of animated cinema and sets the tone for
much work to follow.

In the live-action prologue, McCay good-humoredly bets a group of
friends visiting his studio that he can produce enough drawings in one
month to make them move in a lifelike manner on the screen. He refuses
the offer of a drink, insisting on water, and calls for supplies for the task
ahead. Helpers bring in ridiculous quantities of barrels of ink and bundles

of drawing paper as McCay sets to work at producing the drawings. He demonstrates a viewing device that shows the drawings in motion, a mechanism on the principles of a mutoscope, rapidly flipping the drawings. Later in the film, John Bunny, Vitagraph's biggest star at the time, pays a visit, and McCay has the film projected for him. Live action still plays a part, though, as the artist's hand appears to begin the drawings, which then take on a life of their own, tentative at first, then with confidence, through the magic of stop-motion filming. This is the same method used to make drawn objects move in animated films: in between each frame or few frames, the drawings change slightly. The drawing process involves much more labor, of course, than just moving objects around between shots. Because McCay's drawings are so finely detailed, they must have taken even more painstaking work than the animated drawings of Emile Cohl, the artist of the Gaumont Company of France. Cohl's films began to appear in America before McCay's and were likely to have been seen by him. *Little Nemo*, like a Cohl film, is filled with metamorphic images, a thing or person turning into something else, as happens in dreams. McCay's figures, however, are drawn with a highly developed sense of perspective. They are solid and they move in depth, although they are without any horizon line to aid the illusion. It is quite astonishing how McCay's drawing of the dragon chariot becomes smaller and smaller as it moves deep into the blank white space, swishing its tail all the while.

Eugene V. Brewster, one of the men visiting McCay's studio in the live-action part of *Little Nemo*, was the editor of the newly established *Motion Picture Story Magazine* (produced by Blackton), which he casually holds up for the camera in the course of the live-action part of the film to get some free publicity. Today's product placement is not new. McCay's artistry became further embroiled in the commerce of publishing outside the context of the film. By the time the film was completed, the newspaper strip had come to a halt because McCay signed with the Hearst papers and the *Herald* got an injunction to keep him from taking the wonderful *Little Nemo* strip with him. On 12 April, McCay's new vaudeville routine opened in New York with this film as part of the act (Crafton, *Mickey* 89–112). The months of work necessary to produce a *Little Nemo* means that it could only have been made outside the system of daily release. The film was designed as a prestige item for Vitagraph, and McKay may have become involved in the hopes of using the film as a part of his vaudeville act. Only after fulfilling that purpose would *Little Nemo* be put to use in the ordinary film distribution circuits, where, like other filmed vaudeville acts, it permitted the wonders of live theater and the vaudeville circuit to be extended to the smallest towns across the country. In the daily demand to fill the theater programs, many a film made chiefly for another purpose would be put to use there. Blackton surely had it in mind to distribute the film as one of the Vitagraph releases when he entered into production of *Little Nemo*, for efficiency demanded that every possible use be exploited.

■ Manhattan Trade School for Girls: The Educational Film

The horrors of the Triangle Waist Company fire called attention to the situation of young women employed in the less skilled levels of the garment industry. The Triangle Company business practices exemplify the efforts to increase efficiency in the manufacture of clothing by employing unskilled workers at very low wages in a kind of assembly-line production, with no chance of promotion to higher-paying jobs. Garment industry jobs potentially provided a better option for young women in the workplace than in the mills and factories, but in practice such workplaces were often sweatshops, and the work was often piecework, sometimes performed by underage children.

The Manhattan Trade School for Girls, a characteristic institution of the Progressive Era, was entirely supported by philanthropy and aimed at improving the lot of immigrant girls or the daughters of immigrants and integrating them into American culture. Established in 1902, the school had the purpose of training unskilled young women without resources for a career in the garment industry. Admittance was competitive, attendance was free, and some of the poorest students received stipends for their living expenses. While basic sewing and cooking courses were taught, advanced courses trained young women to operate machinery and perform more intricate tasks as dressmakers and milliners, providing some possibilities for advancement, although many students probably would end up in the lowliest jobs in workplaces like the Triangle Waist Company.

Manhattan Trade School for Girls bears no production company name and survived in the archives of George Eastman House as a 28 mm print. This film stock, like the later 16 mm stock, was made of nonflammable ingredients, for use in educational institutions where the fire safety regulations that governed the projection of nitrate film did not exist. However, the 28 mm camera, invented by Pathé in France, was not yet available at the time of the film's initial release, meaning that *Manhattan Trade School for Girls* would have been made in the standard theatrical 35 mm. At the time, educational films were in demand by those theater managers who sought to

Documentary-style depiction of women learning labor skills forms the core of *Manhattan Trade School for Girls*.

incorporate uplift into their programs and gain respectability for the business. Educational films were not as popular with the wider audiences, however, and soon ended up being shown chiefly in schools, clubs, and churches. For that reason, it is likely that this film was shown first in the higher-class cinemas, later to be relegated to the educational venues and transferred to 28 mm safety film for that purpose.

The professionalism of the production indicates that it was probably made by one of the major Trust companies, Edison or Vitagraph, for example, on behalf of the school, which then would have used it to promote the raising of funds. Sponsored films were made by most of the establishment production companies (those in the Trust) on behalf of good Progressive causes. The marks of professional production are evident in the style of *Manhattan Trade School for Girls*: it is carefully lit and photographed, with a variety of camera angles, and varies close views of various tasks with panning shots to show the extent of the operation. With very few exceptions, the participants avoid looking at the camera, unlike most nonactors of the period. The Edison Company made a lot of sponsored films for social and educational purposes, but Edison films, unlike this one, usually enlisted interest in the educational subject through a fictional story. This film is more persuasive in its message because it does not use fiction, but instead personalizes the message by following four girls from their admittance through training and graduation to job placement. At the same time we are shown groups of girls learning the same tasks as the individuals, carrying the narrative from the particular to the general and back again, as the camera position varies from close views to medium and long shots.

Jennifer Bean, in her commentary on *Manhattan Trade School for Girls* for the DVD release *Treasures III, Social Issues in American Film* (National Film Preservation Foundation), and Scott Simmon, in his accompanying notes, both call our attention to the words "Good Taste" on the lesson plan chalked up by the teacher. They are right to emphasize this message. Good taste, we may learn from the words of the school director, means "simple" and "refined" as opposed to "gaudy" and "showy." It was considered essential for a school that was training young immigrant girls from southern and eastern Europe to understand and adopt the values of the dominant white Protestant culture, not just for their work in the garment trade, but as future citizens of America. We might expect that such values were needed for the upper levels of success in the garment industries, in order to cater to the tastes of the middle and upper classes. However, the list of courses titled "factory laws, tenement house laws, child labor laws, and trade unionism" are of particular significance here. They are characteristic of the values of the Progressive Era. While it seems likely that most of the graduates were expected to be employed in the trades only for a limited number of years before marriage, these young women were learning how to fend for themselves. The reformers had every confidence in their ability to shape, control, and order the inchoate mass of America's huge immigrant population as, in this film, they trained these young women to enter the working world as self-reliant citizens.

■   ■   ■

Order, efficiency, control, progress: these were the goals of the Progressive Era and of the established members of the motion picture industry, the Motion Picture Trust. In this year, there was widespread confidence in their ability to achieve these goals.

NOTE

1. The others were *The Guerilla* (1908), *In Old Kentucky* and *The Honor of His Family* (1909), *In the Border States, The Fugitive,* and *The House with Closed Shutters* (1910), and, in this year, *His Trust* and *His Trust Fulfilled,* filmed prior to *Swords and Hearts.* Two more films followed: *The Battle,* later in the year, and *The Informer* (1912).

1912

Movies, Innovative Nostalgia,
and Real-Life Threats

RICHARD ABEL

"FEDERAL SUIT TO DISSOLVE THE PICTURE 'TRUST'": so read the headline story in "Motion Pictures and Photo Plays," the *New York Morning Telegraph*'s Sunday supplement of 18 August. Two days earlier, the U.S. attorney general had filed a suit against the Motion Picture Patents Company (MPPC) and two dozen "Allies" for violating the Sherman Anti-Trust Act. The suit charged that "the defendants determined to destroy competition between them, to monopolize commerce relating to the motion picture art, to exclude all others and carry on commerce according to the terms of the unlawful combination which they were to create." Other events, of course, gained far greater attention in the general press. In April, on its maiden voyage, the *Titanic* collided with an iceberg in the North Atlantic and sank within hours; of the 2,200 passengers and crew, fewer than 700 survived. This was but one of several shocking disasters or sensational clashes early in the year that ranged from the deaths of Captain Scott and four others as they returned from a successful South Pole expedition to the "Bread and Roses" strike of textile workers led by the Industrial Workers of the World in Lawrence, Massachusetts, in which police killed several strikers. The year also included major political events, from the growing public campaign for women's suffrage to the presidential election, in which Theodore Roosevelt ran as the Progressive Party candidate, after failing to wrest the Republican Party's nomination from President William Howard Taft, thus allowing the Democratic Party nominee, Woodrow Wilson, to win the general election. This was also the year of the dance craze, from wildly vigorous dances with animal names like turkey-trot and chicken scratch (their ragtime derivation had racist overtones) to elegant ballroom dancing, in which Irene Castle's simple, lightweight dresses inspired looser, more comfortable clothing for women off the dance floor. Although the U.S. antitrust suit against the MPPC seemed minor in the context of many of these events, it would have major repercussions for the film industry over the next few years; yet, even in this year, it signaled that the industry was undergoing a number of significant changes.

One of the more germane changes was the growing strength of the "Independents"—and their own efforts to "monopolize" film distribution. The Motion Picture Distributing and Sales Company (Sales) had cornered the market in releasing the product of most companies not part of the MPPC and now rivaled the General Film Company, the MPPC's own distribution affiliate. Through more than fifty rental exchanges, Sales could release four to five reels of film per day, serving one-third of the motion picture theaters across North America. Internal dissensions, however, provoked the company's break-up in the spring, with many of its members, led by Carl Laemmle, joining a new company, Universal Film Manufacturing, and the others hastily reorganizing as Film Supply. Each company soon had the capacity to release three reels of new film per day. Yet further disputes and realignments continued into the summer: the New York Motion Picture Company (NYMP), for instance, left Universal after a bitter battle over the Bison-101 trademark and reorganized its production units according to three new brands—Kay-Bee, Broncho, and Keystone. Within months after NYMP had negotiated a distribution deal with Harry Aitken's Mutual Film, the latter was strong enough to take control of nearly all its partner's distribution rights. By year's end, Universal and Mutual, along with General Film, had created something like a closed market for distributing different variety packages daily of three to five films.

Since single-reel and split-reel films were the mainstay of all three distributors, most exhibitors, from small nickelodeons to large picture theaters seating 1,000 or more, could offer continuous shows that changed daily, very like a newspaper, whether their shows also included vaudeville acts or illustrated songs. Although exhibitors continued to use company brands or trademarks to promote their shows, two other strategies emerged as means of securing regular audience attendance. One exploited the growing popularity of movie personalities or stars. Exhibitors increasingly used stars' names in their local newspaper ads: G. M. "Bronco Billy" Anderson and John Bunny seem to have been invoked more frequently than any others. *Motion Picture Story Magazine*, the first fan magazine, opened each monthly issue with a "Gallery of Picture Players," full-page photographs of a dozen individual stars. In January, the magazine sponsored one of the first popular picture player contests, won by Vitagraph's Maurice "Dimples" Costello, with Anderson and Mary Pickford among the top ten. Companies like Vitagraph also offered "souvenir postal cards" of their stars, which could be purchased through the mail or at a local theater box office. The other strategy was the film series that involved a single, recurring character in separate, autonomous stories. There were comic series like Essanay's Alkali Ike (with August Carney) and those of Vitagraph starring Bunny; most prominently, there was Essanay's Broncho Billy western series starring Anderson. Edison introduced an influential variation on the format with monthly episodes of *What Happened to Mary?* (starring Mary Fuller), also serialized in *Ladies' World*, a mail-order mass magazine.

Pathé developed a particularly reliable series strategy with its "visual" newspaper, *Pathé's Weekly*. This much-imitated newsreel combined several kinds of nonfiction film that had become viable during cinema's first decade—*actualités* or topicals, news events, travel films, sports films, industrials—into a single-reel format that could be renewed each week. *Pathé's Weekly* typically comprised from six to ten "short scenes of great international events of universal interest from all over the world," which were occasionally described in their entirety in local exhibitors' newspaper ads. The week of 20 May, for instance, the Colonial (in Des Moines) advertised the following (with one misspelled location):

New York, N.Y. Eight thousand Suffragists . . . parade through the city.

Melbourne, Australia. The strike of the street railway employees. . . .

Coovaller, Ore. The Cadets of the Oregon Agricultural College are reviewed. . . .

Belfast, Ireland. Bonar Law, M.P., speaking to 100,000 Loyalists. . . .

Pawhuska, Okla. A cyclone sweeps from Mississippi through this section of Oklahoma, killing 18 people and injuring many more.

Alicante, Spain. The Spanish sovereign visits the city. . . .

New York, N.Y. The Evening Mail Modified Marathon Race. . . .

London, England. Sir Francis Howard reviews a detachment of English troops.

Camden, N.J. The Chinese protected Cruiser, Fei Hung . . . is launched. . . .

Paris, France. The advance styles in Summer Millinery show wide diversity. . . .

The last item on Paris fashions was a consistently recurring item in *Pathé's Weekly* and always targeted "the ladies" in the audience. Throughout the year other newsreels appeared—*Gaumont Weekly* (through Film Supply), *Animated Weekly* (through Universal), and *Mutual Weekly*—but Pathé's newsreel remained the favorite. By year's end, picture theaters across the country were advertising the newsreel as "Pathé's *Famous* Weekly," without the slightest sense of hype.

Single-reel and split-reel films may have remained the backbone of the business throughout the year, but multiple-reel film production, distribution, and exhibition was developing rapidly. Two significant distribution policies developed for feature films were the roadshow system, whereby larger legitimate theaters were rented for the special screening of a feature film and higher prices charged for the limited engagement, and the state rights system, which involved producers selling off regional rights for distribution of individual features to distributors who then booked the film in a variety of theaters within a geographically defined area. After Monopol Film established the viability of these distribution strategies with Milano's five-reel *Dante's Inferno* in late 1911, a host of companies emerged to release more foreign imports as well as nonfiction features, primarily outside the orbit of General Film, Universal, and Mutual. Feature & Educational Films (Cleveland), for instance, had great success with Éclair's French crime thrillers, from *Zigomar* to *The Auto Bandits of Paris*, the latter based on the Bonnot gang that had received wide coverage in U.S. newspapers. In the wake of the *Titanic* disaster, World's Best Films (Chicago) promoted the sensational elements of Great Northern's *The Wreck of the Aurora*. French-American Film (New York) combined two Film d'Art "classics," *Camille* (with Sarah Bernhardt) and *Mme Sans Gêne* (with Gabrielle Réjane) into a five-reel package that could be exhibited together or in consecutive programs. That spring both *Capt. Scott's South Pole Expedition* and *Paul J. Rainey's African Hunt* opened roadshow and state rights engagements that would run more than a year. By midyear, even General Film had to modify its release schedule to include at least one weekly "special feature," half of them foreign imports such as Pathé's *The Orleans Coach* or Cines' *The Lion Tamer's Revenge*. In August, in a bid to link the cinema more closely to the theater, Famous Players Film (newly formed by Adolph Zukor and Daniel Frohman) began to distribute the French-British adaptation of Emile Moreau's *Queen Elizabeth* (starring Bernhardt) through highly profitable roadshow and state rights engagements. Slightly later, *Cleopatra*, an American adaptation of another French play (starring Helen Gardner), was even more heavily promoted in the trade press and local newspapers.

Arguably the most significant multiple-reel films coming from U.S. manufacturers, however, were sensational melodramas, particularly westerns and Civil War films. In the early part of the year, NYMP set the standard with its Bison-101 Indian pictures, produced and perhaps directed by Thomas Ince and released on a regular biweekly basis. From *The Indian Massacre* to *The Lieutenant's Last Fight*, these films were marked by spectacular battle scenes and unusual stylistic effects and were startlingly ambivalent in depicting the confrontation between white settlers, cavalry soldiers, and plains Indians. The break-up of Sales and ensuing struggle between NYMP and Universal, however, halted their production and distribution that summer. The crisis gave Warner's Features, among others, the opportunity to fill the gap with westerns like *The Peril of the Plains*. That fall, Indian pictures reappeared in even greater numbers. Universal-Bison became known for those starring Mona Darkfeather; Broncho and Kay-Bee combined to release at least one acclaimed western per week, from *The Sergeant's Boy* to *The Invaders*. In conjunction with reenactments of battles that continued to commemorate the fiftieth anniversary of the Civil War, the two units also produced a similar series of historical "war pictures." Previously, Kalem and Biograph had been best known for their Civil War films, but nearly all were single-reel films, even in this year, from *A Spartan Mother* (with a specially arranged score) to *The Informer* (starring Pickford and Henry Walthall). Those now were challenged by spectaculars such as Broncho's *Sundered Ties*, which resolved the conflict between North and South in a "romance of reunion," and Kay-Bee's *Blood Will Tell*, which depicted the war's bleak devastation through the ironic action of a Southerner who mistakenly shoots his own son, in disguise, riding to rescue the family.

Finally, newspapers began to establish a mutually profitable arrangement with motion pictures through two different formats. One was the Sunday page that recognized the movies as no less important for readers than the theater, the arts, or literature. The *Cleveland Leader* had introduced the format in December 1911, but Ralph Stoddard, the editor, only made it a definite fixture roughly a year later. Stoddard's Sunday page included not only ads for local picture theaters and film rental exchanges, but also columns of industry information, capsule reviews, and profiles of the city's exhibitors. The *Baltimore News* began printing its own Sunday page in November, and, within the next six months, more than a half dozen other newspapers would follow suit. The second was the syndicated column devoted solely to the movies. The Scripps-McRae newspaper chain introduced this format, also in November, with a column written by its "movie expert," Gertrude Price. Price offered "personality sketches" of current actors, the majority of them young women, often described as active, independent figures, unencumbered by either husbands or children. In newspapers such as the *Des Moines News*, the column appeared almost daily (occasionally on the front page); in others, at least once a week. However frequent, Price's syndicated column had an unusually wide circulation nationally through Scripps's United Press Association.

Broncho Billy's Christmas Dinner: The Cowboy Film Series

Broncho Billy's Christmas Dinner marks a turning point in the westerns that G. M. Anderson was making for Essanay. Several years earlier, George Spoor had set up his partner with his own production unit to film comedies, melodramas, and especially westerns. Favoring a peripatetic form of shooting, Anderson led his unit through a series of locations—in Colorado (Morrison) and Texas (El Paso) before "settling" in California (Santa Monica, Santa Barbara, Redlands)—where he wrote, directed, and starred in such well-received films as *Under Western Skies* (August 1910) and *The Sheriff's Chum* (April 1911). In the summer, the team moved to San Rafael, north of San Francisco, where *The Stage Driver's Daughter* (October) and *Broncho Billy's Christmas Dinner* were shot; then, after a short sojourn near San Diego that winter, Anderson returned to the San Francisco area and constructed a permanent studio east of the city in the small town of Niles, which he and his team would occupy for the next four and a half years. *Broncho Billy's Christmas Dinner* may not have been the first Essanay film to bear that name, but it was the first of an increasingly regular Broncho Billy series to be released throughout this year. In parallel with other series, whether in film or pulp fiction, Anderson played a recurring character type—a "good badman"—yet in autonomous stories that rarely bore any relation to one another or suggested any change in the character from film to film. The film's release also coincided with efforts to transform Anderson into his cowboy character, blurring any distinctions between the two. Essanay was just then kicking off a campaign to promote Anderson as the "most photographed man" in the business—that is, one of first recognized movie stars. In several northeastern Ohio steel towns, exhibitors seized on the campaign to advertise "Essanay's Great Western Thrillers" with a more "in-your-face" nickname for the star, "Bullets" Anderson. This threatening alternative may have been one reason that Essanay released so many more Broncho Billy titles as the year went on, as if to reclaim the character as its own brand.

In *Broncho Billy's Christmas Dinner*, a small-town sheriff is sent a poster of Broncho Billy (granting him immunity if he turns himself in) just before his daughter prepares to leave for college on the local stagecoach. Meanwhile, in some woods, Billy waits patiently with his horse for the stage to come by, planning to rob its passengers. The stage driver is delayed, however; drunken cowboys spook the horses, and the stage careens off (with the daughter), rushing wildly by the surprised Billy. Racing after the stage, he gets close enough to clamber aboard, grab the loose reins, and bring the horses to a standstill. So grateful is the sheriff's daughter that she invites him to join her family for Christmas dinner; before he can say no (he eyes the stage cashbox), she drags him off and home. Awkward and apparently unfamiliar with such occasions, Billy finally confesses his identity to the sheriff, who quickly accepts him, grateful for his "good deed," and introduces him to family and friends. The *New York Dramatic Mirror* reviewer found the "thrilling ride on [the] stage coach . . . as exciting and realistic as anything of its character ever shown in pictures." The surviving archive print confirms this praise: the scene is marked by some deft framing and editing, including an unusual high-angle midshot/long shot taken from a camera mounted atop the stagecoach and behind Billy as he struggles with the reins of the racing horses. Other trade press stories at the time heightened the thrill of this scene by reporting that, despite breaking an ankle during filming of the runaway stagecoach, Edna Fisher (the sheriff's daughter) "continued acting during three subsequent scenes without revealing the extent of her injuries." Yet the *Mirror* reviewer was equally impressed by the acting "in the quieter moments" near the end, as when a pensive Billy is washing up in the right foreground space of a small room, while the family and other guests cluster around a Christmas tree visible through a doorway in the background.

The Broncho Billy series was unusually popular in Europe, especially in Great Britain and Germany, where Essanay had branch offices. Anderson's phenomenal appeal—what the English called the "irresistible charm of personality and the breezy, easy, infectious humour . . . of [this] magnetic man"—gave credence to Essanay's own boast, furthered by some newspapers, that Broncho Billy was the first American "world famous character-creation." In the United States, that appeal ranged widely, at least according to *Moving Picture World*, taking in the masses in the "gallery," young boys, and, in New York City, "the ladies." In contrast to Bison-101's spectacular westerns, Anderson developed Billy as a heroic figure along the lines worked out in such films as *Broncho Billy's Christmas Dinner*. That is, he often first appeared on screen as either an outlaw or "social bandit," or else as a cowboy between jobs, and never as a rancher, entrepreneur, or any kind of property owner. If this characterization sustained his appeal to working-class audiences and boys, other attributes attracted a middle-class audience. For Billy usually underwent a transformation, through "moral and psychological conflict," in Andrew Brodie Smith's words, into a respectable, "ethical role model" (58, 134). Anderson himself, it is worth pointing out, underwent a rather different transformation when he dropped his real name of Max Aaronson for a more anglicized one. By incorporating Christian themes of moral uplift, self-sacrifice, and redemption, the films—other examples include *Broncho Billy's Bible* (June) and *Broncho Billy's Last Hold Up* (August)—often (and somewhat ironically) evoked the ideals of evangelical Protestantism. Although never strictly a parent, his character sometimes served as a surrogate father, as in *Broncho Billy's Heart* (November), making him an appealing figure to mothers as well as children. In short, the Broncho Billy series became incredibly popular by hewing to "traditional, middle-class ideals of morality, manhood, and character," without totally erasing the figure's initial appearance as "a stoic, isolated male."

The Grit of the Girl Telegrapher: The Railroad Thriller

New technologies of transportation and communication, such as the railroad and telegraph, were inextricably bound up with early motion pictures. They often served a narrative function, of course, but, more important, they created "a new topography [overturning] previous conceptions of space and time through new thresholds of speed," as Tom Gunning so concisely puts it, a topography that was uncannily congruent with the development of a flexible system of spatial and temporal relations in American fiction films ("Systematizing" 27). This congruence was especially notable in a certain kind of sensational melodrama that was relatively common in the early 1910s: "railroad thrillers." The company best known at the time for specializing in "railroad thrillers" was Kalem. Most of these Kenean Buel produced in and around a permanent studio that company had constructed in Jacksonville, Florida (as an alternative to Los Angeles). Although some were "school of action" Civil War films, the majority had more contemporary subjects. Exemplary of these latter "railroad thrillers" is *The Grit of the Girl Telegrapher*, which not only bears a strong resemblance to a later popular Kalem series, *The Hazards of Helen* (1914–1917), but also was re-released as part of that series in March 1916. The film's two-part story is set in the small town of Oreland, where Betty (Anna Q. Nilsson), the telegrapher, and her father seem to run the local railway station and also manage a boarding house. Betty has a fiancé, a railroad detective, who departs on a day trip just as "Smoke Up Smith, a notorious car thief," gets off the same train and, smiling, lights a cigar. A message alerts Betty to Smith's presence, and she uses the ruse of a blindman's bluff game near the schoolhouse to catch him with a pair of handcuffs. Betty now sends a message about Smith's capture to the detective, requesting his return, but Smith escapes.

In the second half of the film, Smith steals an engine and Betty pursues him in another, aided by a stoker who gives hers greater speed. Now she crawls along the steam boiler to the cowcatcher, couples the two engines together, clambers over the coal car, and captures Smith a second time. Initially, the film uses cut-in close shots to reveal crucial details: Smith in profile, shaving off his mustache before exiting the train; Betty snapping the handcuffs on his outstretched hands; and Smith picking the lock on one handcuff while Betty taps out the message that seems to resolve the narrative. It also economically deploys alternation in the editing to simultaneously introduce Betty and Smith, then the detective's departure and the thief's arrival. In the second half, of course, alternation becomes dominant and the editing pace increases; with one exception, the chase is conveyed entirely in shots taken from cameras mounted on the moving trains—positioning the spectator in the very midst of the action. Accentuating that positioning are high-angle midshots that alternate between Smith and Betty in their respective engine cabins. Economical shifts in framing finally privilege Betty's heroic action at the climax: in midshot, she climbs out the engine cabin window; in full shot/long shot she crawls forward from the cabin to the front of the engine; in a tracking full shot, the pursuing engine is coupled to the other's coal car, and she scrambles aboard; and, in a repeated high-angle shot that concludes the chase, Betty stands on the coal car in the foreground, with her revolver aimed at Smith cowering in the background cabin.

In making Betty the principal agent of this story, *The Grit of the Girl Telegrapher* joins a surprising number of sensational melodramas that focus on active heroines, from "cowboy girl" westerns like Vitagraph's *How States Are Made* or Solax's *Two Little Rangers* to "girl spy" Civil War films like Kalem's *The Two Spies* or *The Darling of the C.S.A.*—the latter of which also starred Nilsson. But these films were hardly anomalies at this time. They had parallels in juvenile series for girls such as *The Motor Girls* or *The Ranch Girls* and in spectacles such as the Miller Brothers' 101 Ranch Wild West live shows—champion riders Lucille Parr and Bessie Herberg even appeared as "poster girls" for the show's acclaimed tour in this year. Such entertainments also coincided with, and implicitly complemented, the activities of the suffragist movement; indeed, some action heroines such as Pauline Bush (Flying A) as well as 101 Ranch Wild West riders were suffragettes. Moreover, early movie stars like Selig's Kathlyn Williams or Kalem's Ruth Roland as well as Nilsson and Bush were frequent subjects of Gertrude Price's syndicated newspaper columns, where they were consistently profiled as athletic young women, unmarried and without children, committed to their work, frank and fearless in the face of physical risk. One of the industry's more successful ploys during this period, Jennifer Bean argues, was "to shift [public] attention . . . to the people who enacted real-life situations," giving "a name and a face to spectacle" (Bean 18). The players' bodies, often put at risk in "real-life" stunts, were as likely to be female as male. In "railroad thrillers" like *The Grit of the Girl Telegrapher*, female actors, like their characters, repeatedly experienced the threat of accident and catastrophe: surviving by performing spectacular feats, they actually thrived on them. Not only, then, did heroines like Betty function as projective sites of fantasy adventure, most likely especially for young women (to the chagrin of one commentator in *Moving Picture World*, who preferred "a womanly, lovable girl"), but actors like Nilsson, as a new kind of active, attractive worker or professional, also could serve as successful role models to emulate. Such figures were probably seen as popular, influential figures of a specifically American "New Woman."

The New York Hat:
The Contemporary Melodrama

D. W. Griffith directed a number of important films for Biograph this year, many of them sensational melodramas of one kind or another: for example, *The Girl and Her Trust*, *The Musketeers of Pig Alley*, and *The Informer*. Several, however, gave unusual latitude to one or another of his favorite actors to develop what Roberta Pearson has called a "verisimilar code" of acting, sometimes to perform alone in an extended scene. An oft-quoted example is *The Painted Lady*, in which Blanche Sweet goes quietly mad at the climax after shooting a masked burglar and discovering he is the stranger with whom she had earlier become infatuated at a church lawn festival. Another is *The New York Hat*, in which the performance of Mary Pickford (already a very popular and highly paid star) is no less striking than Sweet's. Promoted as "a dramatic comedy of New England life and character," this film is much less a serious "psychological study of character" than a light, charming story of contemporary life in a small New England town that, despite some broad satirical touches, is exceptionally affecting. Notable for being Pickford's last film for Griffith and Biograph before she left the industry, however briefly, to enjoy stage success in David Belasco's *The Good Little Devil*, it also was Anita Loos's first produced screenplay. Not only does the film ground its fairy tale romance between the local minister and his young ward in a verisimilitude of the ordinary, it also deploys the threat of censure, through misperception, to complicate the romance and then dissipates the threat with a "hat trick" that implicitly validates a very modern desire for consumption.

In the film's opening scene, a dying woman makes a secret bequest to the minister (Lionel Barrymore), asking that he use the small sum of money she has saved ("My husband worked me to death," her letter reads) to buy her daughter (Pickford) "the bits of finery she has always been denied." Soon after, the daughter shyly asks her father for a new hat and is refused. The local millinery shop has just received an extravagant new hat from New York; when the minister notices her and other young women admiring it, he remembers her mother's bequest. Later he shocks her with the gift of the hat, and several "ladies of the church" begin to spread gossip of an imagined scandal. The gossip quickly reaches the father, who seizes the hat and destroys it in a rage. The daughter runs to inform the minister ahead of her father and the Church Board, who are determined to accuse him, but the accusations falter when he reveals the mother's letter. Unexpectedly, the minister now proposes marriage, and, once again stunned, the daughter shyly accepts, with her chagrined father's consent. This story is shot and edited with an assurance that requires none of the techniques associated with Griffith's sensational melodramas. Instead, the film relies on Pickford's performance, especially her handling of articles of clothing and her facial expressions in relatively close shots. Particularly striking is the scene in which she looks at herself sadly in a wall mirror as she gently puts on an old black hat "that sits on her head like a small half-baked pancake" (according to the copyrighted synopsis). Another comes shortly after, when she takes her one and only black glove, doubles it over one hand, and, her head held high (and hatless), walks with small mincing steps to town, in an effort to dispel any sense that she is without finery. Others involve Pickford in relation to the new hat—as she looks in the shop window and surprises herself, admiring it; as she dozes in a chair, her right hand tracing its outline in the air and then seeming to gently place it on her head; as she nearly faints away after opening the hatbox, lovingly puts the hat on, admires herself in the mirror, and vainly tries to repress her pleasure; and finally as she stands stunned, hugging the dismembered remains of what she once so desired.

In one sense, *The New York Hat* follows the patterns of domestic melodrama analyzed so influentially by Peter Brooks. That is, its characters assume the "primary psychic roles [of] father, mother, child"; the "family romance" narrative is blocked by a misperception that threatens to destroy the virtue "inherent" to those characters; and the narrative is resolved, the family restored, only when that misperception is corrected (Brooks 4, 32). In this case, the blocking agents are gossiping, envious, straitlaced women, along with a domineering skinflint of a father—all caricatured as New England stereotypes. More interesting is the position that the minister is asked by the mother to assume—that of a "good father" in opposition to the "bad father" who has worked his wife to death. In the end, through the revealed letter, the mother seems to sanction her daughter's marriage as the shift from one father figure to another. Crucial as is the moral and religious authority of a benevolent patriarch in restoring the film's family, his authority also seems to come from an invisible fairy godmother. Equally intriguing is the role that consumption or consuming desire plays in this film. Here, the small town is linked to the metropolis not through the railroad, telegraph, or telephone, but through circulating commodities—in this case, the hat. Reaching into the countryside and redefining the rural life of this and other small towns is the desire fostered by a consumer economy becoming so characteristic of modern urban society. Specifically, a consuming desire for fashionable clothing is what principally defines the young women in the film, and most especially the poor shy daughter. Unlike *The Painted Lady*, any hint of approbation about this is confined to the least sympathetic characters and dissolves away almost magically, more quickly than the hat itself. Indeed, the minister and daughter are first joined together by the prominently displayed hat as they stand in front of the shop window, his desire seemingly spurred by hers for the hat. In the end, her own desire thwarted (for the moment), the daughter seems on the verge of becoming the primary desirable object herself, in a more literal "hat trick" substitution, but the film's final intertitle, "An unexpected trust," veils that; as if still guided by the absent mother, the minister's proposal (and the daughter's uncertain response) points to a chastely companionate marriage—perhaps with more "finery" to come.

▬▬▬ *The Cry of the Children:* The Social Problem Film

Spurred by continued labor unrest and muckraking articles that exposed the dreadful working conditions in factories and farms alike, Progressive reformers focused on the most vulnerable laborers, children, who made up one-sixth of the workforce in America by the turn of the century (Blanke 38). A national debate on the exploitation of child labor erupted early this year. Among the means of propaganda and persuasion involved in this debate, not unexpectedly, were motion pictures, from films allegedly concerned with workplace safety, like *The Crime of Carelessness* (sponsored by the National Manufacturers Association), to working-class melodramas or "social problem" films. The National Child Labor Committee, established in

1904 to promote the rights of "children and youth as they relate to work and working," already had used the indelible photographs shot by Lewis Hine to publicize its work, so it was not unusual for the agency to cooperate with Edison Manufacturing to produce the one-reel *Children Who Labor* (February). Representative of the film industry's general position, which promoted the cliché that capital and labor needed each other to prosper, the film individualizes capitalist greed and then solves the social problems it creates through neither the workers' action nor government intervention, but a factory owner who realizes and remedies his "mistakes." Two months later, Thanhouser released *The Cry of the Children* (in two reels), a much less sanguine working-class melodrama, that W. Stephen Bush lauded in a special review in *Moving Picture World* as "the boldest, most timely and most effective appeal for stamping out the cruelest of all social abuses" ("Social"). In one of its ads, the company even quoted Theodore Roosevelt (as if he endorsed the film): "When I plead the cause of the overworked girl in a factory, of the stunted child toiling at inhuman labor . . . when I protest against the unfair profit of unscrupulous and conscienceless men . . . I am not only fighting for the weak, I am fighting also for the strong."

The Cry of the Children takes its title and tone, elegiac but also sentimental, from a poem by Elizabeth Barrett Browning, lines from which appear in the film's prologue and epilogue intertitles. Early one morning a family of textile workers goes to work in a mill, leaving their youngest child, Little Alice (Marie Aline, the "Thanhouser Kid"), at home, desperately trying to protect her from having to work. After the owner and his wife briefly tour the mill, the latter spots Alice fetching water from a stream and is enchanted by her radiant good nature. The wife offers to adopt the child, but Alice chooses to stay with her father, mother, two sisters, and brother. The workers strike for higher wages, but the owner refuses to meet their demands; when the family is forced to return to work, the mother is too weakened by hunger to go back. Having to replace her, Alice now decides to accept adoption, but is scornfully turned away, her appearance coarsened by labor. Soon stricken by exhaustion, Alice collapses and dies. Walking slowly home from the cemetery, the numbed family encounters the owner and his wife in their car, and now the wife can only reproach herself and refuse her husband's comfort. Shot and edited rather conventionally for the most part, the film is nonetheless of interest for its surface verisimilitude. The mill interiors and exteriors are done on location, and, except for Alice, the family can scarcely be differentiated from the other workers. The family's two-room dwelling is cold, cramped, and sparsely furnished with cheap furniture and utensils (interior and exterior spaces, however, don't always match). The final cemetery encounter occurs on snowy ground among barren trees, accentuating the pathos of the child's loss. The film also ends with an unusual series of flashback images, dissolving out of the shot in which the factory owner takes his wife's hand, moving through an elliptical reiteration of Alice's brief life and death, and dissolving back into the initial shot as the wife pulls away from her husband, who seems slightly exasperated. Their differing responses suggest no remedy for the family's working conditions; not even the wife's sense of shame will transform her husband into a benevolent capitalist.

"Any motion picture portraying deplorable social conditions is . . . an agent of good," Bush declared, especially one that had the temerity to "kill off" a child actor like the Thanhouser Kid; wherever *The Cry of the Children* was shown, he hoped, "converts to the necessity of thorough child labor reforms will be made by thousands" ("Social"). The impetus for what Bush calls "necessity" was the Federal Bureau established earlier in the year by Congress and President Taft—a body that immediately proved ineffectual because it was given no authority other than simply to investigate child labor conditions. Whether or not the Thanhouser film, along with Edison's, actually did have any direct impact on public discourse is unclear, but in June Massachusetts became the first state to enact a minimum wage law for women and children and Congress itself extended the eight-hour workday to all workers receiving federal contracts. The film definitely was used by unions and radicals: Steven Ross discovered in the *New York Call* that, on 26 August, Bronx socialists rented the Rose Theater for an evening program that included *The Cry of the Children*, *The Merchant of Venice*, socialist-produced newsreels of the Lawrence strike, other short films, and sing-alongs (106). More than a thousand men, women, and children thronged the theater, confirming labor activists' sense that producing and exhibiting motion pictures could be an effective part of their political work. *The Cry of the Children* also served as a valuable presidential campaign argument, as Bush had predicted, when the Democratic candidate, Woodrow Wilson, cited the film as an illustration of the Taft administration's failure to adequately address the "social problem" of child labor.

▨▨▨▨▨▨ *Queen Elizabeth:* The Multiple-Reel Historical Film

In September, *Billboard* claimed that "novelty foreign pictures [were] exceedingly popular," and nothing demonstrates that more clearly than *Queen Elizabeth*. New York exhibitor Adolph Zukor and Broadway producer Daniel Frohman founded Famous Players Film expressly to distribute this film, a three-reel adaptation of one of Sarah Bernhardt's recent stage roles. The Emile Moreau play had been a flop in Paris, and, to recoup her financial losses, Bernhardt agreed to reenact the role for a French-Anglo-American company, to which Zukor contributed major funding in exchange for rights to distribute the film in North America well before it would be released in France. After previewing the "artistically tinted and toned" film in New York for "a large and enthusiastic gathering of newspaper men and critics" and getting the MPPC to license its release, Famous Players adopted a combined roadshow and state rights strategy of distribution, modeled partly on what had worked so well for *Dante's Inferno* the year before. The company also Americanized the film by commissioning Joseph Carl Breil to compose a special orchestral score for its exhibition. On 12 August, *Queen Elizabeth* opened at the Powers Theater in Chicago for a five-week run (tickets cost between twenty-five cents and one dollar); by early September, it was playing in Marcus Loew's seventeen theaters throughout New York City—each of which, on average, drew "two hundred dollars a day more" than usual. For the next several months, on the added strength of excellent reviews and a front-cover illustration for *Photoplay* (September), Famous Players booked the film for roadshow engagements, usually for a week, at a range of legitimate theaters throughout the Midwest and, through state rights licensees, in major picture theaters throughout the Northeast and elsewhere. Zukor and Frohman's plan was to use the substantial profits from *Queen Elizabeth* to produce a series of feature-length American films, but unexpected difficulties in production and distribution soon brought the company close to bankruptcy.

The film focuses exclusively on the legendary "romance" between the aging queen and the youthful Essex (Lou Tellegen, the star's young lover at the time), who incites her jealousy by having an affair with the Countess of Nottingham, whose husband, in turn, frames Essex with a counterfeit letter. Essentially a melodrama of intersecting, duplicitous love triangles, the scenario follows the conventions of the well-made play. The first reel establishes Essex as the queen's favorite in a scene that includes a brief staging of Shakespeare's *The Merry Wives of Windsor* (Falstaff escapes detection for an amorous dalliance by hiding in a laundry basket), but it concludes with a fortune-teller who prophesies Elizabeth's unhappiness and Essex's doom. The second reel works out the intrigue between Essex and the Countess and Earl of Nottingham, climaxing in a public court scene in which the queen confronts Essex with the incriminating evidence (from which, unlike Falstaff, he cannot escape). The third then stages a series of spectacular moments as the predicted catastrophe falls on Essex, the countess, and

Essex (Lou Tellegen) kneels before Queen Elizabeth (Sarah Bernhardt) in a production still from *Queen Elizabeth*. *Photoplay* cover, September 1912.

eventually Elizabeth herself. Unlike most American (and French) films of the period, *Queen Elizabeth* adheres to an older tableau mode of representation, partly in order to highlight its historical accuracy (a point W. Stephen Bush stresses in his *Moving Picture World* review). The producers insisted, for instance, on using at least a dozen set decors from the theatrical production, including "dresses, armor, and furniture." The costumes alone contributed greatly to the emphasis on spectacle—the last one worn by Bernhardt, for instance, is a long ermine robe "with sleeves so widely bell-shaped that when her arms are horizontally extended, the bottom of the bell reaches the knees." The narrative also is fully articulated in no fewer than twenty-six intertitles, most of them quite lengthy, so that the action within the full shot/long shot tableaux largely illustrates a set of prior verbal texts. Moreover, several intertitles explicitly make a claim for historical accuracy (just as Griffith would do later, in *The Birth of a Nation*), particularly those exhibiting the queen's "authentic" signature in two documents: Essex's commission to quash an Irish rebellion and his "death warrant."

Although American audiences may have been drawn to the film as a history lesson, it is more likely that they were lured for other reasons. One was to see "the world's greatest actress" in a performance that did not rely, as had her frequent tours, on her extraordinary voice, speaking French. Instead, as the *Cleveland Leader* put it, audiences could attend to her "marvelous acting . . . her facial expressions and the 'business' that . . . conveyed the story." Another reason was the striking scenes of spectacle that marked the film's final reel. In one, the queen stands with her back to the camera, in the foreground, watching through a full-length window as Essex, in the background, passes from left to right toward the Tower; when the executioner comes on behind him, she orders the curtains drawn—so that the entire scene appears to be a theatrical tableau, one she can barely abide, staged by the queen herself. In the last scene, she deliberately stages an even more spectacular moment—her own death. Before an enormous pile of cushions just in front of the throne, Bernhardt stands unsteadily, surrounded by servants, sips an offered cup of wine, shakes her head at her image reflected in a mirror, stretches her arms out, suddenly clutches at her breast, staggers, recovers momentarily, and then pitches face forward into the cushions. Initial ads displayed a morbid fascination with this last reel, spinning it with sensational lines such as "MURDER" and "Sarah Bernhardt Is Going to Die!" One final reason for *Queen Elizabeth*'s success may be how well it coincided with the ever-increasing efforts to reestablish close bonds linking the United States with Great Britain. Reacting to the alleged threat of mass immigration from southern and eastern Europe at the turn of the last century, many writers had constructed a shared Anglo-Saxon heritage—historically, culturally, and especially racially—that seemingly erased the hostilities of a century or more earlier. Whether intended or not, *Queen Elizabeth* exploited that heritage by reimagining an age of chivalry and knighthood (often invoked by writers as a model of virile, Anglo-Saxon masculinity), transplanting the French production to London (where the film was shot), and "unmanning" the historical Elizabeth to remake her as an emotionally tragic woman.

▬▬▬▬▬ *The Confederate Ironclad:* The Civil War Film

The Civil War was commemorated in a variety of ways during what was called the "Golden Jubilee" years of 1911–1915. There were countless newspaper and magazine stories, editions of histories and photo albums, reenactments of famous battles (stage-managed by veterans), and local historical pageants that included war episodes. As a popular subject, the Golden Jubilee celebrations provided a crucial impulse and context for the production and marketing of so many Civil War films during these years. Whereas Civil War films from Biograph tended to focus on domestic or family-oriented stories that traced a trajectory of departure, sacrifice, and return (reworking a stage melodrama tradition), those of Kalem and Selig tended to follow the "school of action" formula of sensational melodrama. Whatever the formula or orientation, however, by this time the majority of Civil War films were "Southern war pictures," with active heroines usually the principal characters, often as "girl spies." With its studio in Jacksonville, Florida, Kalem was in the forefront of producing such films as *A Spartan Mother* (March) and *The Drummer Girl of Vicksburg* (June). Perhaps inspired by Bison-101's multiple-reel westerns, the company began giving greater emphasis to spectacular scenes in its own two-reel Civil War films such as *The Siege of Petersburg* (July) and *The Darling of the C.S.A.* (September). Although only one reel in length, *The Confederate Ironclad* (October) combines spectacle elements of Kalem's previous films—mass attacks, locomotive chases, bridge burnings—with the novelty of a climactic river gunboat battle. Ads for the film highlighted these sensational scenes; in the *Minneapolis Journal,* the Confederate ironclad was even turned into a fantastical creature, a freakish "sea monster." It is likely, as Scott Simmon suspects, that the film's ironclad is a replica of the *Merrimack*, constructed for a commemorative reenactment, around which Kalem simply devised a melodramatic story (*Treasures* 10). Finally, the film had the added attraction of a commissioned piano score (by Walter Cleveland Simon), which belongs,

Lieutenant Yancy (Guy Coombs) and his "Southern sweetheart" (Miriam Cooper) allow Elinor (Anna Q. Nilsson) and a Union officer to escape in the final shot of *The Confederate Ironclad*.

Martin Marks writes, to "the earliest series of fully written out American film scores known to survive" (*Treasures* 10).

The Confederate Ironclad begins with a rivalry for the affections of Lieutenant Yancy (Guy Coombs), pitting his "Southern sweetheart," Rose (Miriam Cooper), against Elinor (Nilsson), a neighbor's orphaned niece from the North. Elinor is a "girl spy," however, and she gets Yancy to reveal the location of the ironclad, which she quickly relays to Union forces. The latter attack and overrun the Confederate forces, but Yancy escapes, discovers the ironclad is low on gunpowder, and rides off to reach a powder train. He and Rose jump into the train's locomotive and elude pursuing Union soldiers; when he is wounded, Rose takes the locomotive's controls, guides the train over a bridge that Elinor has set afire, and uncouples one burning flatcar just before it explodes. The gunpowder delivered, the ironclad does battle with Union gunboats and triumphs. Yancy captures Elinor, but Rose persuades him to be "a generous foe" and allow her to escape on horseback with a Union officer. The film makes an exemplary display of Kalem's impressive camerawork and economical editing. The first is noteworthy in the shot of Rose and Yancy's first meeting on a foreground platform overlooking a big rail yard, in high-angle long shots of a diagonal line of Confederate cannon confronting the Union attack, in long shot/extreme long shots of the powder train looming over the Confederate soldiers in the left foreground as Union horsemen ride in from the right background, and in the shot of Rose running back over one flatcar, uncoupling the burning flatcar, and running forward and off camera before it explodes. The editing is deft in the integration of long and close shots during the locomotive run, notably during the scene when Rose guides it over the burning bridge. In contrast to the rest of the film, the climactic gunboat battle seems awkwardly handled (at least to twenty-first-century eyes). Yet in the context of reenactments involving the *Merrimack* (which most audiences would not have viewed), the scene may have worked effectively because it reproduces the historical phenomenon of spectators watching such battles from the safety of the shore. Moreover, the film tries to include the audience here by having Rose, Yancy, and Elinor serve as stand-in spectators.

The Confederate Ironclad represents another instance of sensational melodrama, like "cowboy girl" westerns and Kalem's contemporary "railway thrillers," whose narratives are driven by active heroines. Although Rose and Elinor are first established as romantic rivals, they quickly become antagonists in the more serious struggle between Confederate and Union forces. Each woman single-handedly drives the narrative's advance at key points, Elinor by revealing the secret location of the ironclad and then burning the railroad bridge, Rose by multi-tasking—bandaging Yancy, controlling the locomotive, and saving enough gunpowder to supply the ironclad. Moreover, it is the southern woman who concludes the film with an act of generosity, with the implication that later the North will owe the South an equal measure of generosity. The film also is representative of many of the period's Civil War films in that it accepts the "nationalist" tradition of historiography, led by the influential work of James Ford Rhodes, that claimed the South's secession was as honorable as the Union's preservation was necessary. That tradition assumed the myth of the "Lost Cause," whose effect was to grant a nostalgic dignity to the suffering and sacrifices of white Southerners during the war, out of which a "new South" might emerge. The widespread acceptance in the North of the Lost Cause ideology and its nostalgia for a vanishing, allegedly honorable past (simply erasing slavery) goes a long way toward explaining the appeal of "Southern war pictures" across much of the United States. As stories of reconciliation, these films presented a cultural "reconstruction" of the South and its subjected white "aliens" (not unlike many immigrants), making them acceptable once again for assimilation within a framework of "national harmony and patriotism." Although later multiple-reel Civil War films tended to tell stories of a resurgent male heroism (now northern as well as southern), which the *Cleveland Leader* pronounced "worthy of exhibition in every school in the country," "Southern war pictures" like *The Confederate Ironclad* also did their part in supporting Dudley Miles's claim, in his famous 1913 essay "The Civil War as a Unifier," that by this time "the war deepened and spread the sense of nationality" (188).

The Indian Massacre: The Multiple-Reel Indian Picture

Among the more popular genres in the early 1910s were westerns of one kind or another: cowboy films like the Broncho Billy series, "cowboy girl" films like Kalem's *The Girl Deputy* (with Ruth Roland), and Indian pictures like Bison's *Little Dove's Romance* (with Mona Darkfeather). Repeated trade press criticism—an example is *Moving Picture World*'s "The Indian and the Cowboy (By One Who Doesn't Like Them)"—denigrated many of these until the multiple-reel Bison-101 Indian pictures that the New York Motion Picture Company began making early this year not only dispelled that criticism but also increased audience interest: everyone now wanted "Wild West pictures." The company promoted its first title, *War on the Plains* (February), as marking a "new era in western pictures"; in a full-page story devoted to its release, the *World* compared it favorably to the latest historical spectacular from Italy, Ambrosio's *The Golden Wedding*, suggesting that the trade press saw such films as noteworthy rivals of the Italian imports that were transforming film distribution and exhibition. This was the first American effort, *Billboard* added, to produce "fictional features" for regular weekly or biweekly release. By the time that *The Indian Massacre* (March) and *Blazing the Trail* (April) appeared, the trade press was absolutely taken with Bison-101 Indian pictures. In an unprecedented four pages in the *World*, Louis Reeves Harrison told the story of *The Indian Massacre*, and he followed that more than a month later with a laudatory overview of "The 'Bison-101' Headliners": "The New York Motion Picture Company is certainly engaged in blazing the trail of artistic achievement so far as depicting battle scenes is concerned, as I have never seen action more vivid and realistic" (Harrison 320).

The Indian Massacre begins in an Indian encampment, where Ravenwing's baby has just died, and at the Browns' settler cabin, where another mother cradles her baby as the father goes off to plow. In the third scene, an Indian hunting party comes upon a white scout they have named "Bad Medicine" who has just shot a buffalo; when they attack, three of their small party are killed. These scenes quickly and economically set up a narrative in which the struggle between Indians and white settlers is driven by parallel desires, each crucial to the other's survival. The first involves food and escalates into an attack on the larger white settlement and a retaliatory massacre of the Indian encampment—hence, the film's ambiguous title. The second involves offspring and during the initial massacre leads to the seizure of Mrs. Brown and her baby, in order to replace the dead Indian child. Just before the retaliatory massacre, however, Ravenwing takes pity on the white woman, secretly returns her child, and allows her to escape. A *New York Dramatic Mirror* reviewer praised these Indian pictures for their "intense figure compositions" and "marvelously clear . . . larger ensembles" (27), and the camerawork in *The Indian Massacre* certainly is impressive. The Indians attack the white settlement in an unusual high-angle, extreme long shot that stresses the choreography of the action, and they later descend on the foreground cabin from over a distant hill in the background. This contrast between foreground and background figures recurs at several other key moments: as the scout first sights several distant buffalo; as the Indian party sights him, in a high-angle long shot; as he fires at the Indians charging him from over a distant hill; and as he and white settlers crawl into the foreground and spring up to attack the Indian encampment. Other long-shot tableaux serve to make the women of the two antagonists parallel victims: in one, Mrs. Brown stumbles among the bodies strewn around the burning cabins; in another, Indian women mourn their dead at the ravaged encampment. In a final long shot tableau, in an indelible image of sacrifice, Ravenwing stands silhouetted on a bare hilltop, her arms raised high to the fragile pole platform on which her dead child rests.

Bison-101 productions like *The Indian Massacre* had a huge impact in exhibition and served not only to promote the Independents as a whole but also to further establish the western as a serious American subject. In Boston, *The Indian Massacre* was given a special advance screening for exhibitors and pronounced big in every sense of the word. In Cleveland, *War on the Plains* reportedly had "crowds waiting for seats" at the downtown Mall ("Latest"). In Lynn, Bison-101 Indian pictures played exclusively at the Central Square over a four-month period and were the sole feature attractions all week in late May and early June. Similarly, in Minneapolis, from late February through June, these "thrilling headliners" played first at the Crystal (usually in four-day runs) and then at the Isis (on weekends), where *The Lieutenant's Last Fight* (June) "arouse[d] the most hardened of moving picture fans" with its depiction of "war in all its realism" ("What's Offered"). That fall, Kay-Bee and Broncho westerns like *The Invaders*

Ravenwing (Anna Little) in silhouette mourns her dead baby in the last shot of The *Indian Massacre*. A production still reprinted in the trade press.

(November) more than confirmed the genre's audience appeal and "educational value," in the words of the *Cleveland Leader,* as "historic subjects that are worthy of exhibition in every school in the country" ("Latest"). Equally popular in Europe, the Bison-101 Indian pictures were the earliest imported American films in regular release that ran more than one reel, putting them in the same category as the Italian, French, Danish, and German multiple-reel films then coming into vogue. That, in turn, enhanced their status not only as a distinctly American product but also as a potential national epic, in which the conquest of the West offered a foundational story of national identity (however illusory), a mythic narrative of origins. In this myth, the "vanishing American" or Indian was an especially salient figure for what Renato Rosaldo has called the "imperialist nostalgia" for the defeated Heroic Other—stunningly epitomized in *The Indian Massacre*'s final tableau (Fabian 32–33). In many of these films, the "vanishing American" served as an emblematic figure of exclusion from, or assimilation into— and, either way, justified—a new "imperial" American nation. Neatly summarized in the narrative trajectory of *The Indian Massacre*, the Bison-101 Indian pictures enacted an ongoing ritual performance of "innovative nostalgia" that, in the new medium of motion pictures, articulated nostalgic imagery within a dynamic framework oriented toward the future.

1913

████████████

Movies and the Beginning of a New Era

CHARLIE KEIL

At what point did the United States become a modern nation? When did the American cinema make the transition from small-scale industry to mass entertainment, from novelty to an accomplished storytelling medium? Such changes are gradual ones and can't be attributed to the events of a single year. Even so, this year assumes particular significance in the development of American society and cinema, because it witnesses a series of transformative moments whose cumulative effect confers upon the year a special status. A new president, propelled by a belief system tied to social improvement and government activism, comes into office; the nation embraces numerous trends ushering in modernity; and, in tandem with the development of a star system and the move to custom-built theaters, motion pictures achieve a new level of national prominence, shedding their reliance on the single-reel format to welcome the advent of the feature-film era. As America moves more decisively into the modern age, cinema also establishes itself, with greater confidence than ever before, as the medium best suited to entertain a nation in transition.

President-elect Woodrow Wilson is inaugurated in March, fortifying the influence of Progressivism within the country. Progressivism, espousing the value of limiting the concentration of capital, of promoting an ideal of collective national self-identity, and of recognizing technology's role in improving society, underwrites many of Wilson's earliest initiatives (Blanke 4). In Wilson's first year in office, a domestic reform package labeled "New Freedom" advocates passage of the Underwood Tariff (aimed at tariff reduction, but also including a provision for a national income tax), and of the Federal Reserve Act (laying the foundations for a central banking system operated by the federal government).

Temperance, suffrage, and civil rights, key issues that will dominate the decade, find variable levels of support from the federal government and the public alike. Even before Wilson takes office, the Webb-Kenyon Act, outlawing the interstate transport of liquor from a jurisdiction where drinking is allowed to a "dry" one, passes, despite a veto by lame-duck President Taft. Sympathy for suffrage is buoyed when an angry crowd denounces a parade of 5,000 women marching up Pennsylvania Avenue the day before Wilson's inauguration. Despite Wilson's reputation as a Progressive, the president thwarts those reformers pushing for more activist legislation (such as limits on child labor and support for farmers). It soon becomes clear that the Wilson administration's Progressive agenda does not extend to African Americans, with the president quoted as saying, "Segregating is not humiliating but a benefit." Such a quote may strike us as particularly ironic in the year that witnesses the death of Underground Railroad legend Harriet Tubman and the birth of a future civil rights pioneer, Rosa Parks.

The modernization of American society continues apace, with a variety of social trends marking the country's growing acceptance of transformative technologies. The principles of Taylorism inform the operations of industry, as witnessed by Henry Ford's newly opened Highland Park plant in Michigan, which speeds assembly of the Model T. Mary Phelps Jacob inaugurates a revolution in women's undergarments when she patents the backless brassiere, which will eventually supersede the constraining corset. The American debut, and immediate popularity, of dancers Irene and Vernon Castle helps usher in lifestyle trends ranging from the ascendancy of the wristwatch as the preferred male timepiece to more physical contact between the sexes on the dance floor. American Francis Ouimet's come-from-behind victory at the U.S. Golf Association Open broadens appeal of the sport, while professional baseball's popularity leads to the creation of a third league, the Federal League. The Actors' Equity Association emerges to secure expanded rights for theatrical performers. A notable number of established female authors publish books this year, including Willa Cather and Edith Wharton, but Gertrude Stein stands apart in her continued experimentation with prose style in *Tender Buttons*. And the modern era announces its arrival with two signal events occurring in that most modern of American cities, New York: the February staging of the Armory Show, which revolutionizes U.S. attitudes toward modernist art, and the completion of the iconic skyscraper, the Woolworth Building, labeled the "Cathedral of Commerce."

A Year of Expansion: Building Theaters, Exploiting Stars, Making Features

Key developments of this year point toward a transformation of the American film industry that will be largely complete by the end of the decade. In the exhibition sector, one sees the initiation of the move toward the so-called "picture palace," theaters built on a grand scale for the express purpose of screening motion pictures. In February, the Regent Theatre, designed by Thomas Lamb, becomes the first so-called "de luxe" theater in Manhattan to devote itself to a program dominated by movies rather than vaudeville. The Regent's management offers printed programs, an eight-piece orchestra, New York's first movie pipe organ, and uniformed ushers. Even so, the Regent flounders in its location at the southern tip of Harlem (home at this time of a largely German immigrant population) until the budding showman Samuel "Roxy" Rothapfel takes over its management in the fall. By all accounts, Rothapfel injects even more allure by spending heavily on a larger orchestra, a more elaborate stage for the screen, and improved projection. His additional enhancements mark the Regent as a sterling example of how capital investments can achieve the goal of uplift that continues to obsess the film industry. As confirmation, here is a representative approving assessment of the Regent under Roxy's control, appearing in a December review from *Motion Picture News*:

> The handsome and comfortable interior of the Regent has much to do with the success of the performance. There is no finer theatre in New York in point of construction, and Mr. Rothapfel's skillful attention to details has given the interior a refinement not to be equalled in a single other theatre here. The audience, it should be noted, while made up of persons living in the neighborhood of the Regent, was of the kind to be found in the best playhouses. Judged by their decorum and sincere appreciation, they might have been at the opera.   (qtd. in Hall 35)

As part of its concerted effort to attract an expanded audience including those persons likely to "be found in the best playhouses," the industry embarks on changes at the production level, designed to further distinguish motion pictures as a special form of mass entertainment. Certain of these innovations are technological in nature, aimed at taking cinema beyond its status as a mute, monochromatic viewing experience. Kinemacolor receives its biggest marketing push this year, though it was first demonstrated publicly in the United States in 1909. The Kinemacolor process consists of "shooting panchromatic black and white film with alternating frames exposed through green and red filters. These filters [are] also alternated in the projection process with the eye synthesizing the images from a color spectrum" (Musser, "On 'Extras'" 169). Kinemacolor proves to be a short-lived novelty, doomed by the need for expensive special projectors, and does not last out the year as a viable commercial endeavor. Similarly, Edison's Kinetophone, an attempt to market "talking pictures" by employing synchronized cylinder records, fails on all levels, offering poor sound quality, inadequate volume, and erratic synchronization in its disappointing debuts in March on the Keith-Orpheum theater circuit.

Far more significant for the long-term development of the industry is the introduction of feature films. Having mastered the one-reel format, many directors chafe against the limitations imposed by the 1,000-foot limit and agitate for longer running times. D. W. Griffith, the period's preeminent filmmaker, completes the four-reel epic, *Judith of Bethulia*, only to see the film's release delayed because the company responsible for distributing the film, Biograph, cannot devise an effective method of delivering a long-form film to theaters. (Griffith will finally part ways with the company, officially resigning in October, after over five years as Biograph's chief director.) Logistical constraints imposed by entrenched systems of distribution prevent established releasing companies from experimenting with feature-length productions. Newer, more flexible concerns lead the way instead. Among the more prominent are Warner's Features, Inc., a reorganized version of a previously established company, and a forerunner of industry mainstay Warner Bros.; the Lasky Feature Play Company, one of whose founders is future studio-era producing titan Samuel Goldwyn; and Famous Players Company, arguably the most prominent of all, especially once it merges with the newly formed distribution company, Paramount Pictures Corporation. Famous Players' canny leader, Adolph Zukor, recognizes that the presence of prominent theatrical stars will help to sell feature-length properties, and so one sees such luminaries of the stage as Minnie Maddern Fiske (*Tess of the D'Urbervilles*) and James O'Neill (*The Count of Monte Cristo*) appearing in the company's early successes.

But even as Famous Players demonstrates a talent for exploiting the growing interest in features, its insistence on casting aging stars from the legitimate theater runs counter to another important trend within the industry: the cultivation of a star system from within the ranks of motion picture performers. For several years, many of the major film companies have made a practice of publicizing their actors' names, and, now, credit titles commonly appear within films. But in this year, studios raise the importance of stars in the promotion of films to an unprecedented level, through advertising campaigns, contests in magazines, the sale of novelty items bearing the likeness of stars, and the coordination of personal appearances, interviews, and profiles. A new era of high-profile contracts and lavish salaries confirms the centrality of stars to the film industry, as Keystone signs vaudeville sensation Charles Chaplin in May, and Marion Leonard is paid $1,000 a week when she forms her own production company. This dependency on stars to sell motion pictures only accelerates as moviemaking activity continues to migrate to the West Coast, and production procedures (and related mechanisms for marketing films) become more systematic in the process.

Despite the growing presence of multi-reel productions, the well-established film genres continue to flourish as single reelers, with release rates exceeding 200 titles each month by mid-year. Everything from marital comedies (*A Matrimonial Deluge* [Lubin], *The Innocent Bridegroom* [Crystal]) to moral dramas (*The Minister's Temptation* [Edison], *The Tiger* [Vitagraph]) to thrilling adventures, typically set out west (*The Trail of Cards* [American], *Pedro's Revenge* [Majestic]), fill the schedules of a burgeoning slate of producers. Filmmakers show increasing confidence in their handling of cinematic style and narrative structure, a confidence that translates into often innovative treatment of proven formulae. But amidst the familiar, novelty also emerges in the last days of December, with the debut of the first installment of the serial *The Adventures of Kathlyn*, following on the heels of 1912's success *What Happened to Mary*. The serial—featuring scenes of derring-do performed by a prominent female star, produced as an open-ended series of single-reel "episodes," and typically released in tandem with a "fictionalization" tie-in published in local newspapers—typifies as well as any form of filmed entertainment the manner in which motion pictures continue to reinvent themselves in this year of change.

A Typical Film: *The Ambassador's Daughter*

If this year merits consideration as a watershed in the history of the American cinema, the advent of the feature deserves recognition as the development with the most long-ranging consequences. Yet the majority of films produced in the year remained single-reelers, and arguably cinematic form achieved a certain stability in its expressive means at the precise moment when features were introduced, bringing with them more changes to the style and narrative of U.S. motion pictures. The large number of 1,000-foot films produced this year afforded their makers an opportunity to experiment, as certain enterprising directors, such as D. W. Griffith, would do in acknowledged masterworks including *The House of Darkness*, *Death's Marathon*, and *The Mothering Heart*. (For analyses of these works in the context of Griffith's late Biograph career, see Keil "Transition.") Overall, the continued reliance on the single-reel format typically translated into increased assurance in handling performance, staging, and editing. This solidified into a set of norms that most filmmakers would employ with min-

imal variation. Analyzing *The Ambassador's Daughter*, a representative production from industry mainstay Edison, offers an opportunity for an in-
depth understanding of the way these norms play out in an ordinary film
from this year.

The narrative of *The Ambassador's Daughter* is easily relayed in the
course of its 1,000-foot length, as the film relies on little more than a situation to propel its complicating actions. The plot involves minimally motivated intrigue, with "foreign conspirators" responsible for the theft of some
important government papers that the title character, Helen, ultimately
helps to retrieve. As will become increasingly common at this time, the narrative depends upon what might be termed a "double causal structure,"
insofar as the daughter's actions are designed not only to undo the villains
but also exonerate her beloved, Richard, who has been falsely accused of
the theft. At the end, the villains are thwarted and the couple reunited. The
film bookends the main plotline involving the theft with scenes establishing the romance between the two protagonists, demonstrating in its own
structure how the couple's relationship envelops the core narrative.

The film's handling of its mise-en-scène is in line with norms of the
period. The performing style is generally understated, with most gesturing
fairly muted and actors intent on interacting with one another so as to reinforce the believability of the depicted fiction. The interplay between Helen
and Richard is sustained via a number of strategies. In the first scene, which
exists only to define their relationship, the two interact through a mock dis-
pute over the lamentable quality of Richard's singing and piano playing.
Helen attempts to school him in more appropriate musicianship, but to no
avail. (The scene relies on Helen's amusing reactions to Richard's off-key
efforts, and one could well imagine that the film would have benefited from
a live accompanist to punctuate this scene with the appropriate musical
flourishes when the film was shown in theaters.) Later, the film will integrate the couple's flirting into the intrigue plotline by having Richard's act
of taking Helen's glove misinterpreted as the possible theft of the documents. This use of a privileged prop not only provides the actors with a
means to convey affection through a shared object, but also signals the
double resolution of the narrative when Richard can finally return the
glove to Helen. The parallels between romance and intrigue are further
emphasized when the foreign conspirators are revealed to be two lovers,
their interactions somewhat reminiscent of those of the main couple.

In terms of staging, *The Ambassador's Daughter* employs a modified version of multi-planar compositions, often placing action in both the foreground and mid-background: in the first shot, the couple retires to a settee

Modified multiplanar staging: the interplay between Helen (Miriam Nesbitt) and Richard (George Lessey) involving a lost glove occurs in the midground while discovery of the theft of a valuable document by her father (Robert Brower) occupies the foreground in *The Ambassador's Daughter*.

in the background once their sparring at the piano in the foreground has ended; in the second shot, the film announces its reliance on multiple planes of action quite self-consciously when, a few moments into the shot, curtains are parted and figures dancing in the background are revealed, both to the characters in the foreground and to the film's viewers; most of the scenes in the ambassador's office involve competing areas of action, balancing activity at his desk near the front of the frame with other bits of business taking place farther back. The film's emphasis on staging extended actions in many of its shots leads to a somewhat longer average shot length than one finds in more action-oriented films from this year. Accordingly, the film's editing rate is fairly steady for most of its twenty-seven shots, though the pace hastens in the film's final sections, when Helen discovers and reclaims the stolen documents. This section also involves the film's only real instance of a type of intra-scene editing, with Helen's viewing of the conspirators intercut with different vantage points of the same action. As is often the case during this period, an instance of a character looking on at narratively significant action necessitates formal strategies distinct from those employed elsewhere in the film as a whole. In this case, the series of

shots showing Helen spying on the thieves involves the film's only examples of mobile framing (a pan) and altered shot scale (as the camera
adjusts to a tighter framing once Helen is able to establish that the conspirators do have the stolen documents).

For the most part, then, *The Ambassador's Daughter* operates within
fairly prescribed stylistic parameters, and this formal predictability comple-
ments the film's familiar story. In turn, the narrative formulae that the film
relies upon reinforce widely held social beliefs. This becomes most obvious
at the film's climax, when Helen's enterprising actions (and inquisitive
gaze) invite retribution from the conspirators, resulting in her imperilment.
Tellingly, even though Helen initially acted to ensure that Richard would
not be wrongly accused, it rests with him to be the true agent of salvation.
In many ways, *The Ambassador's Daughter* prefigures the narrative pattern-
ing of the serial, wherein the intrepid heroine may initiate the action, but
must ultimately depend on a male figure to put matters right. The measure
of independence accorded women, both onscreen and off, remained limited, by narrative convention in the former instance and by legislation in
the latter.

Women at the Wheel: *Matrimony's Speed Limit* and *Suspense*

The Ambassador's Daughter's typicality also extends to its focus on a female
protagonist: many films from this period feature a heroine at the center of
the story. Prominent on the screen, women still played a more circumscribed role behind the scenes. Most female labor was confined to work in
the craft areas, such as wardrobe and editing. Even so, a number of women
were beginning to make their mark in the higher profile realm of direction
or writing for the screen. Some, such as Gene Gauntier and Mabel Normand, parlayed their status as stars into expanded control of the properties
in which they performed. Two who established their reputations as true
hyphenates, writing and directing their own films, were Alice Guy Blaché
and Lois Weber. Guy, the head of production at Gaumont in France at the
end of the previous decade, had come to the United States with her husband in 1907, working for the U.S. branch of Gaumont before founding
her own company, Solax, in 1910. Weber, also under hire at the American
arm of Gaumont while Guy was there, functioned as a writer, director, and
actor for the company, often in collaboration with her husband, Phillips
Smalley. She continued working at a number of studios before settling at
Universal during the year. In fact, this year marks a turning point in these

two directors' careers: Guy's activity as a director would diminish from this point onward, culminating in the eventual dissolution of Solax by 1920, while Weber's output continued to draw acclaim until she became the highest-paid filmmaker in the country by mid-decade. Guy's *Matrimony's Speed Limit* and Weber's *Suspense* give evidence of how each of these directors invested the conventions of the day with a sensibility that rendered their films distinctive. In this instance, both directors employ the oft-used device of the last-minute rescue in ways that foreground the roles women typically play in such scenarios of imperilment.

Matrimony's Speed Limit highlights Guy's attraction to the comic potential of marital misunderstandings, already showcased in *A Comedy of Errors* (1912) and *A House Divided*. The latter film, likely filmed at the same time as *Speed Limit*, renders the prospect of divorce humorous by featuring a couple that stays together in the same household but refuses to communicate verbally. In *Matrimony's Speed Limit*, on the other hand, Guy focuses on the process leading to marriage, using the premise of a time-limited inheritance to hasten the prospective groom's choice of a mate. Unbeknownst to the man, however, his former fiancée has engineered this scenario to ensure that he will marry her. The film's race to the rescue thus thrusts the woman into the figurative driver's seat, as she commandeers a car to rush her to her beau's side—with a minister in tow—in time for her to take her place as the rightful bride. Guy comically inverts the standard situation of the last-minute rescue so that the woman is put in the position of "saving" the man, not from bodily harm but from an ill-chosen alliance with any number of strangers.

What drives the narrative contrivances forward is the constant pressure of money. The man, Fraunie, decides that he must call off his engagement to Marian because a bad investment has crippled his earning power. Marian offers him her considerable wealth (thrusting bank books and financial documents in his face as proof), but these only remind him of his own failure. Once the promise of the inheritance arrives via telegram, the prospect of financial security motivates Fraunie's every action, but the knowledge that the windfall will elude him once the deadline has passed invests his desire to propose with a manic intensity. The satirical thrust of *Matrimony's Speed Limit* skewers two commonly held social beliefs of the time: first, that a man should control his financial destiny; and second, that the root of marriage should be romantic love. The film systematically rejects the first premise, by asserting throughout that Marian has the means to control Fraunie's actions, whether he knows her to be the source of that control or not. (Interestingly, the telegram Marian devises as part of her ruse informs

Fraunie that the inheritance that hangs in the balance derives from his aunt, still identifying the source of the riches as a woman.) And the questioning of the second asserts itself with each ill-advised proposal Fraunie makes to a variety of unsuspecting women. The inappropriateness of his selections escalates with each example: he moves from a washer-woman to an unattractive spinster to a resistant passerby to a veiled woman who eventually reveals herself to be an African American. Though she seems as perplexed as the others to be so propositioned, she is the only one that Fraunie himself rejects as an unsuitable choice, showing that the divide of race is the one obstacle that cannot be overcome, even in the pursuit of financial advancement.

Matrimony's Speed Limit crosscuts between these episodes of deromanticized offers of marriage and shots of Marian careening through the streets, rushing to ensure that *she* becomes Fraunie's bride before noon. Guy stresses the temporal pressure that frames both Fraunie's quest for a mate and Marian's search for Fraunie by inserting no fewer than eight close-ups of Fraunie's watch, as the minute hand advances on twelve o'clock. In this she parodies the conventions of the race to the rescue that had become familiar to viewers by this time. When Marian arrives in time for the marriage to take place, Fraunie has all but given up, lying down on the road and inviting his own demise. Still unaware that Marian has orchestrated the contrivance designed to ensure that their nuptials occur, he willingly submits to the impromptu ceremony. Guy provides a witty visual commentary on this degraded example of "true love's union" by showing a steamroller advancing on the couple's vehicle as they embrace.

Suspense offers what seems at first glance a much more predictable scenario, reproducing the standard woman-in-distress situation that had characterized the most famous of the race-to-the-rescue screen incarnations. It owes a particular debt to Griffith's *The Lonely Villa* (1909), itself a remake of a Pathé film from a year earlier, *The Physician of the Castle*. The narrative ingredients could not be simpler: a woman (played by director Lois Weber), stranded alone in her remote home once her maid quits, is menaced by an intruding vagrant, who eventually forces himself into the room in which she has barricaded herself and her infant child. The woman's only hope of salvation is her husband, who rushes to save her once he is alerted to her plight by telephone, this before the burglar breaks off communication by cutting the line. Where *Suspense* differs from its forebears is in the stylistic details, and, ultimately, how these shift the focus to the woman's plight, thereby endowing the last-minute rescue with more than just a kinetic charge. Arguably, *Suspense* is the first version of such a rescue that suggests, from the woman's point of view, what is at stake when an intrusion of this nature occurs. Earlier treatments tended to highlight the (male) rescuer's ingenuity or determination, framing the rescue as a test of a man's ability to protect that which belongs to him. *Suspense* redirects the viewer's attention toward male aggression and female fear, repositioning the rescue as an instrument designed to render domestic space safe for its chief inhabitant.

The film carefully builds up a sense of the woman's isolation and entrapment. When the maidservant deserts the house, she leaves a note explaining that she can't tolerate living in such a "lonesome" place. Once the woman discovers the maid's absence, she moves from one space to another, establishing the expanse of the house (as well as the distance the intruder will have to traverse to find where the wife has sequestered herself once she discovers his presence). Her home does not function as a sanctuary, but only as a reminder of her vulnerability: her second-floor bedroom window offers her a vantage point on the tramp's entry into the house, rendered as a frightening overhead close-up of his upturned face; the telephone that she uses to notify her husband is rendered useless when the tramp uses the kitchen knife he finds to disconnect the line; and her barricaded bedroom door offers little resistance to the intruder's insistent and violent act of smashing through the wood (also conveyed as a tight framing of his hand, wrapped in a protective bandana, thrusting into the bedroom). This latter moment constitutes the climax of the film and the third shot in a remarkable four-shot sequence that emphasizes the wife's sense of helplessness in light of the tramp's violent attack on the most pri-vate of domestic spaces, the bedroom. The sequence begins with a shot of the tramp ascending the stairs heading for the bedroom, his steady progress culminating in his face passing directly toward the camera, which results in a looming extreme close-up, an effect quite unusual for this era. This is fol-lowed directly by a shot of the woman clutching her baby and retreating to the point farthest from the door. The door, barricaded by a dresser holding a vanity mirror and vase, is nearest to the foreground, and the subsequent, aforementioned shot of the tramp breaking through the door is a closer framing of this left side of the bedroom, still retaining the mirror and vase. When his fist bursts through, it topples the vase from the dresser top, emphasizing the degree to which his forced entry destroys the sanctity of the woman's personal space. The fourth shot, also closely scaled, shows us another part of the bedroom, the area occupied by the wife and baby. She is shown screaming in reaction to the violation, and the concerted effect of three close-ups in such rapid succession lends the moment an emotional

A distinctive triptych shows three related spheres of action at a pivotal moment in *Suspense*. Director Lois Weber plays the woman in peril, Valentine Paul her husband, and Sam Kaufman the intruder.

intensity that relates directly to the woman's sense of vulnerability and panic.

Running parallel to the events depicting the woman's escalating endangerment are her husband's efforts to reach the home to save her. Before the race to the rescue begins, the film employs a self-conscious triptych composition to relate the woman, her husband, and the tramp, all three occupying distinct spaces. In the first use of the triptych, the woman receives a call from her husband telling her that he will be home late from work; at this point, she is unaware of the tramp's presence outside the home, and her sense of relative safety, shared by her husband, is rendered ironic by the inclusion of the tramp within the composition. The second use, actually a sequence of three variations on the same triptych, separated by dialogue intertitles, involves the woman informing her husband of the tramp gaining entry to the house. While the action in the two sectors depicting the woman and her husband remains virtually the same, the portion that shows the tramp varies considerably, as he moves from the exterior of the house to inside. More to the point, his progress is registered as a series of three elliptically connected shots, the first showing his feet over the door mat where the key has been hidden, the second his face at the door, and the third nothing more than a dangling telephone cord. The triptych seems an inspired way to place the woman and tramp in proximity even before he is physically close to her, but equally to suggest how the causes of the woman's distress propel the husband to action.

The cutting of the cord ends any telephone communication and initiates the actual race to the home, a rescue effort further complicated by the husband stealing another man's car for his vehicle. This results in the husband himself being pursued by police, so that the race involves the threat of his own capture, a delay that would seal his wife's doom. Rather than relying on predictable imagery of vehicles shown speeding down streets, *Suspense* often depicts the chase from the perspective of one of the two automobiles involved. Of particular interest are those moments when the camera is positioned within the husband's car: the closely framed shots capture the pursuing police from the vantage point of his rearview mirror while he looks distractedly over his shoulder. Rather than conveying a sense of speed, these shots offer a rather claustrophobic sense of imminent capture, with the police car often within arm's reach of the pursued vehicle. Tellingly, the emphasis on the mirror relates these shots visually to the bedroom space with its prominently positioned vanity mirror. In its insistence on the shared vulnerability of husband and wife, *Suspense* downplays heroics to convey the sensation of threat to the marital bond from an external source.

Suspense and *Matrimony's Speed Limit*, each in its own way, demonstrates how the race to the rescue, though traditionally aligned with the thrills of an action-oriented cinema, could still be employed for other ends, be they lighthearted social critique or the embodiment of psychological stress. Weber and Guy were not alone in mining such conventions for unexpected effects, but few other directors treated situations affecting women with the same sensitivity.

Moviemaking on the Screen: *The Evidence of the Film* and *Mabel's Dramatic Career*

When cinema was little more than a novelty, one could find occasional examples of motion pictures that depicted the filmgoing experience, typically for comic effect (such as *Uncle Josh at the Moving Picture Show*, from 1902, or 1904's *The Story the Biograph Told*). By the early 1910s, filmmakers were responding to the pervasiveness of their own medium in slightly different ways, either by extending the dimensions of the earlier Biograph title to incorporate the phenomenon of stardom, as one finds in *Mabel's Dramatic Career*, or integrating aspects of the filmmaking process even more fully into the developing narrative armature of the single-reeler, as in *The Evidence of the Film*. Viewed together, these films provide their own evidence: that film in all its facets was now sufficiently known and accepted as a part of mainstream entertainment that to invoke it spoke to a shared cultural experience.

In the previous year, Mack Sennett, who had trained at Biograph under Griffith, quickly established his studio, Keystone, as one of the most popular producers of a particular type of knockabout comedy known as slapstick. Keystone comedies feature an endless array of flailing bodies, thrown objects, and breathless chases. Equally important to Keystone's approach, however, is a spirit of exaggeration and parody, and in *Mabel's Dramatic Career*, particularly the second half, the parodic impulse extends to dizzying levels, as the film looks to the Keystone brand itself for inspiration. If the first half of the film offers much to elicit humor, especially those moments when Mabel Normand attacks anyone who crosses her with a fervor bordering on the maniacal, the latter section, depicting her improbable transition to modern movie star and the reaction of her erstwhile swain (played, inevitably, by Sennett himself) to her onscreen exploits, crosses over into the realm of self-reflexivity.

Mabel plays a maid who has been rudely rejected by her employer once he finds himself inadvisably smitten by a city girl. Her response, in the Pirandellian logic of the film, is to leave the country and become the type of film star who could then be featured in a film like *Mabel's Dramatic Career*. In the first of the film's many self-referential moments, Mabel, in moving to the metropolis, happens upon the Keystone Studios and decides that the company will become her future employer. The film initially portrays this as a foolhardy mission, confirmed by the reactions of those on the set where Mabel auditions. Her elaborate displays of silent film acting are met with barely contained mirth by the Keystone personnel, including studio mainstay Ford Sterling. But Mabel's efforts are only inappropriate when she aspires to a mode of performance unsuited to her own abilities (and, as it turns out, the studio of her choosing). Her prospects improve when her audition ends in an inadvertent pratfall, for this reveals Mabel's true potential as a performer. To become useful to Keystone, Mabel the maid must abandon any pretense toward legitimate acting and release the physical energy within her that was already on abundant display in the film's first half. To put it another way, in this scene the actress Mabel Normand must convey the persona she has already established for herself in a series of Keystone comedies in order to allow the Mabel of the diegesis to become the Mabel of Keystone fame. The humor resides in the fact that Mabel the

Discovering that his former fiancée, played by Mabel Normand, is now a Keystone star (menaced by Ford Sterling) is more than Mack Sennett can bear, in one of many reflexive moments in *Mabel's Dramatic Career*.

maid need do nothing to become Mabel the Keystone star, whereas the actress Mabel Normand had to carefully craft the comic figure that became popular within the Keystone formula, resulting in creations like Mabel the maid. In effect, Mabel the maid provides us with a parodic version of Mabel Normand's own route to stardom in one single extended take. If this scene works to merge the fictional Mabel with the star persona of Mabel Normand, a subsequent scene set in a movie theater will depend equally upon their separation.

That second sustained scene of parodic humor occurs some time later, when the suitor views a screening of a film featuring Mabel, now established as a Keystone regular. In an extended variation on the Uncle Josh premise, Sennett models all the expected reactions of the untrained film spectator. Appalled by the sight of his Mabel endangered by the villainous Sterling, Sennett grimaces, shouts out, lunges, and finally brandishes a gun, ending the projection of the film by shooting directly at the screen. The scene alternates among three views: that of Sennett, surrounded by disgruntled audience members, and looking outward toward the image projected before him; the reverse field of the same setting, with the back of Sennett's head shown closest to the camera, and the projected image beyond; and the inside of the projection booth, where the amazed projectionist is finally forced to flee when the images on the screen prompt a flurry of gunshots from one overwhelmed patron. By alternating among these spaces, the film confirms the totality of the viewing experience, incorporating the apparatus of projection, the screened image, and the gullible spectator. Not only does this render the credulity of the Sennett character all the more comical, but it also fully transforms Mabel's status. She ceases to be an inhabitant of the world that Sennett still belongs to, having become instead a fiction, nothing more than shadows on a screen. By emphasizing the various perspectives on the viewing situation, this scene reinforces the barrier between lived reality and filmed performance, and if Sennett's character has trouble adjusting to the difference, the audience for both the film that he is watching and for *Mabel's Dramatic Career* recognizes it immediately. The film-within-a-film strategy makes clear to the viewer that by becoming a movie star, Mabel has left the workaday world of mops and droopy-eyed suitors to become a fantasy, untouchable and remote. Even so, this idea is qualified once one realizes that her transformation into a *Keystone* star still attaches her to the realm of the mundane, insofar as the slapstick universe of the studio readily incorporates the world of the film's first half.

In the film's coda, one additional shift occurs. Sennett, having thrown the site of projection into havoc, determines to seek revenge on Sterling by seeking out the villain on his home turf. What catches Sennett by surprise is the film's final joke: Sterling has married Mabel, and they are the happy parents of two children. The fantasy life of Mabel the screen star now takes on another dimension: by ascending to the ranks of motion picture actress, Mabel has also attained the romantic goals she so desperately wished for as a servant. (Her distress at being jilted by Sennett was compounded by the fact that he had given her a ring just prior to rejecting her for the city girl.) Surrounded by the domestic comforts of family and (relative) fortune, Mabel the star, even when offscreen, exists in a world forever separate from that of her former suitor. In a comic variation on an iconic melodramatic situation, Sennett can do nothing more than look on, the window framing Mabel's domestic bliss a version of the movie screen he viewed her inhabiting previously. As a substitute for the rain that would typically drench the longing outsider, mirroring the tears in a moment of perfect pathetic fallacy, the film provides a much ruder means of reinforcing the faux pathos of Sennett's situation: a man living above the spot where Sennett stands douses him with a bucket of water. In the world of Keystone comedy, every resolution must involve the equivalent of a sock to the jaw.

In *The Evidence of the Film*, the invocation of filmmaking and film viewing is far less self-referential, and the processes on display integrated into the narrative flow of the film in a more thoroughgoing fashion. In fact, one could argue that the entire film is engineered to showcase the moment when the titular evidence can be displayed on screen, rendering cinema itself integral to the resolution of the narrative, but more broadly, showcasing the veracity of a medium that can offer a record of reality more persuasive than personal protestations. When asserting cinema's value, *The Evidence of the Film* makes its case in the most systematic manner possible, incorporating all three aspects of the filmic process—shooting, printing, and projection—and aligning each to a comparable stage in an investigation—recording, discovery, and verification. The story has little need for actual detectives—their central role is to be our surrogates in the viewing of the film-within-the-film—simply because film has assumed its role as the ideal instrument of the law. In the campaign for film as uplift, few motion pictures operate more economically than *The Evidence of the Film*.

The film's narrative works toward the exoneration of an unjustly accused innocent, dependent on the mute and incontestable testimony offered by the filmic record. This youngster, a courier framed by a corrupt broker who switches the contents of the envelope he hires the boy to deliver to a client, is saved by his twofold connection to motion pictures, one circumstantial, the other biological: first, the broker's actions happen to be captured by a movie company shooting a scene in the same space where the switch occurs; second, the boy's sister works for the processing department of that moviemaking company, providing her access to the incriminating imagery. As the evidence moves from the status of profilmic event—coincidentally occurring within the purview of a camera's viewfinder—to projected record, technology remains integral, confirmation of cinema's impartiality. Unlike the duplicitous broker, who must engineer an elaborate charade, deceiving witnesses who then testify to convincing but ultimately untrustworthy appearances, cinema need only be itself to tell the truth. The camera that records the switch, the take-up reel that holds the valuable strip of celluloid depicting the wrongful act, and the projector that puts the evidence on the screen for all to see: collectively, these instruments confirm that the truth-telling nature of cinema lies precisely in its independence from human intervention. One finds André Bazin's dictum concerning cinema's link to the perceptual real writ large in the argument put forward by *The Evidence of the Film*: we believe in the cinema precisely because we know that its technology can operate free of our control (13). To this validation of technology's truth-telling capacity, the film offers one additional complementary formal overlay: when we see the projected footage of the broker's actions, our vantage point is now equivalent to that of the camera that recorded him, the shift in perspective afforded by the combination of changed camera position and editing. For the film to convince us of what the diegetic camera saw, its own camera must possess a ubiquity of perspective that allows us to compare what we thought we saw to what actually occurred. In this way, *The Evidence of the Film* redoubles its assertions of film's truth-telling (or truth-showing) capacity. Its title is capable of two meanings, and both are realized: film as a medium constitutes a form of unassailable evidence, but equally, this film has demonstrated that motion pictures possess the rhetorical skill to mount a case for their own social utility. The ability to convince spectators of the value of filmgoing through the seductive procedures of formal operations would become one of the legacies of the American cinema from this point in the industry's history onward.

"Six Reels of Thrilling Realities": *Traffic in Souls*

Traffic in Souls's status as one of the year's most important releases derives both from its engagement with a controversial social problem and its extended running time. As an early feature that focuses on the issue of the illegal trade in forced prostitution, *Traffic in Souls* demonstrates more force-fully than any other film produced this year how cinema's dual function as a site of leisure-time activity and a representational form could place it firmly at the center of public debates. Opening in New York in late Novem-ber at Joe Weber's Theatre, *Traffic* proved an immediate runaway hit, and is largely credited (or blamed) for igniting an explosion of similarly themed "white slave" films that would crowd movie houses into the following year. Response to the film was mixed, with supporters suggesting that it could aid reformers in spurring greater public vigilance concerning the evils of pros-titution, while critics charged that it offered a sensationalized view of the problem without offering productive insight into its causes.

The split nature of the film's reception finds an echo in its production origins. Clearly the film was conceived as a commercial proposition, hatched by filmmakers associated with Universal who recycled elements borrowed from a film released earlier in the year by the company, entitled *The Rise of Officer 174*. Even so, the writer of both films, Walter MacNamara, was approached by the president of the Immigrant Girls' Home in New York City, Mrs. S. M. Haggen, who hoped to use motion pictures as a way to edu-cate newly arrived immigrant girls of the threat of white slave traffic (Brownlow 73–74). (Pamphlets and the like had had little effect, as most of these young women could not read.) Though Mrs. Haggen's original vision of the film was not realized in the version of *Traffic in Souls* that resulted, publicity for the film traded on its ostensible link to reform-minded concerns for the victims of white slavery. The issue had been receiving considerable attention for some time, and by this year, public interest reached its apex. A series of plays featuring the "slave trade" appeared on Broadway, bearing such explicit titles as *The Traffic*, *The Lure*, and *The House of Bondage*. While inviting controversy, they also brought in large audiences, whose enthusiasm only increased when police raids heightened the notoriety of these theatrical treatments of prostitution. In the summer, the city's Bureau of Social Hygiene released a study entitled *Commercialized Prostitution in New York City* authored by George Kneeland, indicating that the urban environment harbored the danger of abduction for unwitting young women, who would then be forced into a life of white slavery (Grieveson, *Policing* 157).

So much public discussion of prostitution raised speculation about the extent of the problem and its probable causes. While many agreed that the widespread existence of slavery rings was probably overstated, and that the roots of prostitution were complex and largely socioeconomic in origin, this did not prevent others from positing that young women were putting themselves at risk by frequenting questionable urban spaces, such as dancehalls, amusement parks, and, ironically, movie theaters. According to these arguments, the increased visibility and social mobility of unattached women, many of them now able to earn the wages that gave them access to commercialized leisure activities, served as the source of their vulnerability. So, when these same young women formed the core of the audience for white slave films such as *Traffic*, the expressed anxiety only doubled.

As popular as these films were—and one could argue that their very popularity helped convince some Broadway theater owners of the viability of switching to motion pictures—their reputation as exploitative sensationalism tarnished further the public profile of an industry striving for respectability (Stamp, *Movie-Struck* 53). For this reason, most industry representatives lashed out at the white slave films, particularly because they feared that these works might well invite official censorship. (Such fears appeared justified, when the follow-up to *Traffic in Souls*, *The Inside of the White Slave Traffic*, found itself the target of police raids only days after opening.) Even so, the National Board of Censorship of Motion Pictures had passed *Traffic*, recommending only minor alterations. When reviewing *Traffic* for *Moving Picture World*, critic George Blaisdell took note of the Board's approval of the film, arguing that "its friends, and among these are the members of the National Board of Censorship, are entitled to ask that the production be seen before it is condemned." In the conclusion of his review,

Blaisdell summed up what would become the standard defense of *Traffic*, aligning the film with Progressive efforts at education:

> There may be diverse opinions as to the wisdom of exhibiting this picture. If such exhibition serve to quicken the official or public conscience in lethargic communities; if it help to preserve to society any one of the "fifty thousand girls who disappear every year"; if it tend to make more difficult the vocation of unspeakable traders, then indeed there have been substantial excuse for the making of this melodrama today.   (Blaisdell 849)

Debate, of course, hinged on "if" a film of this nature would help prevent the scourge that it represented, or merely profit through its exploitation. Certainly Blaisdell's choice of the term "melodrama" to describe the nature of *Traffic*'s treatment of the white slave traffic is apt. Despite the initial prompting by Mrs. Haggen, who only wished for a filmed document of the threat the white trade posed, and despite Universal's publicity campaign, which explicitly tied its production to the agenda of such reform documents as the Kneeland report, *Traffic in Souls* was designed as entertainment first and foremost, replete with daring rescues, violent shoot-outs, and intimations of brutality.

Much has been made of the film's distinctive structure, wherein the first third, aside from introducing the main characters, devotes most of its attention to a semi-documentary account of how a slave ring abducts its targeted victims: one a young woman from the country, and the other a pair of Swedish immigrant sisters. For the most part, the film's central characters are tangential to this portion of the film, as it attends much more consistently to the process used by the slave ring to deceive unsuspecting women. Similarly, the film's remainder makes no further reference to these naifs, concentrating instead on a different case of abduction involving the sister of the film's heroine. Ben Brewster, in an exacting analysis of the film's narrative structure, has remarked that the film's first third functions akin to a "separate two-reeler" (Brewster 43). One might note further that the semi-documentary quality of this part of the film quickly cedes to an approach indebted to the detective genre for its remaining reels. And, just as the semi-documentary section is somewhat uneasily yoked to the more patently melodramatic narrative that follows, so too is an ostensible Progressive intent grafted onto an overt investment in heart-pounding action. The uneasy alliance of the two is suggested most economically in Universal's ad copy on its poster, which promises "six reels of thrilling realities" (Grieveson, *Policing* 159).

Traffic's main narrative line involves two sisters, Mary and Lorna Barton, the latter typically referred to as "the Little Sister" in many prints.

Mary, immediately identified as the responsible sibling, works with her sister in a candy store, their inventor father incapacitated and unable to care for the family. Mary's boyfriend, Officer Burke, has been central to the bust-up of one brothel, and when Lorna is abducted and held captive in another, Mary and Burke join forces to free her. A central clue emerges when Mary is hired as a secretary for Trubus, whose humanitarian organization is actually a front for his white slavery operation. Through a Dictaphone, a communication device connected to the office below, where most of the financial transactions central to the slave ring occur, she overhears the voice of the "cadet" who abducted her sister. Using her father's invention, she and Burke are able to record incriminating conversations between Trubus and his henchmen, resulting in a successful police raid on the brothel where Lorna is trapped and the full exposure of Trubus's double life.

Traffic in Souls reveals its moral agenda in the way it frames the white slavery problem through this narrative line. First, by making Lorna the victim of the abduction plot, the film suggests that her irresponsibility contributes to her downfall. Unlike the young women abducted in the first portion of the film, Lorna does not have the excuse of ignorance of a strange urban center's geography and customs, and cannot be duped into entering the brothel on false pretenses. Instead, she is lured by her own willingness to engage in questionable social activities, made most explicit when she visits a dancehall with the cadet pretending to be a suitor. While accepting a dance with the cadet's comrade, Lorna provides her "date" with the opportunity to drug her drink. Anonymous dancing partners, an environment where the mingling of the sexes is encouraged, the ready availability of liquor—all these mark the dancehall as precisely the type of space a sensible young woman would not think of visiting. (On this score, the film is emphatically silent on whether motion picture theaters would qualify as another such questionable urban space.) Contrasted throughout to Mary, Lorna lacks her sister's sense of moral groundedness. The film affirms Mary's worthiness by giving her a suitable romantic partner in Burke and by emphasizing her worried response to the cadet's approach to Lorna. Unlike her unwitting sister, Mary remains vigilant throughout, a woman who knows how to comport herself within an urban environment that offers a multitude of temptations for the unguarded.

Even more revealing is the film's decision to make the mastermind behind the depicted traffic ring a respected reform-minded figure, whose front for the organization is named the International Purity and Reform League. Suggesting that reform hypocrisy and unbridled greed stand behind the existence of the white slave traffic, the film opts to target a specific cause for the social ill of prostitution, rather than explore the possibility that multiple forces might contribute to its existence. Such a strategy facilitates solving the problem through conventional narrative patterns of detection and exposure. In this, the film is particularly emphatic, punishing Trubus severely: not only is his ring smashed, but so too are his social aspirations. By the film's conclusion, Trubus has been imprisoned, seen his daughter's engagement cancelled, lost his wife, and, finally, taken his own life. The devastating fall of Trubus from his previous position as a "higher up" is sealed by the film's representation of his suicide as public information: where once his daughter's engagement plans were the toast of the society pages, now his scandalous decline is fodder for the news section of the daily edition, with the paper itself shown discarded in a trashcan. Those chiefly responsible for restoring moral order are the police, personified by Burke and portrayed as men of honor and action. In this, the film refutes, or at least ignores, one of the planks of Kneeland's report, which indicated that police corruption facilitated the expansion of the white slave trade. As Lee Grieveson has pointed out, "The film offers a culturally affirmative vision that directly contradicts evidence in the real world" (*Policing* 164).

As much as *Traffic*'s narrative formula insists on a moral universe where the righteous prevail, its formal operations also suggest how cinema, as an instrument of modern technology, can aid in the restoration of order. Many critics have noted the importance of the Dictaphone to the film's plot: Mary Barton enlists her father's invention to translate the signals of the Dictaphone into wax cylinder recordings that will expose, by technologically produced evidence, the previously clandestine operations of Trubus and his henchmen. According to the logic of *Traffic in Souls*, modern technology can be an instrument of good or evil, depending on its user. And, as *The Evidence of the Film* also demonstrated, cinema is the ultimate instrument of revelation, its combination of omniscience and incontrovertible facticity rendering it the most persuasive of recording devices. The possible drawbacks of modernity are offset by the power of cinema to right social wrongs. Nowhere is this more evident than in the film's relentless reliance on crosscutting, an editing strategy that stitches together the various narrative strands in a tight causal weave, but that also brings the disparate spaces of *Traffic in Soul*'s story together for the audience to view. As Tom Gunning has pointed out, the film's editing patterns constitute its own version of surveillance and supersede the powers of human vision ("Kaleidoscope" 52). Ultimately, *Traffic*'s reliance on crosscutting reinforces the intricacy of the networks of crime depicted while arguing for cinema's superiority as a medium for recording and revealing those networks.

In its trumpeting of cinema's technological superiority as an instrument of improved moral vision, *Traffic in Souls* embodies the Progressive belief in technology's capacity for social betterment. At the same time, its effective use of crosscutting to enhance the visceral force of its violent episodes of action and to draw out the salacious implications of its instances of female entrapment (such as the threatened whipping of the Little Sister) point to how the medium could stir audiences with little regard for Progressive aims. At this pivotal moment in the medium's development, as cinema continued its drive toward increased length and expanded cultural influence, the success of *Traffic in Soul*'s approach indicated how effectively engineered entertainment could prevail over social commitment. In this year of transition, however, the possibilities still remained open, even as the formal mechanisms and representational power of the medium solidified and the nation looked increasingly to motion pictures as a source of distraction rather than edification.

1914

Movies and Cultural Hierarchy

ROB KING

> In the Classical world years played no role, in the Indian world decades
> scarcely mattered; but here the hour, the minute, even the second is of
> importance. Neither a Greek nor an Indian could have had any idea of
> the tragic tension of a historic crisis like that of August 1914, when even
> moments seemed of overwhelming significance.   (Spengler 176)

The words are Oswald Spengler's, from his monumental history *The Decline
of the West*, and they suggest clearly the degree to which this year marks a
critical moment in the global entry into modernity. Few years define so
keenly the divergent historical experiences of Europe and the New World.
The assassination on 28 June of Archduke Franz Ferdinand, heir to the
Austro-Hungarian throne, triggers a flurry of diplomatic ultimatums in
which the rapidity of modern communications precipitates war across
Europe within weeks. In America, meanwhile, the ever-accelerating pace of
industry points instead toward the maturing capitalism of a new economic
order, consolidating already unprecedented levels of mass production and
communication. By the end of the year, the Ford Motor Company is able to
manufacture a Model T in just ninety-three minutes. Annual advertising
revenues ($682 million) nearly triple the figures from 1900, as new pro-
motional strategies emanate from the commercial sphere. President
Woodrow Wilson's policy of neutrality, proclaimed in August, helps maintain moderate inflation rates, and American society holds course in its transition from a producer- to a consumer-oriented economy.

Underlying this transition is a significant reshaping of relations between
culture and class, what might be described as the shift from a hierarchical
cultural order that once reinforced social divisions to a commercially driven
"mass" culture that has begun to obscure them. One indication of these
changes is the middle-class ballroom dance craze, as satirized in movies
such as the Keystone Film Company's *Tango Tangles* and Pathé's *The Tango
Craze* (in which a young man dances unstoppably after being bitten by a

"tango microbe"). The popularization of new steps derived from working-class dance hall culture—including the fox-trot, introduced this year—is a symptom of a middle class breaking from gentility and experimenting with expressive modes of public conduct (Erenberg 146–75). Another is the modern cabaret, which, despite it murky origins in the rathskellers of urban vice districts, has by now become a prominent urban institution, nowhere more so than in New York: dance partners Vernon and Irene Castle open their Sans Souci cabaret this year and the Shuberts begin operations at Chez Maurice atop the Winter Garden Theater. Yet this receptivity to working-class cultural practice fails to translate into political terms, and the year witnesses the stalling of radical politics on several fronts. On 20 April, company leaders at John D. Rockefeller's Colorado Fuel and Iron Company in Ludlow call in National Guardsmen to break an ongoing strike, resulting in the deaths of twenty-four men, women, and children. The campaign for women's suffrage has suffered a setback with Congress's vote against enfranchisement the previous year, although the debate continues unabated on the nation's movie screens—both pro (e.g., the eight-reel *Your Girl and Mine*, sponsored by the National American Woman Suffrage Association) and con (e.g., Pathé's lurid five-reeler, *The Militant Suffragette*, a picture protested by Nebraska women's groups).

Few cultural practices occupy as central a place in the consolidation of modern mass culture as the cinema of this period, as industry leaders expand upon commercial strategies for increasing the movies' audience base. The star system gains strength as a system of motion picture publicity, with J. Warren Kerrigan and Margarita Fischer topping a poll of *Photoplay* readers in June. English-born comedian Charles Chaplin debuts at Keystone in the one-reel *Making a Living*, and ends the year signing with Essanay for a $1,250 weekly salary, a tenfold increase over his Keystone paycheck. Meanwhile, Mary Pickford continues to win popular and critical acclaim for her appearances for Adolph Zukor's Famous Players Film Company (e.g., *The Good Little Devil*, *Tess of the Storm Country*, and *Behind the Scenes*). Her sobriquet, "America's Sweetheart," is also coined this year. The growth of a movie-fan culture fuels new relations between film and print media, as, by now, many newspapers have begun publishing weekly pages devoted to movies and their stars, all of which is "eagerly gobbled up by the reader," according to *Moving Picture World* (Abel 8). By the end of the year, newspaper tie-ins have become an established part of the industry's promotional practices, initiating strategies of media convergence that lend further economic support to the new cinematic culture industry.

In terms of industry structure, the year marks a threshold between different institutional frames for corporate control. The Independents are clearly succeeding in their struggle against the Trust, and several MPPC members start distributing multiple-reel productions outside the General Film Company (e.g., Selig's nine-reel *The Spoilers*, distributed through the state rights system). In fact, the ascendancy of the feature film—production of which increases by over 500 percent this year—motivates a whole series of changes in the industry's economic organization. New companies are being formed specifically to handle the distribution of multireel films— Lewis Selznick's World Special Films Corporation (founded November 1913) and William Fox's Box Office Attraction Company (January 1914), among others. Prestigious "picture palaces" are opened—notably, in New York, the Vitagraph Theatre on 7 February and S. L. Rothapfel's Strand on 11 April—as exhibition sites for feature programs catering to an upscale clientele. Although the outcome of this transitional period remains unclear, the pages of the trade press are filled with predictions and prognostications. Perhaps, as Carl Laemmle prophesizes in July, the public will soon become "satiated with features" and will return its enthusiasms to variety programs of one- and two-reel subjects (185). Perhaps demand for both kinds of product will stabilize in a two-tier hierarchy of exhibition in which, as augured by critic W. Stephen Bush, "One class of theaters will use mostly single reels, the other will use mostly features" ("Single" 36). Or perhaps the days of the single-reel film are numbered. "It seems it is the general sentiment of the people," observes one exhibitor. "They want to see features or productions produced in more than one reel" (qtd. in Bowser 212).

■ "A Desire for the Uplift of the Industry": The Paramount Picture Corporation, the American Middle Class, and *What's His Name*

No doubt the most famous of the new feature organizations—and, as it would transpire, the most enduring—was the Paramount Picture Corporation, a distribution concern announced to the trade press in May, with W. W. Hodkinson as president. Formed from the affiliation of three feature producers—the Jesse L. Lasky Feature Play Company, the Famous Players Film Company, and Bosworth, Inc.—the new concern was launched with the lofty ambition of "supply[ing] the exhibitor with a program of such advanced standard as to elevate . . . the exhibiting branch of the industry in all parts of the world" ("Feature Producers Affiliate" 1268). In a brief press statement, the heads of the three producing concerns described their motivation simply: "A desire for the uplift of the industry and the further prestige of the feature film" ("Feature Producers Affiliate" 1268). "Uplift," in this context, implied escaping the stigma of the film industry's largely lower-class audience, and it involved exploiting high or "highbrow" culture as a model for filmmaking practice. Each of the producing members accordingly brought the sanction of cultural hierarchy to the birth of the enterprise. Famous Players already owned film rights to the stage productions of Charles Frohman; Lasky was just completing arrangements for the productions of David Belasco; and Hobart Bosworth brought to the lineup an exclusive contract with Jack London. Bringing these organizations together, the reasoning went, the Paramount combination would achieve a corporate basis for industry uplift based on the cultural cachet of the feature film.

Of course, Paramount was hardly unique in these ideals—other "highbrow" feature organizations launched this year would include Dramatic Successes Feature Co., Playgoers' Film Co., and Colonial Productions—but it was the most successful in leveraging cultural capital into industrial might. On Hodkinson's system, films were to be distributed on a percentage basis, with Paramount receiving 35 percent of ticket sales. Exhibitors, meanwhile, had to contract for the full year's worth of films (initially, 102 features) and were prohibited from acquiring films from other distributors. Paramount's regularized, nationwide system of company-owned exchanges represented a decisive departure from the haphazard state rights system and, as such, pointed the way to the future vertical integration of the industry. At the same time, the very expense of the Paramount program supported the nascent picture palace trend: higher admissions and seating capacities were essential if Paramount's program was to make financial sense for the exhibitor.

Thus, in a profound sense, was cinema's emergence as big business tied to the goal of uplift. Yet this twinning of culture and commerce also generated unlooked-for effects, as market forces declassified and transformed genteel cultural standards, at Paramount and elsewhere. The dilemma of uplift, as film historian Sumiko Higashi has argued, was that filmmakers who sought the aura of art for their product ultimately—and unwittingly—helped transform "high" culture into a mechanically reproduced, commercial product, thus paving the way for categories like "middlebrow" (32). In the same way, the picture palace entrepreneurs who sought to attract genteel audiences to their "temples of the motion picture art" were, in so doing, fueling the growth of a new middle-class lifestyle in which older standards of distinction gave way to the commercial pleasures of city nightlife. Theaters like the Strand took their place, not alongside such venerable institutions as the Boston Museum of Fine Arts, but rather as part of the showier firmament of cabarets, nightclubs, and lobster restaurants wherein the social formalism of the Victorian era was ceding to a newly expressive middle-class culture (Erenberg 5–59). Highbrow culture was in some sense the alibi beneath which a new ethos was developing: older standards of taste and distinction remained implicated in middle-class culture, only now more as consumer options than as exemplars of character.

Few could have been more aware of this than the new generation of motion picture entrepreneurs who marketed cinema's uplift during the mid-1910s. The pattern was exemplified by showman Jesse L. Lasky, who came to film following a successful career as a producer of cabaret shows catering to New York's smart set and who promoted one of his vaudeville revues, "At the Country Club" (1908), as featuring "Twenty-six unusually stylish and costly costumes . . . worn by four stunning show girls, and . . . an equal number of hats of the most dazzling and modish creations" (Oberdeck 207). The Paramount program itself took color from the new taste for extravagance when it arranged in the fall to release the output of the Oz Film Company, recently established by children's author and department store design expert L. Frank Baum. Advertised as a "whimsical extravaganza," Oz Film's first picture for Paramount, *The Patchwork Girl of Oz* , owed less to the legitimate stage than to the scenography of musical comedy, sharing a common denominator in Orientalist exoticism and beautifully attired chorines. Fantasy here outmatched gentility in a film structured around extravagant set-pieces and visual effects, establishing a pattern that would be continued in subsequent Oz releases and, elsewhere on the Paramount program, in Famous Players' Christmas special, *Cinderella*, with Mary Pickford.

One film that neatly dramatizes the changes in middle-class culture during this period is the Lasky Co.'s *What's His Name*, one of three adaptations of George Barr McCutcheon's work produced by Lasky this year (the other two being *Brewster's Millions* and *The Circus Man*). An author who sold millions of copies of novels set in the fictional kingdom of Graustark—even inspiring a short-lived genre known as "Graustarkian"—McCutcheon was, like Lasky and Baum, peculiarly representative of the modern taste for opulence and fantasy. Yet *What's His Name* (1911), apparently written during a period of personal crisis, took a self-reflexive step by exploring the impact on genteel ethical standards of a consumer-oriented society. The basic situation of *What's His Name* examines this in gendered terms, tracing the upending of domestic stability that occurs when a woman abandons familial responsibilities for a public career as a Broadway star, a scenario apparently inspired by Minnie Maddern Fiske.

What's His Name, then, is a film about domesticity and theater in middle-class culture, an emphasis that accounts in part for the pronounced interiority of the film's mise-en-scène. (As one critic observed, it was a "rather unusual fact about the film" that "nearly all the scenes are interiors" [Rev., *Motion Picture News*].) More specifically, it is a film that uses the contrast between domestic and theatrical space as a way of addressing the changing role of women in middle-class families. As Mary Ryan argues, the development of Victorian middle-class consciousness had rested on an idealized conception of femininity as moral guardianship, whereby women were to preside over the home as a site for the inculcation of genteel values (145–229). Yet that conception had, by the late nineteenth century, been challenged by the growth of a consumer culture that allotted women new roles as shoppers, drawing them from their homes into a public realm of department stores and shopping emporia. Theater, too, became a facet of that culture, as matinees and evening performances offered women a public place of their own, where they could go without escort and "stop on the way home for ice punch and cream-cakes" (Butsch 390). This feminization of theater (as Richard Butsch terms it) even provided a framework within which young women's aspirations for a public career and independence could take place, as exemplified by the title protagonist of Theodore Dreiser's *Sister Carrie* (1900) or by the many chorus girls who embodied modern femininity at musical comedies and revues.

The impact of consumer ideology on genteel culture was thus, in part, to replace the middle-class woman's private role as nurturing housewife with new public status as a shopper and matinee aficionado. It is this contrast that becomes the chief structuring motif of the film version of *What's His Name*. The director, Cecil B. DeMille, here on only his third picture, clearly establishes the disparity between home and stage in an early scene when the young wife and mother, Nellie, pausing from her household duties, looks out of her apartment window. Cutting to Nellie's point of view, DeMille fills the screen with a poster, presumably across the street, publicizing "A Great Musical Comedy" featuring "40 Girls," before cutting back to Nellie as she sighs. This shot-reverse shot locates the theater beyond the confines of domestic drudgery as a focus for Nellie's dreams of escape; and it establishes an editing pattern—from home to theater and back again—that becomes a formal principle throughout the film, as DeMille repeatedly uses contrast edits to emphasize Nellie's neglect of domestic duties. Thus,

Movers point and laugh at a "God Bless Our Home" sign, while a dejected Harvey (far right) gives up his apartment in *What's His Name*. Courtesy Academy Film Archive.

when Nellie attends the show that evening, leaving her daughter Phoebe with a nanny, DeMille inserts three cutaways showing the nanny treating Phoebe uncaringly. Later, Nellie has become the "Rage of New York," but keeps her husband, Harvey, a secret by ensconcing him and Phoebe in an out-of-town home in Tarrytown: the film here juxtaposes scenes at the Tarrytown home where Harvey lovingly cares for Phoebe with sequences in the theatrical dressing room where Nellie flirts with wealthy admirers. If the former is a space for the bond between father and daughter, the latter is a place made for social show, not for family life at all.

The film's subsequent progress charts the literal dismantling of domestic space that results from Nellie's maternal neglect. The destruction begins on Christmas Day when the millionaire Fairfax, with whom Nellie has begun an affair, visits Harvey's home to demand that he agree to a divorce, resulting in a scuffle in which the Christmas tree is toppled. The next day, Nellie sends movers who take away the furniture, even carting up a "God Bless Our Home" sign. DeMille's emphasis on an interior mise-en-scène here produces a visual metaphor for family breakup, as the space of the Tarrytown parlor is thrown into increasing disarray, eventually stripped bare of furnishings. Finally, domestic space disappears altogether, when

Harvey and Phoebe are forced to leave home to tramp their way back to their rural hometown, yielding the only sustained exterior sequences in the movie.

As Sumiko Higashi argues in a superb analysis of the film, *What's His Name* is usefully seen as a cinematic translation of domestic melodrama, a theatrical form pioneered in the late 1880s through the collaboration of playwright Henry C. DeMille (Cecil's father) and producer David Belasco. A rewriting of melodrama for America's genteel middle class, DeMille-Belasco productions like *Lord Chumley* (1888) and *The Charity Ball* (1889) had translated contradictions in domestic ideology into the ethical quandaries of society drama. "As a sermon," Higashi writes, "domestic melodramas conveyed the message that middle-class apprehension about the eclipse of the privatized home . . . was not unfounded in an age of commercialized leisure" (45). In *What's His Name*, that sermonizing function rests largely upon DeMille's use of editing to construct a moral perspective. The use of parallel editing has throughout implied an omniscience reflecting moral condemnation; but, as the film moves toward its climax, so too do the moral contrasts grow stronger. Scenes of Harvey and Phoebe sheltering in an empty train not only suggest the Holy Family in Bethlehem (as Higashi notes), but are intercut with scenes of Nellie in Reno entertaining actresses and arranging for her divorce. Finally, Phoebe falls dangerously ill and Nellie's maternal reawakening can begin: she breaks with Fairfax and leaves to rejoin her family. DeMille ends the film on a chiaroscuro tableau depicting Nellie and Harvey reunited over their bedridden daughter.

What's His Name thus culminates in an unambiguous reaffirmation of an older, Protestant family ethic in keeping with the film industry's drive for respectability. Perhaps unsurprisingly, trade periodicals that lobbied for the refinement of motion picture art were unanimous in judging *What's His Name* exemplary. It was a technically "perfect piece of work" and "a picture of unusual merit"; more to the point, it had "a philosophy that the average spectator will like" (Rev., *Motion Picture News*; Rev., *Moving Picture World*). That "philosophy" suggests clearly the degree to which older standards were implicated in the industry's bid for middle-class appeal; yet it also indicates the degree to which those standards were losing ground against modern consumer values. Indeed, for audiences less committed to a genteel worldview, this year would provide a number of pictures that offered a quite different take on the themes of *What's His Name*. One group of these, in particular, would constitute the most distinctive—and certainly the most profitable—of the year's new trends.

■ "A Romance of Adventures": The Serial Craze, Mass Marketing, and *The Perils of Pauline*

A genre of filmmaking often seen as symptomatic of this transitional period, the action-packed serial enjoyed a terrific boom in popularity this year. The mold was cast by Selig's thirteen-episode *The Adventures of Kathlyn* (beginning December 1913)—which made the daring exploits of an athletic "serial queen" (in this case, Kathlyn Williams) central to the format's appeal—and was emulated many times over in subsequent months: in Pathé's *The Perils of Pauline* (March) and *The Exploits of Elaine* (December); in Universal's *Lucille Love, the Girl of Mystery* (April), *The Trey o'Hearts* (August), and *The Master Key* (November); in Thanhouser's *The Million Dollar Mystery* (June) and *Zudora* (November); in Lubin's *The Beloved Adventurer* (September); and in Kalem's *The Hazards of Helen* (November). Typically released in episodes of one or two reels over a period of three or more months, the serial was an economic bonanza for exhibitors unable or unwilling to shift to features: the very words "To be continued"—supervening at an appropriately exciting moment—virtually guaranteed repeat attendance, sustaining the viability of the short film program in the face of the growing market for feature films. "This is where the picture will be successful from an exhibitor's point of view," noted a reviewer of *Perils of Pauline*. "It assures him of return patronage, and return patronage means money, which spells success" (56).

Like the multiple-reel feature, the serial depended upon the medium's growing capacity to tell stories: it was, in the words of one critic, "the logical outcome of the storytelling power of the films." Yet in its structure it stood apart as *sui generis*, less an evolutionary step toward the feature film than an alternative narrative commodity at a time of changing exhibition practices. Central to the serial's distinctive form, as it would develop, was the famous "cliffhanger" structure, predicated on a continual deferral of closure in a system of (seemingly) endless reversals and catastrophes. This had not always been the case; indeed, the earliest serials—such as Edison's *What Happened to Mary?* (1913) and *The Adventures of Kathlyn*—tended to favor relatively self-contained episodes, with each installment simply linked by an overarching premise (characteristically, a conflict over the heroine's inheritance). By the end of the year, however, virtually every serial installment would end on a suspenseful pitch of excitement. (Film historian Ben Singer cites Pathé's *Perils of Pauline* as the transitional serial in this respect, with most installments presenting complete adventures while others left the story hanging [210].)

It is often noted, in fact, that the serial replicates the psychology of commodity form: story events become leveled and interchangeable, their primary function simply to whet the viewer's appetite for more. Not for nothing, then, did the serial also mark a watershed in film advertising: far-reaching and unusual campaigns were a *sine qua non* for generating the sustained public interest on which serials depended. From the start, a common form of ballyhoo was the contest in which viewers competed for cash prizes by writing in answers to the serials' mysteries. One popular example inspired by *The Perils of Pauline* offered entrants twenty-five thousand dollars for providing speculative answers to episode-specific questions like "What did the Mummy say?" or "What was the aged man's message?" When Thanhouser ran a similar contest offering ten thousand dollars for the best ending for its *Million Dollar Mystery*, the editors of *The Movie Pictorial* cashed in with a series of "Helps to the Solution of the Million Dollar Mystery," supposedly written by a real detective, William J. Burns. But the centerpiece of these new promotional strategies—a turning point in relations between moving pictures and the national press—was the prose-version tie-in published simultaneously in newspapers. Here again it was *The Adventures of Kathlyn* that set the mold: in what was reported as a "mammoth and novel" plan involving the cooperation of Selig-Polyscope and a newspaper syndicate headed by the *Chicago Tribune*, a full-page story version of each biweekly installment of *Kathlyn* was published in some forty-five newspapers each Sunday prior to the new episode's release ("Mammoth"). Prose versions of films had appeared in the nation's newspapers before—as early as November 1911, the *Tribune* had begun publishing a "Photoplay in Story Form" in its Sunday "Features" section—but the scale of the Selig campaign was nonetheless something new.

Such co-production strategies represented an important step in constructing a mass audience for cinema. The example of the *Tribune* is again instructive: in an excellent local study of *Kathlyn*'s promotion in Chicago, Barbara Wilinsky has shown how the *Tribune* effectively pooled its audience with Selig's by providing unprecedented coverage of the serial. Whereas the *Tribune*'s "Amusements" section had only rarely offered movie listings heretofore, it now began publishing full listings of locations at which the serial was playing; at the same time, it placed teaser ads in its pages and ran prominent stories on the serial's success. The Chicago paper thus joined its largely middle-class readership to the film industry's working-class audience base to make *Kathlyn* a hit of unexpected proportions. Indeed, such was *Kathlyn*'s success—more than four times the number of prints of the serial were released in Chicago than for any film previously shown there—

that hardly a serial would thereafter be made without some kind of newspaper involvement. Pathé jumped on the bandwagon for *The Perils of Pauline*, developed in conjunction with William Randolph Hearst, whose papers continued the pattern of publishing full-page prose versions the day before each episode's release. Next was *Lucille Love, the Girl of Mystery*, for which Universal contracted with the A. P. Robyn Newspaper Syndicate to publish installments in forty dailies nationwide. By the end of the year—with newspaper serializations of *The Million-Dollar Mystery* ("200 leading papers"), *Trey o' Hearts* ("eighty dailies"), and *Zudora* ("500 leading newspapers") either recently completed or still in process—it was no doubt difficult to find a paper that wasn't somehow hitched to the serial craze.

No less important as marketing tools, however, were the stars themselves, the serial queens who embodied adventurous lifestyles both onscreen and, according to fan magazines, in their off-camera pursuits. At a time when the motion picture star system was just coming into effect, the serial queens were paradigmatic of the extent to which fan publicity fused stars' personal identities with their screen personas. Week after week, fans learned that these women not only displayed tremendous daring during filming, but that they carried their taste for high-octane adventure into their daily lives. Kathlyn Williams, for instance, was reported to be fascinated with "the strange sensation of flying through space" and was "the first woman ever to fly in a hydro-aeroplane" ("Kathlyn the Intrepid"); Pearl White, meanwhile, was a former trapeze artist, a "pretty fair swimmer," and an "athlete" who had "aeroplaned often" ("Real Perils of Pauline" 59–64). Indeed, as Shelly Stamp has argued, serials were particularly well suited to the operations of a nascent star system, since their prolonged stories facilitated continuing audience fascination with a single screen persona and, in the process, sustained the production of multiple fan magazine profiles and other consumer tie-ins (*Movie-Struck* 141–53). (There was, for instance, a "Kathlyn waltz," "Kathlyn tango pumps," and even a "Kathlyn Williams perfume," advertised as the "crowning attribute to a woman's loveliness.")

As the work of recent historians suggests, these stars and their onscreen roles seem to have appealed in particular to the young working women who formed the core of the new movie fan culture. No less than *What's His Name*, the serial queen phenomenon constituted a discourse on changing ideals of womanhood, albeit from the vantage point of a modernizing star system that offered consumer images of "personality" for audience identification. For working girls negotiating their own entry into the public sphere, serials supplied hyperbolic tales of female power whose plots allegorized the changes they were experiencing in their own lives. A common story formula, for example, was to mark the heroine's independence from the outset of the narrative through the death or loss of a father figure: Kathlyn's adventures begin when her father is kidnapped, Pauline's when her guardian dies. The woman's story opens, then, with a release from familial bonds that is also, frequently, a refusal of marriage. As Pauline bluntly states in the first episode of *Perils*, in defiance of her dying guardian's hopes that she marry his son, Harry: "It may be that I shall consent to marry Harry some day, but you know my adventurous spirit and my desire to live and realize the greatest thrills so that I can describe them in a romance of adventures."

Yet, if the serial narrative thus typically begins with a rupture of familial obligations, it is with their reimposition that the tale commonly ends: "heredity and lineage come to assume central importance in virtually all of the plots," writes Stamp, "and marriage, though initially forsaken, usually marks the conclusion of [the] young woman's escapades" (*Movie-Struck* 144). The narrative of *The Perils of Pauline* is exemplary in this regard, taking place in the space "between" two familial obligations—to Mr. Marvin, whose death frees Pauline to give rein to her "adventurous" spirit, and to Harry, marriage to whom abruptly ends her adventures in the serial's final episode. It is only in the period between these patriarchal bonds that Pauline encounters her "perils," repeatedly fighting off the murderous designs of her guardian's secretary, Owen, who is plotting to take control of her inheritance. Pauline's "romance of adventures" thus occupies the interstices of another story—her passing from father (figure) to husband—and is sustained only so long as she defers her obligations to patriarchy. Each episode, moreover, replicates this structure in microcosm: at the beginning of each installment she places herself outside the orbit of male control—usually by embarking on a solitary excursion into peril, whether participating in a daring hot-air balloon ascension, competing in an automobile race, or testing her hand on a motorboat—only to be returned to it at the end, typically by being saved by Harry. Adventure, for Pauline, exists only outside patriarchy's purview, and is bought, ironically, at the cost of inevitable return to its strictures, whether through rescue or, ultimately, marriage.

There is thus a paradox operating across the structure of serial narrative, in which ideologies of female agency are often coupled with expositions of female victimization and dependency, in *Perils* as in other serials from this period. In the same breath as these films exploit female derring-do as commercial spectacle, so also do they serve as cautionary tales about the "perils" that await women who venture outside of wedlock and family.

Posters for *Perils of Pauline* frequently offered sensational depictions of female victimization. Courtesy Academy of Motion Picture Arts and Sciences.

One way to describe these seemingly contradictory operations—this coupling of power and peril—would be in terms of what has been called the "utopian" dimension of mass culture, the capacity of mass cultural texts both to engage and to repress liberatory fantasies, offering purely imaginary resolutions to real social contradictions (Jameson 9–34). As an early example of a genuinely "mass" cinematic text, the serial may have provided just such a utopian venue—both a site for articulating dreams of empowerment that remained unfulfilled in the social world *and* a means of deflecting those desires into a consumer cycle of fan magazines and media tie-ins.

If, then, the serials' conservative implications arguably differed little from those of *What's His Name*, still the mode of cultural expression differed substantially. Whereas the DeMille film looked backward to the prescriptive moral standards of genteel culture, the serial pointed to a modern mass culture that drew utopian energies from popular forms. Whereas the former had intertexts in a tradition of domestic melodrama that offered sermons to genteel audiences, the serial had origins in the cheap, working-class "ten-twenty-thirty" melodrama, where sensationalism had long outmatched an overt moralizing function. Indicative of the diversity of filmmaking practice during this period, the serial and the feature film thus inhabited separate terrains, both industrially and ideologically. In what follows, this chapter examines how sensationalism exerted an impact on other aspects of film culture this year.

"The Impossible Attained!" The Challenge of Feature-Length Slapstick and *Tillie's Punctured Romance*

What, then, of the nondramatic genres, of the comedies, scenics, and newsreels that remained essential components of both variety and feature programs? The advent of the feature film must have been a cause for particular uncertainty in these fields, a challenge to their market position and profitability. Whereas, earlier in the decade, the single-reel production had been the standard commodity for the industry as a whole, the rising tide of multiple-reel dramas had begun to introduce a disparity. Dramatic filmmaking was increasingly geared to feature length, while the nondramatic genres remained short: comic and nonfiction manufacturers would have to respond or face marginalization.

There was, however, scant uniformity to those responses. The newsreel's changing fortunes are touched on in the next section of this chapter. As for the travelogue, the viability of the multiple-reel format had, in fact,

An advertisement for *Tillie's Punctured Romance* in *Motion Picture News*, 23 January 1915.

already been established two years previously with the astonishing—and, even by this time, continuing—success of the five-reel *Paul J. Rainey's African Hunt* (1912). Multiple-reel slapstick, by contrast, remained un-explored territory, the general assumption being that comic pleasure could not be sustained beyond a single reel. "Nor do we believe that multiple reel comedy will ever successfully rival the short snappy comedy of a thousand feet," opined *Moving Picture World*'s Stephen Bush. "On the screen as in the newspaper and on the stage brevity is the soul of wit" ("Single" 36). Con-siderable interest was generated, then, when it was announced in May that the Keystone Film Company—the industry's leading slapstick manu-facturer—had begun work on a series of multiple-reel comedies featuring musical comedy star Marie Dressler. "Under any circumstances the venture was a gamble," recalled studio head Mack Sennett (184); and, although the planned series never transpired, the enterprise did result in *Tillie's Punctured Romance*—the first six-reel comic feature in motion picture history and a film that, on its release, was hailed as a "masterpiece of the slapstick art."

"For any producer to tackle a six reel humorous number was daring, to say the least," commented one reviewer, "[but] the temerity of the makers has been amply justified" (Rev., *Motion Picture News*).

The language is revealing: multiple-reel slapstick was "daring," it was a "gamble" that required "temerity." Why such a gamble? The problem becomes clearer when it is recalled that slapstick was a form with roots in the plebeian style of variety and burlesque humor and, as such, belonged to an aesthetic mode that foregrounded sensationalism over storytelling refinements. (The ideal variety act, suggested vaudevillian Wilfred Clarke, was one with "no time for plot. . . . Each sentence should create a laugh, so as to never allow the ball to stop rolling" [Jenkins 78].) Vaudeville's "nut acts," "bone crunchers," and "knockabout" clowns exemplified a comic aesthetic predicated not on narrative coherence, but on the cumulative impact of violent pratfalls; and, by the early 1910s, the Keystone Film Company had become the major cinematic repository for this style of comedy. Sennett's decision to initiate the production of multiple-reel slapstick was thus one that promised paradoxically to mix modes, twinning the "high" with the "low." Formerly associated with conceptions of uplift, the feature format was here being appropriated as a vehicle for the slapstick comedy to which uplift had always been opposed. *Tillie's Punctured Romance* would consequently challenge, rather than affirm, the cultural hierarchies that allotted priority to the feature drama as the industry's "prestige" commodity. It would be, almost of necessity, a subversion of the genteel connotations of the feature format, an ideological rewriting that satirized the narrative conventions through which feature filmmakers made their films conform to the ethical precepts of middle-class culture. Not only would the film defy critical consensus on the viability of feature-length slapstick; it would also burlesque the gentrifying ambitions that had given rise to the feature film in the first place.

From the outset, the film establishes a playfully deconstructive take on the clichés of cultural hierarchy, appealing to familiar formulas of cinematic "respectability" only to stand them on their head. Thus, at the beginning, a title card announces "Marie Dressler," who, out of character, steps from behind a curtain and bows to the camera. A strategy for capitalizing on the legitimacy of stage versus film, such "curtain" openings were not uncommon in feature films of this period (indeed, *What's His Name* begins in very similar fashion). Taken here, the opening would seem to suggest continuity with Dressler's stage successes, a suggestion sustained as a dissolve next transforms the star into "Tillie," the hulking and homely yokel she had made famous in the two-year run of the musical comedy *Tillie's Nightmare*

(1910). But the appeal to such safely middle-class registers is immediately undercut when a second dissolve commences the narrative proper, showing Tillie in front of a farmhouse from which her father exits: he kicks her in the butt, and the film is immediately launched into an excruciatingly rough style of slapstick, extreme even by Keystone's standards. Dressler was well known for her famously broad performance style ("an actress whose main aim is to make herself a monstrosity," was how one theater critic described her), but her appearance in the Keystone film remains remarkable for its raucousness (Lee 174). Kicking, foot-stamping, and even brick-throwing provide the comic appeal of the film's opening reel, a style of violent comedy that led the Chicago board of police censors to demand extensive cuts. The respectable appeal to theatrical intertexts with which the film begins is thus little more than a cover for the sheer slapstick spectacle that ensues. The film is, in fact, less an adaptation of the play *Tillie's Nightmare*, with which it shares little in common beyond Dressler's performance, than a freeform slapstick interpretation of the lyrics to the show's hit song "Heaven Will Protect a Working Girl," which recount the story of a "village maid" who is enticed to the city by a villainous gent, played in the film by Keystone's newest star, Charlie Chaplin.

The clichés of cinematic "refinement" receive another drubbing later in the film, in a self-reflexive scene in which the city gent, having stolen Tillie's money, visits a nickelodeon with his girlfriend (Mabel Normand) and watches a (fictitious) Keystone film, *A Thief's Fate*. The action of this film-within-a-film precisely mirrors the events of the framing narrative, causing the two protagonists to point out their similarity to the characters on the screen. As such, moreover, it establishes a pointedly satirical adaptation of the form of D. W. Griffith's 1909 *A Drunkard's Reformation*, a temperance play that had depicted the moral reawakening of an alcoholic father who attends a play about the evil of drink. Exemplifying earlier attempts to establish the motion picture as a vehicle for moral sermonizing, Griffith's film had been a landmark in early cinema's inscription in genteel social discourse. As Tom Gunning has argued, *A Drunkard's Reformation* "not only proposes theater as a moral and didactic medium, but it also draws attention to film itself as the vehicle of [a powerful temperance lesson] to the audience" (*Griffith* 170). Yet it is precisely the reformist content of Griffith's film that Sennett's version deflates. Following the Griffith film, Sennett continually cuts between the action on the screen and Mabel and Charlie's alarm at the film's parallels to their own lives; unlike *A Drunkard's Reformation*, however, the characters' reaction to what they see hardly constitutes moral reawakening. Mabel mischievously provokes her boyfriend by pointing out his similarity to the screen villain; Charlie gleefully turns the tables by indicating her resemblance to the villain's girlfriend; both become increasingly restless when they notice a mysterious character sitting beside them; and both flee the theater in open panic when they spot a sheriff's badge on his vest. What they have learned from the film is the imminent possibility of being caught, not the moral consequences of their wrong-doing—and as their continued misdeeds will prove, this hardly counts as "reformation."

But it is in its approach to narrative that the film establishes its clearest distance from the standards of the feature film, ultimately abandoning any pretense to storytelling unity for a focus on disjunctive slapstick and performative virtuosity. In his astute *Motography* review, Charles Condon summed up the film's attitude to narrative as follows: "The plot is a substantial one and if emphasized would become a good comedy-drama, but in its treatment here it merely furnishes a background for individual action, a frame-work upon which the members of the cast hang innumerable laugh-provoking mannerisms." This approach is nowhere more evident than in the film's final two reels. By this point, the city slicker has forced Tillie into a hasty marriage, after learning of her inheritance from a rich uncle, and the newlyweds host a formal party to celebrate their "Entrance into High Society." Of all the scenes in the film, the party is not only the longest (occupying most of the fifth reel and almost a third of the sixth), it is also the most devoid of substantive plot developments. Throughout much of the sequence, the film's causal progression stops dead to allow Dressler and Chaplin to perform their specialties—burlesque dancing on Dressler's part, roughhouse violence on Chaplin's. For these scenes, Sennett subordinates the film's visual style to the demands of foregrounding comic performance: Dressler and Chaplin are kept front and center in the frame, their actions often directed frontally toward the spectator (as in a vaudeville perform-ance). Narrative space is transformed into performance space and plot development is supplanted by a focus on bizarre comic spectacle.

But this is only the beginning of the film's final abandonment of narrative order. Tillie catches her husband spooning with Mabel (who has entered the party disguised as a maid) and the film immediately launches into an extraordinary eight-minute chase sequence. The basic principle here is one of accretion: Sennett multiplies lines of action and events, building the film toward a climactic tumult of comic spectacle. "Believe me, the work of assembling that last reel was some job," Sennett confessed in a *Chicago Tribune* interview. "There were over 300 scenes [i.e., shots] in it, and they all had to be put together logically, and so that none of them overshadowed any other. . . . Had to have perfect balance and cooperation, and it sure was some work getting it" (Kelly). As usual, the Keystone cops appear; but, in this case, there are four separate groups, each associated with a different mode of transportation—one group in an automobile, one on foot, one group in a motorboat, and one in a rowboat. Character after character tumbles into the ocean as the chase leads onto the Santa Monica pier—first Tillie, then the carload of policemen, then two more policemen when a wave upsets the rowboat. Three times Tillie is hauled out of the water and dropped back in before the police successfully lift her onto the pier. "What we want is straight going action," Sennett explained. "We can't stop to go back and we never repeat. . . . That's the way in 'Tillie's Punc-tured Romance.' It started with the simple little scene on the farm and then grew from a spring into a brook, into a river, into the ocean" (Kelly). What mattered most to Sennett was not closure but climax—the "ocean" as both setting and metaphor for a cumulative burst of frenetic action in which plot interest and development are finally swept away. In the end, the film provides only the most cursory of resolutions: a drenched Tillie returns her wedding ring to Charlie; Mabel rejects him too; and, doubly spurned, he faints back into the arms of a waiting policeman. The narra-tive ends as Tillie and Mabel embrace, weeping in sympathy over the city slicker's infidelities.

That such a film nonetheless proved a major popular and critical hit indicates clearly that "low" cultural forms could be successfully marketed to the growing mass audience. Distributed on a state rights basis, *Tillie's Punc-tured Romance* debuted in mid-December at prominent theaters nationwide, breaking attendance records in houses from Pittsburgh to Los Angeles. The critic for the *Motion Picture News* described the picture as a "masterpiece" and "six thousand feet of undiluted joy." "At the private showing," he related, "case-hardened reviewers . . . laughed until the tears streamed down their careworn faces" (Rev., *Motion Picture News*). Many critics also complimented Keystone's success in sustaining its slapstick style within the longer format. It was "a much enlarged, a de luxe edition of Keystone burlesque," argued one reviewer, which "set a fast pace for a six-reel journey and ended with a sprint" (Rev., *New York Dramatic Mirror*). Nor was *Tillie's* success the only indication of cross-class enthusiasm for Keystone comedy. In the same month as the six-reel feature's release, the managers of Delmonico's restau-rant—a mecca of New York's elite nightlife—decided to screen Keystone's *Dough and Dynamite* as a treat for Christmas customers. Earlier in the year, Roxy Rothapfel had selected a Keystone comedy—Roscoe Arbuckle's *A Bath House Beauty*—for the gala opening of the Strand in April, and a number of

Broadway palace theaters had, by the fall, begun following Rothapfel's lead. Evidently, the very business practices introduced in the name of uplift—the picture palace, the multiple-reel feature—could also serve as channels through which low cultural forms, like slapstick, were being popularized among upscale audiences. New business models thus outstripped their original ideological formation; there was no way to cater to middle-class tastes that did not also open the door for the "trickle-up" diffusion of more disreputable styles and genres. Yet, even as older cultural boundaries began to blur, events abroad were creating opportunities for synthesis on a truly global scale, certain to alter the conditions of mass culture's ideological construction.

▪▪▪▪▪▪▪▪ "Gruesome Aspects . . . Vividly Depicted": War and the Culture of Sensationalism

The development of new technologies of mass communication, Paul Virilio reminds us, has historically been inseparable from the spread of machine warfare. Perhaps no year occupies a more central place in that trajectory—even within Virilio's own writings—than this one. The global crisis revealed, with unimpeachable clarity, that communications technology had become a major factor in diplomatic affairs and that popular response to political and military events was now, as a result, dangerously accelerated. A historian of turn-of-the-century modernity argues that the diplomatic crisis that precipitated World War I was brought about by the very "volume and speed of electronic communication" (Kern 275–76). A historian of the telephone likewise notes how "all the world's telecommunications facilities," which should have been put "to peaceful uses, were [now] set to the frantic uses of war" (Robertson 116). The American cinema, too, participated in this relay of information; and this chapter concludes by looking at the increased production of newsreels during this period and the assumptions that shaped their representations of contemporary events.

This was not the first time this year that the film industry had involved itself in war. One of the few military conflicts before World War II to receive extensive motion picture coverage was the Mexican Revolution, which began with the 1910 uprising against dictator Porfirio Diaz. The Mexican filmmaking industry was one obvious beneficiary of that revolution, gaining in size and confidence as audiences flocked to see actuality footage of their country's upheavals. (For instance, thirty-three new theaters opened in Mexico City in 1911 alone, following the outbreak of the conflict [Paranagua 1].) But, by this year, a number of U.S. production companies were also exploiting the revolution's commercial potential, sending correspondents south of the border to capture their own images of war: the Selig-Hearst news service, Universal's *Animated Weekly*, and the Pathé newsreel all dispatched cameramen to Mexico that summer. Certainly among the most curious developments in this respect was rebel leader Pancho Villa's decision to sell motion picture "rights" to the conflict to the highest bidder, eventually striking a deal with the Mutual Film Corporation. Signed in Juárez on 3 January, the contract stipulated an initial payment to Villa of $25,000 plus 50 percent royalties, in return for which Villa guaranteed to provide "moving picture thrillers" in any way "consistent with his plans to depose and drive Huerta out of Mexico." "It's a new proposition, and it's been worrying me all day," explained Mutual president Harry Aitken to the *New York Times*. "How would you feel to be a partner of a man engaged in killing people?" ("Villa"). Despite heavy publicity, however, the Mutual films were not successful, disappointing audiences with a lack of actual battle scenes. The "thrillers" Villa had contracted to provide turned out to be "timely, but not very thrilling," according to the critic at *Motion Picture News* ("Special Film Reviews").

What strikes the contemporary reader here is the openness with which the Villa footage was publicized and even critiqued in terms of "thrills," rather than for its potential news value. Nor was Villa's vanity project unique in this respect. If the newsreel made substantial advances during this year, then this was not because of renewed interest in cinema's journalistic potential but because news offered the rarer pleasures of thrills intensified by authenticity. Early motion picture newsfilm producers saw their primary role not so much as to provide educational information as to supply sensational visualizations of news events, after the pattern of the cheap nineteenth-century "story papers." The launching (in March) of the *Selig-Hearst News Pictorial,* to take one example, was no more promoted as "news" than had been Selig's previous newspaper co-production, *The Adventures of Kathlyn*; instead, what was offered was "battles, riots, wrecks, massacres, holocausts—in fact, sensational happenings all over the world" ("Selig-Hearst Pictorial"). In early June, the industry's leading news producer, Pathé-American, responded with its own "epoch making innovation"—the launching of the first daily newsreel—announcing a worldwide network of stringers with "a keen scent for interesting events." Here, too, however, it was the immediacy of the information, not its quality, that counted for most: "In the morning a man can read of some event going on in the world," trade press readers were informed, "and then the same afternoon . . . he can go to see the event in motion pictures" ("Pathé").

The early newsreel was thus revelatory of the way in which sensation-alism, as an aesthetic mode, opened onto broader issues of politics and nation. Far from being the mindless escapism that most genteel reformers assumed, popular sensationalism provided a pattern of comprehension that even framed political discourse. The world war, when it erupted, was eas-ily cut to that pattern; it was, according to trade advertisements, the "reign-ing sensation of the World" and "Christendom's Greatest Catastrophe," and new newsreel services eagerly sprang up to cater to public demand for "authentic" scenes of war. The paradox, however, was that actual footage of the conflict, when it was forthcoming, was rarely adequate to the sensa-tional claims made on its behalf. In general, military authorities forbade any filming at the frontline, forcing filmmakers either to rely on footage shot far from the action or to recycle older releases. Only infrequently did news cameramen even come close to capturing combat footage, as when Univer-sal's *Animated Weekly* acquired two hundred feet showing the capture of a scouting party prior to the siege of Antwerp.

Extant footage, though difficult to date with accuracy, tends to confirm the difficulties faced in filming actual combat. Later in the conflict, Brigadier General Edgar Russell of the U.S. military's Photographic Section explained the problem: "When conditions are good for fighting they are, of necessity, poor for photography, and vice versa" (Mould and Berg 54). Accordingly, most genuine surviving images come from behind the lines and consist of a predictable succession of troop inspections, training maneu-vers, tent pitchings, distant shell explosions, and home-front dignitaries. In some instances, filmmakers exploited editing techniques learned from fic-tion cinema to create the impression of actual combat engagement—for example, by intercutting anti-aircraft training scenes with images of flying planes and the "resulting" battlefield explosions. Such rudimentary fabrica-tions testify to an impulse to generate sensationalism through implied causality, though in general the impression left by surviving footage is of causes without effects and vice versa. The key, evidently, was in the ren-dering, and the newsreel floundered on its inability to render war footage as a sufficiently thrilling narrative.

The fictionalization of war—both in faked newsreels and in fictional war features—was the predictable response to the actual war's failure to live up to expectations. Newsreel producers soon began staging battle scenes, and sensationalism outmatched authenticity as a criterion for news reportage. In a letter to Carl Laemmle, John Tippett, Universal's London representative, stated categorically that all combat films shown in America had been faked: "Anything you see in America of any consequence is fake.

. . . Cameramen are absolutely forbidden to go anywhere near the points of interest" ("All War Pictures Fakes"). A flood of fiction features, some imported, answered to the demand for what one distributor termed "blood and thunder" business—for example, *With Serb and Austrian* (Austro-Servian Film Company), *The War of Wars* (Ramo), *The Ordeal* (Life Photo Film), and *Lay Down Your Arms* (Great Northern), the latter advertised as "all the gruesome aspects of war vividly depicted." If the dichotomy of fiction versus fact collapsed so quickly in war coverage, then this was because factual events failed to keep pace with the cinematic market in thrills.

Ultimately, the war would provoke a major rethinking both of American cinema's civic role and of its place in the global film market. With respect to the first of these, the industry soon learned the pitfalls of addressing politically sensitive subject matter: police efforts to ban war films took place in San Francisco, Los Angeles, and New York, while the State Department itself participated in investigating Life's *The Ordeal* for possible violation of the country's policy of neutrality. Such attitudes were quickly internalized by the industry's trade press, which began warning exhibitors against "partisan war films," urging that "the screen ought to remain neutral or pro-American which is much the same thing" ("Facts and Comments"). If the outbreak of war raised the possibility of a politically engaged, civic role for cinema, then it was a role that the industry chose to disavow, preferring the commercial safety of mass appeal to the divisiveness of ideological debate. More eagerly pursued, however, were new opportunities for international market dominance, as industry leaders realized that the European crisis promised long-term export gains. A steep decline in film production in the warring nations resulted in a spate of headlines in the U.S. trade press declaring that "American Makers May Profit Largely by This Calamity" or suggesting ways for "Cashing In on Europe's War." "There have always been foreign markets," declared Arthur Lang, export manager of the Nicholas Power Company. "The war has, however, done two things. It has forced the attention of our manufacturers on these markets, and it has made it far easier than it ever was before to introduce their goods into these markets."

■ ■ ■

Thus, as the year rounded to a close, external and internal developments combined to open unforeseen prospects for cinematic mass culture, as new business models and export opportunities put the American film industry firmly on the path toward global hegemony. Some features of the new pattern emerge clearly from the foregoing discussion, for example, the ascendancy of modern consumer standards, the repackaging of popular sensationalism for a cross-class audience, and the avoidance of a political role. If the industry still gave lip service to a cultural hierarchy that placed aesthetic refinement at its summit, it increasingly gave precedence to a competing hierarchy that celebrated material abundance and the thrills of popular sensationalism. Cinema's development in this key transitional year thus reflected less a process of uplift, as is sometimes claimed, than a complex cross-breeding of aesthetic traditions that abolished the distinctiveness of "high" and "low" and helped in the formation of a new, commercially driven mass culture. Whatever cinema achieved in subsequent years would be born from this dissolving point of traditional class and aesthetic hierarchies.

1915

Movies and the
State of the Union

LEE GRIEVESON

The United States marks the completion of the Panama Canal with two international expositions in California, celebrating the remarkable technological achievement of the creation of a passage across the continent between the Caribbean Sea and the Pacific Ocean. The expositions seek to fashion a national self-identity marked by technological advancement and a new position of hemispheric and international leadership. The canal radically reduces the time it takes to transport trade across the United States (shortening the route from coast to coast by as much as 8,000 miles and thirty days). Business and government forces use the canal to conquer South American markets, contributing significantly to the emergence of the United States as the world's dominant economic power, and extending the influence of "the American way of life" in South American countries. (The occupation of Haiti on 3 July is further evidence of U.S. imperialist ambition.) At the expositions, in San Diego starting in January and San Francisco in March, the idealization of an American modernity of technology and commercial and governmental expansion is figured in particular through exhibits of industrial advancement. On display is a model of the canal itself and, the most popular exhibit, a replica of the recently created moving assembly line at the Ford Motor Company, which greatly speeds up production time of each new Model T. Watching the creation of an automobile from start to finish, crowds witness the new power of industrial organizations to compress time, manage and discipline the bodies of workers, and increase profits accordingly. Ford celebrates the manufacture of its one millionth Model T in October; other technological advancements this year—including notably the first transcontinental telephone call from Bell Telephone—further solidify the compression of space and time and enable the circulation of information and capital.

Yet other developments threaten this image of American modernity, both at home and abroad. The excursion steamer ship *The Eastland* sinks in

Chicago in July, killing 844 people. Women march in record numbers (estimated at 40,000) in New York City to demand the rights of citizenship, responding to the rejection of a proposal in the House of Representatives and in New York State to extend the vote to women. Likewise, African Americans continue to demand an end to racist practices and representations. "Gathering clouds along the color line," to use journalist Ray Stannard Baker's words, play out in various arenas: protests occasioned by the film *The Birth of a Nation;* a sickening tide of lynching, which reaches an all-time high in this year (seventy-nine African Americans are murdered in this way; 10,000 African Americans march in New York City in July to protest this); the segregation by President Woodrow Wilson of federal government employees; the white-led celebrations when the African American boxing champion Jack Johnson is defeated in April. Xenophobia and racial violence are not directed solely at African Americans, however, as perceived racial and ethnic differences solidify more broadly throughout the nation. In August, a Jewish factory owner named Leo Frank, who had been framed for the rape and murder of a young girl, is convicted by a jury amid an environment of sensationalism and public fury, then abducted by a mob from Atlanta's state penitentiary and lynched. Fifteen thousand people go to see the corpse.

Abroad, the conflict in Europe is brought closer to the United States in May by the German sinking of the British passenger liner *Lusitania* off the coast of Ireland. Among 1,198 passengers who perish are 128 American civilians. Wilson immediately initiates a tense stand-off with Germany over its use of submarine warfare, which is seen to contravene the accepted code of war and of maritime rights. Whilst the policy of neutrality continues, debates about military preparedness flourish, leading to the resignation of Secretary of State William Jennings Bryan, who regards Wilson's position as one that will inevitably lead to war. Indeed, preparedness plans are proposed to Congress in December.

The year sees a number of notable literary works that would become significant film adaptations in future years, such as L. Frank Baum's *The Scarecrow of Oz,* John Buchan's *The Thirty-nine Steps,* and Edgar Rice Burroughs's *The Return of Tarzan.* Theodore Dreiser's novel *The Genius,* banned by the New York Society for the Suppression of Vice, tells a semi-autobiographical story about a young artist's relationship with several women, probing shifting attitudes toward art and morality. Its modernist sensibilities and rejection of moral norms are shared by other cultural works of this year, perhaps most notably T. S. Eliot's poem "The Love Song of J. Alfred Prufrock" (published in June in *Poetry: A Magazine of Verse,* edited by Ezra Pound), and in Charlotte Perkins Gilman's feminist novel *Herland,* which imagines a utopian society entirely made up of women who radically transform social, familial, and political relationships. This year also marks the initiation of the production of what artist Marcel Duchamp called "readymades," that is, ordinary manufactured objects that, when signed, become works of art. Once again, the year was poised between conservative traditions and modernist rejections of those traditions, rejections that would reshape the world.

In relation to the film industry, the first day of the year epitomizes the synergy of the atavistic and the modern that marks the social and political history of the year. On 1 January, a twelve-reel historical epic called *The Clansman*, directed by D. W. Griffith, is previewed at the Loring Opera House in Riverside, California. Announced in advertisements in the local press as the "greatest of all motion pictures," the film was, the *Riverside Daily Press* reports, duly applauded "long and loud" (qtd. in Lennig "Myth"). Critics declare it a harbinger of developments in film production, film form, and "the advancement of film art," and its exhibition in opera houses and large theaters as symptomatic of the newfound respectability of cinema. The day after the film's launch, columnist Louis Reeves Harrison announces that the coming year will see the development of the "ten-reel photodrama," or what he calls "photopera" (43). While Harrison's prophesy of a shift toward longer feature films exhibited with original music will be partially fulfilled in the coming twelve months, the related development he calls for—the connection of film to high cultural forms like opera—proves more complicated. Griffith's film, renamed in early February *The Birth of a Nation*, exemplifies these complications. Counterbalancing praise for the film, a flurry of criticism and controversy focuses principally on the film's racist representation of the nation's history and of African Americans' place within it. Watching the film later in the month of January, at another special preview screening, the National Association for the Advancement of Colored People (NAACP) criticizes the film for its "vicious" and racist account of African Americans in the Reconstruction era, inaugurating a campaign against the film that will gather many supporters and run throughout the year and beyond.

Around the same time *The Birth of a Nation* is being previewed and fought over, the Supreme Court hears its first case involving the film industry. The decision it renders is probably the most crucial one in the history of American cinema. Mutual, a large distribution company, had challenged the constitutionality of the Pennsylvania and Ohio state censor boards. The boards dictate that all films shown in the states must be inspected beforehand by a board of censors empowered to block exhibition if found to be "sacrilegious, obscene, indecent or immoral."[1] Having lost its cases, Mutual files an appeal with the Supreme Court, and the Court agrees to hear the cases together in January. Lawyers for Mutual argue that the company is entitled to invoke the protection of the state constitutional guarantees of free speech and freedom of publication. At stake here is the question of how, or indeed if, cinema can participate in the public sphere of common debate (like the press) and thus how it can be rendered consistent with the remit of government to preserve the body politic. The justices deny Mutual's claims and their conception of the function of cinema. "It cannot be put out of view," Justice Joseph McKenna writes, "that the exhibition of moving pictures is a business, pure and simple, originated and conducted for profit, like other spectacles, not to be regarded, nor intended to be regarded by the Ohio Constitution, we think, as part of the press of the country, or as organs of public opinion" (*Mutual* 244). Moving pictures thus become the only medium of communication in the history of the country to be subject to systematic legal prior restraint. Cinema is discursively constructed as a realm apart from the press and its engagement with controversial and topical issues (Grieveson "Policing").

Many reformers and members of the legal community applaud the decision of the Supreme Court. It is, however, challenged by many associated with the film industry. *Moving Picture World* publishes numerous articles bewailing the decision and its potential effects. Griffith, too, takes issue with the decision and its conception of cinema. In a pamphlet privately published late in the year entitled *The Rise and Fall of Free Speech,* he argues that the decision will damage the role and future development of cinema. Many others argue that cinema can be utilized to engage with contemporary social issues and problems. Indeed, cinema proliferates in various spaces, outside theaters (in schools, churches, YMCAs, and so on). The medium is adopted by many who think it can become a crucial educative device: by industrial organizations explaining and proselytizing for new commercial and industrial processes; by government departments to explain government policy; by political groups (feminists, labor groups, for example) to argue for political change; and by filmmakers engaged with contemporary social problems like crime, gangsters, temperance, and poverty. Films of this year reflect on current events, including *The Battle Cry of Peace,* telling a story of an unprepared America attacked and devastated by a foreign invader, and the documentary *History of the Great European War. Prohibition* narrates a tale of the deleterious effects of alcohol, participating in the temperance debates that flourish in this period. *The Silent Plea* dramatizes the financial problems of a widow trying to bring up young children, directly making an argument about unfair tax practices. Cinema is, then, inextricably entangled with public debates this year, in terms of production, representation, exhibition, and response. The Court's attempt to divorce cinema from the world—inspired, ironically, by concern over its place in that same world vis-à-vis censorship—will be only partly successful.

Louis Reeves Harrison's prediction of the dominance of "photopera" will also prove only partly accurate for this year. Multi-reel feature films do become more prevalent (a total of 447 films of at least five reels are produced [Singer "Feature"]). Amongst these are films that seek to connect to a high cultural intertext, such as *Carmen,* starring opera singer Geraldine Farrar, or a series of films produced by the company Famous Players drawing on literary intertexts. Mary Pickford is hired at great expense by Famous Players (the production wing of the distributor Paramount) and stars in a number of films, including *Mistress Nell, Rags,* and *Madame Butterfly.* Other notable feature films include *Ghosts,* based on the play by Henrik Ibsen, *The Italian,* about immigrant life in New York City, and *The Warrens of Virginia,* set during the Civil War. Alongside the gradually accelerating production of features, movie palaces are constructed in increasing numbers (detailed throughout the year in a column entitled "At the Theaters" in *Moving Picture World*). And movie studios, the production plants, are constructed too, including, most notably, Universal City, a huge new studio complex in California that opens in March to considerable fanfare in the trade press.

Yet while the production of feature films is on the increase, figures suggest that they constitute only 10 percent of film production this year (Singer "Feature"). Short films, those of three reels or fewer, make up 90 percent of film production, and their production continues to rise, though less steeply than before and less dramatically than feature film production. Many continue to argue that shorts should be central to the industry and/or that a rounded film program, including shorts and a feature, is critical to the provision of an evening's entertainment. Charlie Chaplin's shorts, including *The Tramp, The Champion,* and *Burlesque on Carmen,* are extremely popular, after he is lured from Keystone to Essanay, given a huge salary, and accordingly hyped in the press (from 2 January onward). Chaplin's stardom, like Pickford's, is increasingly important to film entrepreneurs attempting to attract mass audiences (Grieveson "Stars").

Births, Deaths, Marriages: *The Birth of a Nation*

The Birth of a Nation is timed to commemorate the American Civil War on its fiftieth anniversary. It appears in the context of other retrospective accounts of the nation's history and supposedly unique identity that proliferates in this year. It also references a more immediate context, that of the war con-vulsing the "old world" edging ever closer to the United States. It begins with a statement of support for neutrality with its first title: "If in this work we have conveyed to the mind the ravages of war to the end that war may be held in abhorrence, this effort will not have been in vain." An allegori-cal ending to the film reinforces this position, showing the God of War fad-ing away to be replaced by the figure of Christ. Griffith talked of the film as a "sermon against the horrors of war."

Griffith's claim for the public role of *The Birth of a Nation,* its status as a "sermon," was elaborated further with claims about its historical veracity and about the role cinema should play in recounting the nations' history. In an article in April, Griffith makes the following announcement about the future of cinema and historical knowledge:

> The time will come, and in less than ten years . . . when the children of pub-lic schools will be taught practically everything by moving pictures. Certainly they will never be obliged to read history again. Imagine a public library of the near future, for instance . . . you will merely seat yourself at a properly adjusted window, in a scientifically prepared room, press the button, and actually see what happened. There will be no opinions expressed. You will merely be present at the making of history.   (qtd. in Silva 25)

The Birth of a Nation's account of the Civil War and Reconstruction period exemplifies this "picturization of history," according to Griffith, and he goes so far as to offer a $10,000 reward for anyone who can prove its inaccuracy (though is unable to respond when the president of the NAACP questions aspects of the film's racist rewriting of history). Woodrow Wilson's *A History of the American People,* written when he was a professor of history at Prince-ton, is quoted in the film (and indeed Wilson's argument about the creation of a unified nation as a consequence of the Civil War supposedly is respon-sible for the change of the film's title to *The Birth of a Nation*). Various scenes are claimed to be based on historical facsimiles, including the theater where Abraham Lincoln is assassinated. Vice crusader Reverend Dr. Charles Park-hurst writes, "This drama is a telling illustration of the possibilities of motion pictures as an instrument of history" (qtd. in Silva 102–03). Wilson sees the film at the White House, and later Griffith implies the president had endorsed its historical account, observing in an interview, "I was gratified when a man we all revere, or ought to, said it teaches history by lightning" (qtd. in Lennig "Myth").

Yet Griffith's conception of the Civil War and Reconstruction period in *The Birth of a Nation,* his sense of a nation reborn through the actions of the Ku Klux Klan, is profoundly racist. It is not uniquely so, to be sure, for the film recapitulates dominant historical accounts of the Reconstruction period like that articulated by Wilson. It is, however, unusually widely seen and influential, and the connection of historical events to fictional events led by racist ideology proves powerful. Shortly before the film is shown in Atlanta late in the year, white Georgians burn a cross atop nearby Stone Mountain. This serves to mark the rebirth of the Klan, a group of vigilantes who take it upon themselves to police moral and social order guided by racist principles and a conservative nostalgia for clear-cut racial hierarchies. Thus Griffith's fictional account of the Klan's role in Reconstruction in the second part of the film, based partly on contemporary historical accounts, helps to reanimate the Klan, which had largely been dormant since the 1870s, and more generally to enable racist discourse and practices.

Closer inspection of the film—at least, the version extant today—reveals a complex articulation of a racial politics that insists on a separation of black and white populations and on the necessary centrality of whiteness to appropriate governance. The presentation of a sexual drama in the film, of the threatened connection of black and white bodies, thus allegorizes a critical political drama. On the one hand, that drama is a historical one, telling a story of the disenfranchisement of black populations, the curtailment of the promises of Reconstruction, and the "necessity" of the vigilante role of the Klan. On the other hand, it is simultaneously a story that is contemporary to the production and reception of the film, as an argument for an exclusionary American polity in the face of gathering black migration northward (the "Great Migration") and the increasing immigration of southern and eastern European migrants to the United States, who are viewed through a perspective that insistently constructs them as racial others.

Take, for example, a scene toward the middle of the second part of the film, a crucial pivot that lays the groundwork for the rise of the Klan and the disenfranchisement of black populations. "Little sister" Flora Cameron (Mae Marsh) leaves her house, Cameron Hall, in Piedmont, South Carolina, to fetch water from a local well. As she walks alongside the white picket fence separating the house from the street, she is watched by Gus (Walter Long in blackface), who had been described in the title sequence as a "renegade Negro," the word marking his betrayal of white slave owners and white mastery. Gus crouches in front of the fence, in the shadows; the lighting and mise-en-scène is expressive of Gus's position outside of a polity imagined in part in the film through the insistent focus on the space of Cameron Hall, whose columns mark it as a grand, classically ordered space. Cameron Hall stands as an idealization of a domestic and political order that is briefly articulated at the opening of the film (notably a scene where

Gus (Walter Long) propositions Flora (Mae Marsh) in *The Birth of a Nation.*

northern visitors are taken from the house to cotton fields behind it, surveying a well-ordered world where slaves dance happily for their white masters); later it is threatened by vigilante black soldiers, in a scene juxtaposed
with Lincoln pardoning the son of the house, Ben Cameron, that seeks to
connect Lincoln to a Christ-like figure of forgiveness and thus to an ideal of
administrative authority and generosity. In the next shot in the sequence of
Flora leaving Cameron Hall, she walks past the end of a fence and into a
wood (it's a different fence, it seems, but the centrality of the fence imagery
is critical in Griffith's construction of this scene and the separation of white
domestic space and its outside). Gus approaches and tells her he is now a
captain in the army and will need a wife. At this, Flora recoils in horror and
runs away. Leaving the fence behind, Flora effectively departs the civilized
space of whiteness to enter a forest symbolically connected to a savagery
that is presented as subhuman. In the extended chase sequence that follows,
Flora is pursued by Gus through a forest until she comes to a cliff, where-
upon she jumps to her death rather than submit to what appears to be a
potential rape.[2] In long shot, Gus appears to howl with anguish.

   When the necessary and "natural" separation of white and black breaks
down, as when Flora ventures outside the white fence protecting Cameron

Hall, disaster inevitably follows. The two mulattos in the film embody the breakdown of this separation. Lydia Brown and Silas Lynch conspire to wreak a terrible crisis for individuals and the nation. Lydia is the house-keeper and the mistress of the northern politician Austin Stoneman. His desire for her, which the film codes as unnatural, influences his political beliefs on the equality between black and white people. An intertitle refers to his desire as "the weakness that . . . blights a nation," thereby referring us back to the title of the film: the nation is blighted by interracial desire and the concomitant destabilization of civility and proper and wise govern-ment. When Austin tells Silas, who becomes a leader in the Reconstruction-era South, that he is the "equal of any man," Silas takes this literally and, like Gus with Flora, approaches a white woman for marriage—Austin's daughter, no less, Elsie (Lillian Gish), who ("naturally") refuses. The scene is remarkable for its representation of lascivious sexual desire: Silas locks Elsie in a room with him as he awaits a priest, kisses her white gown, and rubs his thighs suggestively, while she hysterically tries to escape. Lighting in the scene aestheticizes the contrast between black and white, putting Silas partly in shadow while Elsie is wrapped in a circle of whiteness (Dyer). Again, the film insists on the connection of interracial desire with dis-ordered, dangerous governance. Indeed, the mulatto is the embodiment of the illicit and dangerous mixing of bodies. As such, these characters stand as symbolic of the division in the nation at large, marking a disturbance in the sphere of the sexual that, because it connects individual bodies to the social body, is for the film necessarily intertwined with issues of national policy and power. It is in this way that the political drama of producing sub-jugated and racialized bodies is allegorized as a sexual drama.

Silas, Gus, and Lydia are united in a common trait—ungovernable emo-tions, a lack of self-control and self-discipline. In this the film is consistent with period discourse, which commonly asserted that mulattos in particu-lar were characterized by ungovernable emotions as a result of their mixed heritage (the joining, it was thought, of the immorality of black people with the ingenuity of white people, articulated clearly in this year in Henry Her-bert Goddard's book *The Criminal Imbecile*). The question of self-control is writ large in *The Birth of a Nation*, for the black control of the South in the Reconstruction period is represented as a despotic, disorganized, and dan-gerous destruction of a regime of civility and order. Griffith thus argues, like other contemporary Reconstruction historians (and indeed policy makers), that the Thirteenth Amendment, freeing slaves and giving them the vote, was catastrophic, as indeed were the Fourteenth and Fifteenth Amend-ments that gave African Americans free access to public facilities.

Whiteness is a prerequisite for the ability to govern self and others. At the black political meetings that lead to a black majority in the South Carolina legislature, signs demand "Equality" and, more specifically, "Equal rights, equal politics, equal marriage." After the election, this agenda is pursued. One scene is critical here, of the South Carolina legislature: introduced by an intertitle claiming the veracity of the representation of the space—consistent with Griffith's attempts to present the film as history, to secure the fictional in the factual—we see black representatives drinking whisky, eating chicken, not wearing shoes. The title "Negro mis-rule" is an important one, for the logic of the second part of the film is to insist upon the incapacity of black characters to offer effective government. In the scene in question, the black representatives pass two pieces of legislation: insisting that "all whites must salute negro officers on the streets" and another that legalizes "the intermarriage of blacks and whites." Here the breakdown of white rule is connected to the disabling of white male hegemony—the need to salute black soldiers—and again to the purported black male desire for white women.

Yet order and white power is ultimately restored, leading indeed to the birth of a nation understood as a commonality of whiteness or, as an intertitle has it, "the common defense of an Aryan birthright" and, correspondingly, the exclusion of black Americans from political participation and presence. The death of Flora is the critical pivot point for this restoration of the state of the union. After her brother, Ben Cameron, finds her at the bottom of the cliff, he establishes Gus's guilt and assembles his Klan brethren to find Gus and punish him. Gus is soon lynched (the extant print shows this only briefly, though it seems more material was shot and widely seen), and Ben and the Klan become a serious force for the reestablishment of white rule. This is further expressed in the plotline surrounding Ben's father, Dr. Cameron, who earlier had been abducted from Cameron Hall by black soldiers and a growing black mob on the streets. He escapes their clutches with the help of some "loyal" slaves, but is pursued by the black soldiers and holes up in a log cabin with his daughter Margaret, some white northern soldiers, and the loyal slaves. At the same time, Elsie Stoneman is threatened by Silas Lynch, who, as we have seen, proposes marriage. The Klan rescues Elsie just in time, before a forced marriage ceremony. Meanwhile, Dr. Cameron and others hold guns over the heads of their daughters, willing to kill them rather than have them taken by the black soldiers. It will not come to that, though, for the Klan arrives just in time, rescuing those hiding in the cabin. Vachel Lindsay, in his new book *The Art of the Moving Picture* (the first English-language book-length example of film theory and criticism), aptly describes the Klan as arriving like a "white Anglo Saxon Niagara" (152). Whiteness sweeps all before it, eradicating the black threat and establishing the conditions for a nation founded and unified on the principles of racial unity—asserting itself now over regional conflict— and the necessity of racial hierarchy.

Three concluding ideas are necessary to the imagination of the nation as coterminous with a particular conception of race and appropriate governance: one, black voters are scared off by the Klan—black presence in the political process is necessarily curtailed; two, a call for the return of African Americans to Africa— Griffith, it seems, shot a conclusion that promoted this "solution" as one devised by Lincoln; and three, a union of white characters—Ben marries Elsie Stoneman and Margaret marries Elsie's brother Phil, thus joining South and North as white civility and marriage secure the birth of the nation. The film ultimately routes its historical account through fictional terrain, connecting its story of the Civil War and Reconstruction— rebirth of a nation as coterminous with a racial exclusivity—to the union of heterosexual couples that so frequently establish the resolution of classical narrative cinema, a form of which Griffith is often seen to be a crucial progenitor. Or, put another way, the film manages a dizzying mix of fiction and fact to uphold fictions of race as fact and so legitimate a culture of segregation mandating the exclusion of African Americans from the privileges of citizenship and the public sphere.

Unsurprisingly, *The Birth of a Nation* and its assertion of the necessity of a segregated culture are controversial from the start, and the subsequent debates about the film mark significant positions in relation to the unresolved question of cinema's own place in the cultural arena. The NAACP denounces the film as a "vicious" misrepresentation of black people that "created race hatred" and that "would likely lead to a breach of the peace" (qtd. in Mast, *Movies* 129). Local censor boards, councils, and mayors prohibit screening the film in cities like Cleveland, Ohio; Wilmington, Delaware; St. Louis, Missouri; Topeka, Kansas; Louisville, Kentucky; and San Antonio, Texas (Fleener-Marzec esp. 66–73, 94–99). The film is at least initially banned by statewide authorities in Illinois, Michigan, Kansas, and Ohio (Gaines 233; Fleener-Marzec 265–68). In Ohio, censors reject the film in accordance with the remit of the state censor board. The film was, they said, "not harmless."[3] Censorship and regulation here sought, in part, to protect vulnerable audiences from dangerous "speech." Its effects were complex, though, for it also positioned cinema as incapable of legitimately engaging with controversial topical issues, just as the justices of the Supreme Court were likewise ruling on the definition of the function of cinema. That it was Griffith who protested this so loudly, to protect his rights to make a film advocating practices of racial hierarchy and segregation, speaks to the paradox of protest in liberal democracies.

Commerce and Its Discontents: *The Cheat*

Other films speak to this context of racist discourses and practices in the delineation of a sense of nationhood built on exclusionary lines. Bookending the year begun by the previews of *The Birth of a Nation, The Cheat* (directed by Cecil B. DeMille for Lasky/Paramount), for example, is released in December and tells a story of a Japanese businessman's desire for a white socialite that results in an act of brutality—branding her with a hot branding iron to connote ownership—that stands in for the act of rape. We are introduced to Hishuru Tori (Sessue Hayakawa), the businessman, at the outset, costumed in a Japanese robe inscribing his mark on an objet d'art, illuminated by the glow of the brazier in a scene tinted red to imply a dangerous sexuality. The film thus begins with an emphasis on a racial otherness that it will ultimately present, like Birth, as ineluctable and insurmountable. Later, dressed in a suit, Tori is shown with the wealthy white women with whom he is friends. One of them, Edith Hardy (Fannie Ward), is an obsessive consumer, a fact that troubles her husband, Richard (Jack Dean), a New York stockbroker, who asks her to wait for his investments to pay off before spending more money. Edith is unable to do so and gambles on the stock market funds she controls as treasurer of the Red Cross (the funds were meant for Belgian refugees, the film's only reference to the events of the war). When that money is lost, Tori offers to lend her the same amount and she agrees—implicitly to exchange herself for the money. The consuming woman becomes the consumable object. Tori's costume at this point symbolically marks—for the film—the dangerous mixing of "East and West": his white tie and tuxedo shirt is covered by a Japanese kimono. Richard's investments, meanwhile, pay off, and Edith goes to Tori with the money, attempting to renege on her deal. When he insists that "you cannot buy me off," a struggle ensues, and he brands her on the left shoulder with the mark of his possessions. He grabs her roughly and asserts again that he is entitled to have her. She shoots him, also on the left shoulder, and escapes. When Richard arrives on the scene shortly thereafter, he finds Tori clutching a piece of Edith's dress, marking the sexual nature of his threat to Edith. Attempting to shield his wife from the crime, Richard assumes blame for the shooting and is tried in court. When a guilty verdict is announced, Edith dramatically intervenes, showing the jury the branding mark given to

Tori (Sessue Hayakawa) pressing his claim in *The Cheat*.

her by Tori, at which the members of the jury leap out of their seats, exonerate Richard, and attempt to attack Tori, thus resembling, as Sumiko Higashi observes, the "lynch mobs that murdered blacks with impunity in a segregationist era of Jim Crow laws" (108).

Outraged white jury members thus seek to uphold the sanctity of the "color line" in a way similar to the Klan in *Birth*. Yet Tori also marks a specific threat, situated as he is in relation to a virulent anti-Asian sentiment that had in the nineteenth century sharply curtailed Asians rights of entry, naturalization, and land ownership and that was further intensified in the early twentieth century in the context of geopolitical anxieties about the expansionist policies of Japan. Japan played a complex role in the American imaginary at this moment. Certainly it was feared for its political power and thus for its threat to American imperial goals (notably in the Philippines and Hawaii). Japanese immigrants and Asians more generally had come to be associated in public discourse on immigration restriction with degeneracy and immorality.[4] Many of the anxieties about so-called "white slavery," the abduction of white women into prostitution, focused upon Asian men, once again connecting race and sexuality at the center of anxieties about a modernity characterized by increased national and global traffic. Yet Japan was also regarded with considerable interest. Orientalist discourse flourished, associating the East with ideals of aesthetics, sensuality, and an intensity of experience. World fairs, including the Panama-Pacific Exposition, exhibited Japanese artifacts. One of the central ideas about "the Orient" at this moment was that it inhabited a premodern temporality, an idea that made it central to the mediation of modernity in the United States in public discourse (Harris; Lears *No Place*).

Cecil B. DeMille's style in his direction of the film, particularly his much-praised innovations in lighting, do indeed frequently present Tori in medium close-up as an object of fascination to be scrutinized, so curiously mirroring Tori's own fascination with objects. Take, for example, the sequence where Tori shows Edith his priceless objects in his "Shoji Room." The mise-en-scène is overwhelmed by beautiful objects—a bronze Buddha, a golden screen, a cabinet full of objets d'art—and the scene is tinted amber and then blue. According to *Moving Picture World,* "the lighting effects . . . are beyond all praise in their art, their daring and their originality" (qtd. in Higashi 111). Once again, like in Birth, aesthetic innovations in filmic discourse take place alongside the articulation of a discourse about the lack of civility and the immorality of culturally dissonant populations. While Tori is first rendered an object of curious scrutiny, of fetishized spectacle, he is, at the end, necessarily separated from respectable and "civilized" white culture, tried and found guilty in the court of public opinion. Commerce, both literal and figurative, between Tori and Edith, between "East" and "West," is necessarily curtailed.

Curtailing commerce is indeed central to the film's articulation of ideas about economy and notably about Edith as a problematic "new woman." United in their marginality from a productive economy exemplified by Richard and his investments—a unity marked visually with their identical wounds—Tori and Edith are positioned as homologous threats to social and economic order that call for appropriate forms of discipline. Constance Balides and Sumiko Higashi, among others, have shown how the film associates Edith with the dangers of overconsumption, with a loss of self-control and surfeit of consumerist desire, which is consistent with wider discourses about the perils of consumerism and the regulation of domestic economy that were articulated in dialogue with the redefinition of the social roles of women as central participants in a new consumer economy (Balides; Higashi). Chastened by her experiences, shamed in court, Edith walks out of the film at its conclusion alongside Richard, back to the domestic sphere, it seems, and an adjustment of her consumerist desires in line with his dictates. To regulate her involvement in the public sphere is also, neatly, to regulate Tori's, for the co-articulation of ideas about race and gender in the film enables a doubled policing of mobility and participation, as it does also in Birth and as it does, historians have argued, in the broader discourses (and practices) of lynching and in the furor around "white slavery." Cultural work here maps out the configuration of the body politic, marking out those whose claims to participation, mobility, and indeed citizenship are worthy.

Citizen Vamp: *A Fool There Was*

One of the central issues in relation to this organization of social and political order is a gendered division of space that had aligned men with public affairs, while relegating women to a private (and ostensibly nonpolitical) realm. Yet many increasingly challenge this division, not only the 40,000 people who march on New York City to demand the right for women to vote. The ramifications of this challenge to the hegemonic gendered configurations of space and citizenship at a moment of profound transformation in the public sphere is played out in films other than *The Cheat.* The serial film *The Exploits of Elaine* merits brief attention here. The serial ran for thirty-six episodes, including two immediate sequels, *The Romance of Elaine* and *The New Exploits of Elaine,* testament to a popularity generated in part by a tie-in with Hearst newspapers and by a strategy of appealing to female audiences. Together, the films show the travails of Elaine, pursued consistently by the "Clutching Hand" and his cohorts, often in ways that directly mimic sexual assault, but rescued through a combination of her own quick-wittedness and, more frequently, by Craig Kennedy, a "scientific detective." In doing so the films mediate the twin poles of independence and dependence, empowerment and imperilment, articulating ideals of the so-called New Woman yet in a way that was consistently shadowed by danger (for more on serial films, see Stamp *Movie-Struck* and Singer *Melodrama*).

Other films mediate the shifting terrain of women in society in distinctive ways. In the social problem film *The Cup of Life,* for example, sisters Ruth and Helen are department store saleswomen. Ruth marries a stable working-class man and becomes a housewife and mother. Helen, fearing the poverty and drudgery of working-class immigrant life, takes "the easiest path" to the rewards of consumer culture by becoming the mistress of several men until she is rejected and dies in impoverished circumstances. Life outside of domesticity leads to tragedy.

Likewise, the emergence of the figure of the "vamp" (that is, alluring, sexually aggressive woman) this year, notably in the film *A Fool There Was,* ties together anxieties about sexual, economic, and indeed ethnic disorder.

The vamp (Theda Bara) triumphing over her victim's wife in *A Fool There Was*.

In the film, a happily married lawyer, John Schuyler, is appointed as special diplomatic representative to England. On board the ship across the Atlantic he meets "the vampire," a woman who seduces and ensnares him, causing him to leave his family and career behind. Toward the beginning of the film we see the vamp toy with other men (telling one of them "kiss me, my fool"); Schuyler is unable to resist her charms and despite the efforts of his family cannot leave her. At the end, he is driven mad by desire and loss, or as an intertitle has it: "Some of him lived, but most of him died." In this way, the vamp as sexually voracious and dangerous woman derails not only domestic order but also law and political order, given Schuyler's status as a lawyer connected to the State Department.

A Fool There Was starred Theda Bara, a name invented by Fox studio publicity—an anagram, they noted, of "Arab Death"—for one Theodosia Goodman. They also invented an entire history for her: she was, they claimed, born in the shadow of the Sphinx, played leads at the Theatre Antoine, distilled exotic perfumes as a hobby, was well versed in black magic, and was identical to the character she played in the film. In reality, she was from Cincinnati. Together, the film and the publicity surrounding Bara mark anxieties about women, sexuality, and disorder that find a locus in the body of the immigrant vamp, a figure of contamination and disorder that must be pushed beyond the borders of society. The film is based on a play by Porter Emerson Browne, in turn based on Rudyard Kipling's poem "The Vampire," and so participates in a broader discourse about the "dangerous" sexuality of women that spoke to anxieties about their changing role in society. Once again, then, cultural work in this year articulates ideals of citizenship and social order that draw precise boundaries of inclusion and exclusion for a public sphere threatened by profound transformation.

Crime and the City: *Regeneration* and *Alias Jimmy Valentine*

One cycle of films this year concentrates directly on the evils of urban criminality and the threat it posed to the social body and the state, building on stories proliferating in urban newspapers and in the nascent study of criminality in the disciplines of sociology and criminology. Pertinent films include *Regeneration, Alias Jimmy Valentine, The Folly of a Life of Crime, The Bridge of Sighs, The Last of the Mafia,* and *Are They Born or Made?* Together, these films participate in discourses about criminality, social control, and urban space. They merit attention here as another articulation of the question of cinema's participation in the circulation of ideas about pressing topical issues.

Regeneration is based on a memoir by former gang member Owen Kildare. The story starts with the death of his mother, leaving him alone in a threadbare tenement in what *Moving Picture World* described as an "accurate" presentation of "the depressing squalor of tenement life on the East Side of New York." Owen watches as her coffin is taken away, and he is then escorted out by the neighbors, though the man in the house is a violent drunkard who beats him. "And so the days pass," a title observes, "in the only environment he knows." Location shooting in the city emphasizes the crowded and squalid nature of that environment. Later, Owen becomes a leader of a criminal gang, "by virtue of a complete assortment of the virtues the gangsters most admire," and organizes a robbery in a saloon. Owen's gang is opposed by a district attorney who has resolved "to sweep the city clean." Together with his friend Marie Deering, the district attorney visits a nightclub known to be a gangster hangout to satisfy Marie's curiosity about gangsters. Recognized by the gangsters, the district attorney is surrounded and threatened, but after an exchange of looks between Owen and Marie, Owen rescues him. Following this, and after listening to a speech about the need for charity in the local neighborhood, Marie sets up a "settlement house" and a relationship between her and Owen begins. Owen helps at the settlement house. He buys Marie flowers. Later, after old loyalties oblige Owen to shelter a gangster, Marie searches for Owen, only to be trapped and threatened by one of his former gang members. Owen and the police rush to the rescue—but too late, for she is shot and killed. Owen returns to the gang hideout to kill the gangster responsible, but the apparition of Marie stops him. Trapped, the gangster looks down to see a rat in a hole (a consistent trope in discourse about criminals, connecting gangsters to vermin and social waste); he is killed by Owen's friend as he tries to escape across washing lines threaded in front of a tenement skyline. At the close, Owen and the friend place flowers on Marie's grave. The flowers consistently associated with Marie connect her to a nature uncontaminated by the city.

Regeneration can be connected to discourses about criminality and the city and in particular to environmentalist discourses about criminality. By the mid-teens, reformers, sociologists, and sociologically oriented criminologists increasingly were focusing on the effects of environment on the development of criminality, delinquency, and, in particular, the formation of criminal gangs. The shaping effects of environment were recognized by many progressive reformers. This suggestion motivated, for example, the establishment of settlement houses in immigrant sections in cities—where (in the main) women would live and work to serve poor and immigrant communities. Academic sociology and criminology took a lead from this environmental perspective. Support was waning for a eugenic criminology that linked criminality to hereditary and thus frequently to ideas about ethnic and racial hierarchies. A significant publication here was the new book by William Healy entitled *The Individual Delinquent.* Together, work within criminology and what came to be called urban sociology were informed by the widespread belief that urban life inaugurated a critical shift in social order, often understood along European models as a shift from *Gemeinschaft* to *Gesellschaft,* that is, from the moral order of rural spaces and social organizations like the family and community to the every-man-for-himself competition and moral disorder of the city (Tönnies).

Regeneration is informed by a sense of the environmental causes of gang-related criminality. Location shooting establishes the importance of the city. The opening of the film in the threadbare and violent tenement in particular emphasizes the environmental factors in pushing Owen toward crime, showing, *Moving Picture World* observed, how the gangster "is the natural product of an unfavorable environment." Owen is connected to a saloon culture that dominates the tenement region, at one point near the beginning moving through crowded streets of the neighborhood to collect a pail of beer for his violent surrogate father and later visiting a saloon and drinking in a nightclub. Counterpoised to the space of the tenement, saloon, and nightclub is the redemptive space of the settlement house. Here the film draws directly on the environmental discourses that sustained the settlement house movement. Informed by this rhetoric, the film has the settlement worker Marie—who in the original book was actually a teacher—help reform Owen, drawing him away from the gang and corresponding underworld spaces toward a role as upstanding citizen.

Owen's reformation is conceived in terms of a realignment with domestic space. The breakdown of domesticity—the death of Owen's mother, the violence of the father surrogate—is seen to lead directly to crime but, the film argues, this can be counteracted by the reestablishment of domestic space, now writ large as the settlement house. Owen's reformation is complete when he helps Marie rescue a baby from a violent father and restore it to its mother. In effect, the expanded domestic space counteracts crime and the gang.

Valentine in *Alias Jimmy Valentine,* based on a short story by O. Henry and subsequent play, likewise ultimately reforms in accord with the ideals of domesticity. After a successful robbery, Valentine fights with one of his gang's members who is guilty of harassing a woman on a train, and the gang member spitefully talks to the police. Valentine is jailed for ten years. (Scenes were actually shot within Sing Sing prison and included footage of the reforming warden there.) Rose, the young woman he saved, happens to visit the prison with her father and recognizes Valentine. Together, Rose and her father work for his release. Once outside prison, Valentine goes to visit them and thank them and eventually accepts a job working for the father in a bank. Two years pass and Valentine has "buried his past life and alias" and is "now a trusted cashier." When a former gang member visits and reminds Valentine of "the old thrills of the past," there is a flashback to various crimes and Valentine becomes increasingly animated. He makes as if he will go with the gang member, but just then Rose enters with her younger brother and sister, and he tells his former accomplice: "I swore to go straight and I'll keep my word." However, the detective who originally arrested him has tracked him down because he is investigating an old case and suspects Valentine. Valentine denies being involved and produces a faked photograph to show he was giving a speech at the time of the crime. Circumstances, however, conspire to reveal his identity. At the bank where he works, Rose's young sibling is accidentally locked into a new safe that is seemingly impregnable. Valentine, watched by the detective and Rose, is able to use his criminal skills to open the safe and rescue the child. At the end, as Rose pleads for Valentine, the detective agrees to let him go, convinced of his genuine reform.

Valentine reforms because of his love for Rose, and his reformation is directly connected to the protection of children and, by extension, domestic social order. A scene shortly after Valentine leaves prison is important here. He goes to a saloon to discuss a potential robbery with one of his gang members, a scene crosscut with Rose reading a story to her younger siblings. Valentine and gang-related criminality is connected to the space of the saloon, commonly regarded and here literally presented as diametrically opposed to that of the home. Valentine's reformation in "going straight" is connected to a movement away from the space of the saloon and toward that of the domestic space exemplified by Rose and her siblings. The detective is accordingly convinced of his genuine reformation when he saves the child at the end. In this way, the film proposes that self-discipline--guided, on the one hand, by the morality of women and, on the other hand, by the State as figured through the police--is necessary to manage criminality.

Conclusion

If my account of this year so far has concentrated on the way cinema intervened in the public sphere—around issues of race, immigration, the changing roles of women, and criminality—it is important to note, finally, that the purpose of providing "harmless" and diversionary entertainment to diverse audiences becomes increasingly central to the goals of film entrepreneurs and to the self-definition of the mainstream industry. The decision rendered in the Supreme Court supports this. Audiences are increasingly sought worldwide. Indeed, the building of the Panama Canal stimulated American shipping and commerce and impacted the global distribution of American films. With the war increasingly affecting European production and distribution, American film producers sought in particular to enter South American markets. The dominance of these markets by European film-producing nations prior to the war had allowed them to amortize expensive productions that would not pay for themselves in these countries' domestic markets (Thompson 41). With the "help" of the war and the Panama Canal, American producers are able to begin to dominate this market by the end of this year (after the stockpile of European films was exhausted); the effects of this would fundamentally alter the balance of power in respect to film production. American cinema becomes a truly global cinema from this point on.

ACKNOWLEDGMENTS

With thanks to Amelie Hastie, Peter Kramer, Tom Rice, Claire Thomson, and Ben Singer for their help with the writing of this essay.

NOTES

1. House Bill No. 322, 80th General Assembly, Ohio, *General Assembly: Legislative Service Commission, Bills, and Acts, 1835–1996*, Box 3552, Ohio Historical Center, Columbus.

2. The extant print is unclear, though some accounts of the screenings this year suggest there was more material to suggest rape and that this was cut in various locales as a consequence of censorship. On these issues see Gaines 219–57.

3. Record of Proceedings of the Industrial Commission of Ohio, Department of Film Censorship, 6 January 1916, General Correspondence 1916–1956, Box 50,736, Ohio Historical Center, Columbus.

4. It is worth noting the fungibility of this conception of Japan, however, for when the film was re-released in 1918 Tori's nationality was changed to Burmese, thus acknowledging the alliance between the United States and Japan during World War I. Geopolitics impacts on film texts, and the world according to Hollywood, in complex ways.

1916

Movies and the Ambiguities of Progressivism

SHELLEY STAMP

American involvement in the European war is debated throughout the year, as the rising death toll overseas causes great consternation. One million casualties are reported at Verdun, over a million more on the Somme, including 30,000 dead in the first half-hour of battle. Millions more die on other fronts. President Woodrow Wilson is reelected by a narrow margin in a campaign based largely on his vow to keep the country out of war. Wilson makes repeated but unsuccessful attempts to mediate the war in Europe. Heralding what would come the following year, the National Defense Act enlarges the standing army and reserve. While staying out of the European conflict for the time being, the United States continues imperialist intervention elsewhere: President Wilson sends 12,000 troops into Mexico pursuing Pancho Villa after his raid on Columbus, New Mexico; marines invade the Dominican Republic, beginning an eight-year occupation; and the United States buys the Virgin Islands from Denmark for $25 million.

Evidence of the Progressive political agenda continues as the Keating-Owens Act regulates child labor laws for the first time, the Federal Land Bank System is created to aid farmers, the Workmen's Compensation Act protects federal employees, and the National Park Service is formed. John Dewey's *Democracy and Education* promotes the view that early education ought to emphasize thinking and reasoning skills over rote memorization and educational authoritarianism. Margaret Sanger opens the first American birth control clinic in New York City, publishing information in English, Italian, and Yiddish. She is promptly imprisoned on obscenity charges, making contraception front-page news across the country. Bastions of American leadership are beginning to change as well. Jeanette Pickering Rankin, a Montana Republican, becomes the first woman elected to the House of Representatives, and Louis Brandeis becomes the first Jewish Supreme Court justice, confirmed only after a long and bitter Senate hearing in which his "oriental" ancestry is questioned.

Icons of modernity are everywhere: New York City revises its building code to allow for "skyscrapers" of unlimited height; the nation's first self-serve grocery store, Piggy-Wiggly, opens in Memphis; the distinctive Coca-Cola bottle shape is released; and the female silhouette changes as well when narrow hobble skirts are replaced by fuller skirts permitting greater freedom of movement.

Cinema becomes an icon of modernity, too. Motion pictures are now the fifth most profitable industry in the country after agriculture, transportation, oil, and steel, an assessment only confirmed by events this year. Charlie Chaplin signs a contract with Mutual Studios guaranteeing him $10,000 per week (when the average American's annual salary is $708); Mary Pickford quickly follows suit with a handsome contract of her own; and Lois Weber inks a deal with Universal making her the highest-paid director in the industry. Power consolidates in Hollywood as production companies Famous Players and Lasky merge, then acquire controlling interest in the distribution arm, Paramount, moving toward a model of vertical integration.

Despite this consolidation, independent production companies continue to form, notably African American–owned outfits like the Lincoln Motion Picture Company and the Frederick Douglass Film Company. Comedian Mabel Normand forms Mabel Normand Feature Film Company and begins filming the feature *Mickey*, but shooting is suspended after she becomes ill. Female screenwriters, who will dominate the industry in the coming decade, rise to prominence this year. Frances Marion's first script for Mary Pickford, *The Foundling*, is produced, marking the beginning of a long association between the two women. Anita Loos pens the intertitles for *Intolerance* and begins writing a series of comedies that make Douglas Fairbanks a star. With her screenplay for *Joan the Woman* Jeanie Macpherson cements her creative partnership with Cecil B. DeMille. Nell Shipman gets her big break this year as well, a starring role in *God's Country and the Woman*, where she also works, uncredited and unpaid, on the film's dialogue, honing a formula she will exploit later as writer and producer.

Censorship continues to loom large for the industry, another measure of cinema's growing influence on the nation. Maryland becomes the fourth state to establish a board of censorship, with bills pending in several other state legislatures and federal film censorship on the table in Washington as well. The National Board of Censorship changes its name to the National Board of Review, suggesting a more moderate reconceptualization of its own role. As the debate about film censorship aims to gauge cinema's psychological and sociological impact, famed Harvard psychologist Hugo

Münsterberg publishes *The Photoplay: A Psychological Study*, one of the earliest scholarly tracts on cinema.

This is the year of what *Photoplay* calls the "Master Film," motion pictures that strive for epic status in their form and the subjects they address (Rev. of *Civilization* 137). Many films speak to the looming European war: *Joan the Woman* begins with a preface where a solider fighting in Europe finds Joan of Arc's sword; Thomas Ince's epic *Civilization* makes a strong case against the horrors of modern warfare; and Ida May Parks's script for *If My Country Should Call* features a pacifist mother who tries to prevent her son from enlisting in the army by poisoning him with her heart medication. *Clansman* novelist Thomas Dixon writes and directs *The Fall of a Nation*, a fear-mongering follow-up to *The Birth of a Nation*, about a German-backed conspiracy to take over the United States by arming its immigrants.

Films continue to address American social problems as well. The last of the white slavery films appear—*Is Any Girl Safe?* and *Little Girl Next Door*—virtually exhausting the cycle. *The People vs. John Doe* intervenes in a growing national debate surrounding capital punishment by dramatizing the year's most notorious criminal case involving Charles Steilow, whose death sentence is commuted just days before the film's release. Cleo Madison directs *Her Bitter Cup*, about a woman who marries an exploitive factory owner's son in order to divert his ill-gotten gains back to the labor force, while *Shoes* makes a strong case for women's wage equity and fair labor practices.

Artists famous for their work in other art forms appear on screen in a move many reviewers herald as cinema's coming of age: soprano Geraldine Farrar stars in *Joan the Woman*, following up her appearance in DeMille's *Carmen* the previous year; Russian dancer Anna Pavlova makes her screen debut in Lois Weber's adaptation of the opera *The Dumb Girl of Portici*; and African American vaudevillian Bert Williams makes a rare onscreen appearance in *Natural Born Gambler*. Screen stars also try their hand in highbrow literary adaptations, with Theda Bara starring in *Romeo and Juliet*. With longer, more elaborate films demanding specially tailored sound accompaniment, Victor Herbert composes an original score for *The Fall of a Nation*, the first composition written entirely for the screen. Spectacular visual effects in *20,000 Leagues Under the Sea* and *Snow White* showcase cinema's growing technical sophistication.

Defending Cinematic Art: *Intolerance*

D. W. Griffith conceives his epic film *Intolerance* following the controversy that surrounded his racist epic *The Birth of a Nation* and the Supreme Court's landmark decision ultimately stemming from that case. As Scott Simmon argues, the film must be seen not only as Griffith's response to the "intolerance" that greeted *The Birth of a Nation*, but also his attempt to defend cinema's status as a legitimate art form, equal to—perhaps even superior to—any other and certainly entitled to be free from the censor's gaze (*Griffith* 11). Motion picture censorship is the first major challenge to the doctrine of free speech in the modern age, Griffith writes in *The Rise and Fall of Free Speech in America*, released just prior to the film. In producing *Intolerance*, Griffith seeks to bring all of cinema's powers to bear on another series of historical reenactments (as he had done with the Civil War in *The Birth of a Nation*), and at the same time demonstrate even more clearly the kind of uniquely cinematic narratives that could emerge, striving to create what could not be achieved in any other art form.

For *Intolerance*, Griffith expands a story he had been working on about striking workers and modern-day reformers to include other examples of "intolerance" in human history. The film begins with this modern story depicting inhabitants of a mill town who are forced to relocate to an impoverished urban neighborhood after a violent strike. The Dear One (Mae Marsh) and the Boy (Robert Harron) meet there, marry, and are then beset by a series of interrelated tragedies culminating in the Boy being sentenced to hang for a murder he did not commit. In what one reviewer calls a "radiant crazy quilt," their tale is intercut with re-creations of three monumental historical events (Rev. of *Joan the Woman* 113): the fall of Babylon, center of ancient civilization, in 539 B.C.; the massacre of protestant Huguenots in Paris on St. Bartholomew's Day in 1572; and the crucifixion of Christ in A.D. 29. Forces of "intolerance" and injustice appear in each story. Treacherous High Priests of Babylon betray Prince Belshazzar, described in an intertitle as an "apostle of tolerance and religious freedom," and the city falls to King Cyrus the Persian. Cunning Catherine de Medici, mother of France's King Charles IX, goads her son into genocide, masking "her political intolerance of the Huguenots beneath the great Catholic religion." And the Pharisees oppose Christ, whom an intertitle deems "the greatest enemy of intolerance." A greedy mill owner and meddling social reformers are cast as their latter-day equivalents in the modern story.

Re-creating these four historical periods proves a monumental undertaking. Enormous sets are erected to replicate the gates of Babylon, ancient Judea, and medieval France. Thousands of extras are employed in spectacular crowd scenes, filmed with sweeping moving camera shots. A pamphlet accompanying the film's release promises a novel visual experience for viewers: "You will see as from a mountain top with one comprehensive glance the four greatest stories of the world's history. . . . You will see the world's greatest paintings come to life and move and have their being before your eyes." More than this, the pamphlet promises a "radically revolutionary . . . handling of dramatic themes" ("Declaration"). The film's structure is, indeed, radically nonlinear. An opening title informs viewers that "you will find our play turning from one of the four stories to another, as the common theme unfolds in each." As Griffith explains further in the film's program notes, "events are not set forth in their historical sequence or according to accepted forms of dramatic construction, but as they might flash across a mind seeking to parallel the life of the different ages." In this last turn of phrase Griffith echoes Hugo Münsterberg, who theorizes that "the photoplay obeys the laws of the mind, rather than those of the outer world." Cinema has "the mobility of our ideas," Münsterberg proposes, and "can act as our imagination acts" (91). *Intolerance* thus attempts two feats simultaneously: it promises to illustrate all of human history, bringing events to life before our eyes, setting them within a comparative structure that exemplifies cinema's artistry while mirroring our own mental landscape.

As essential as the film's four interlaced narratives are to its construction, no definitive print of *Intolerance* exists, since Griffith would continue to cut and recut the film during its initial run, and then three years later would release stand-alone versions of the modern and Babylonian stories as *The Mother and the Law* and *The Fall of Babylon*. Nonetheless, versions of the film currently available still provide a strong sense of the intricate narrative tapestry Griffith intended. Intercutting between the four stories allows both pointed comparison and sharp contrast. Scenes of the Friendless One, forced to rely on a sexual liaison with the head musketeer to support herself in the city, are juxtaposed with the marriage market in ancient Babylon where, a title explains, money generated from the sale of beautiful women is given to "homely ones" as dowries so that they too can be married and (by the film's logic) protected from sexual exploitation. Perhaps most spectacularly, plans for the Boy's execution are intercut directly with Christ's crucifixion and, more generally, with the fall of Babylon and the St. Bartholomew's Day Massacre.

Ultimately the activities of the modern-day reformers, described as "the vestal virgins of Uplift," are compared with genocide, crucifixion, and the destruction of ancient civilization. An intertitle describing the reformers as "modern Pharisees" makes clear their association with the priests who hound Christ in the Judean story, all "equally intolerant hypocrites." Their reform efforts are also juxtaposed with scenes of Catherine de Medici's

The Dear One (Mae Marsh) fights with reformers trying to take her baby in *Intolerance*.

orchestration of the Huguenot massacre, suggesting a larger historical problem with female leadership. In the modern story, scenes of the do-gooders
zealously closing bars, dance halls, and brothels are intercut with Christ's
efforts to halt the stoning of an adulteress. "He that is without sin among
you, let him first cast a stone at her," Christ proclaims, clearly pronouncing
judgment on the do-gooders. Though the Dear One and the Boy are their
primary diegetic targets, the women clearly represent for Griffith the modern forces of "intolerance" that castigated *The Birth of a Nation*.

Intercutting within the modern story itself also sets the reformers
against the consequences of their own actions. After the reformers close
bars, dance halls, and brothels, we see shots of bootlegging and street prostitution: the women's efforts have not eradicated these vices, merely forced
them underground where they breed crime and vice. When the uplifters
seize the Dear One's baby, on the pretext that it will be better off, we see
how misguided these efforts are: instead of being at home with its loving
mother, the infant is warehoused in an industrial-looking nursery run by
inattentive "hired mothers." The damage wrought by these do-gooders is
the logical consequence of Progressive-era governance overtaken by a feminine hand, or so Griffith makes clear in a pamphlet he circulates with the
film's release. Griffith ties the film's reformers to contemporary suffrage

campaigns and his fears about gender equality. Female leaders would require us to "surrender all personal liberties" that would lead to a return to a "puritanical form of government," he writes, ". . . a selfish paternalism that would legislate the joy out of life."

Connecting the four narrative threads is the recurring image of a mother (Lillian Gish) rocking a cradle accompanied by a quotation from Walt Whitman's poem "Leaves of Grass": "Out of the Cradle Endlessly Rocking. Uniter of Here and Hereafter—Chanter of Sorrows and Joys." The woman's dress does not identify her with any historical era depicted in the four stories and she is placed against a plain black background, lending the image a quality of timelessness. Punctuating the different stories, the image reminds us of the continuity of human history, an idea already enforced by the parallels between the different stories. But it also emphasizes another mode—the circular cycle of birth and death and the constancy of maternal love alongside the egregious examples of human cruelty depicted. "Today as yesterday, endlessly rocking," an intertitle explains, "ever bringing the same human passions, the same joys and sorrows." Vachel Lindsay will call this image the film's "key hieroglyphic" ("Photoplay" 76). The figure of eternal motherhood contrasts sharply with female characters who drive the narrative elsewhere in the film, both the single heroines in each narrative (the Dear One, the Mountain Girl, and Brown Eyes) and their female adversaries (murderous Catherine de Medici, the meddling reformers, and the Friendless One whose machinations endanger the Dear One and the Boy).

All four narrative threads converge in the film's final moments, bringing with them the inevitable: the fall of Babylon, the crucifixion of Christ, and the St. Bartholomew's Day massacre. In the midst of these grand tragedies lies one ray of hope: the Boy's death sentence is commuted at the very last instant and he is reunited with the Dear One, suggesting the possible triumph of the forces of good against intolerance. Despite the recurring cycles of destruction and misery it illustrates, the film finds room for hope in the end. A final coda sequence depicts an imagined future when prisons and warfare are eradicated "and perfect love shall bring peace forevermore." A fortress-like prison dissolves into a field of flowers, soldiers lay down their weapons, and children frolic around a cannon, now so obsolete it is overgrown with plants and vines. In the final vision, a cross of light appears in the sky above a battlefield. One last image of the mother rocking the cradle of humanity concludes the film. So while the three historical stories suggest inexorable human cruelty, the film's closing moments evoke the possibility of transformation. Cinema, it appears, is the instrument through which to imagine this change.

With *Intolerance*, then, Griffith aims to prove not only the uniqueness of cinema, but also its superiority as an art form. Cinema can reproduce events in human history, even the most monumental of events, as no other medium can. Cinematic storytelling can mirror human thought like no other art form. And perhaps most spectacularly, cinema has the capacity to visualize previously unarticulated human longings—for peace, justice, divine intervention. So while *Intolerance* bills itself as "a story of love's triumph over adversity," it is ultimately about the redemptive power of cinema itself.

■ Cinema's Editorial Page: *Where Are My Children?*

While Griffith tackles stories of the ages in his quest to establish cinema's great artistic potential, Lois Weber, equally committed to proving cinema's unique status as *the* modern art form, takes on one of the year's most controversial social issues—legalizing birth control—in her film *Where Are My Children?* The film takes its place alongside a series of Weber's releases this year on key social issues like capital punishment, women's wage equity, and drug addiction. She believes cinema can be the equivalent of a living newspaper, capable of bringing discussions of complicated cultural questions to life. For Weber, this project involves not simply elevating cinema's cultural cachet during the years of its new-found popularity, but also uplifting its audience, speaking to them in a "voiceless language" capable of engaging some of the era's most vital problems. "I'll tell you what I'd like to be," she says, "and that is, the editorial page of the Universal Company" ("Smalleys").

Disseminating contraceptive information of any kind remains a felony during these years. Still, *Where Are My Children?* seeks to engage cinema and its patrons in the national debate sparked by Margaret Sanger's crusade to legalize family planning, or "voluntary motherhood," as she calls it. And the film does so at a critical juncture—less than a year after the U.S. Supreme Court has denied motion pictures protection under the First Amendment. No director other than Weber, one commentator suggests, would tackle a subject like birth control "from the intellectual standpoint and hope to make a commercial success of it" (Black 199).

Where Are My Children? combines a dramatization of the legal battles surrounding contraception with a more intimate portrait of marital struggles over reproduction. District Attorney Richard Walton (Tyrone Power), the central figure in both plotlines, comes to favor family planning while trying a doctor accused of circulating contraceptive information to impoverished women. Yet, while prosecuting another doctor for performing abortions,

Edith (Helen Riaume) collapses after Richard (Tyrone Power) confronts her in *Where Are My Children?*

including one that killed his own housekeeper's daughter, Richard discovers that his wife, Edith (Helen Riaume), and her society friends have been using the doctor's services to ensure that they remain childless. His climactic cry, "Where Are My Children?" accuses Edith and her set of murder.

Unlike Sanger, who argues that all women ought to have access to safe and legal contraception, *Where Are My Children?* advances an argument that poverty-stricken women should practice birth control to limit the size of their families, while women of wealth and "good breeding" like Edith Walton are selfish if they choose to remain childless, a condemnation the film underscores by having the women resort to abortion rather than birth control. In doing so, the film advances a eugenics argument tied to racist and classist fears about "race suicide" not uncommon in birth control movements at the time. Faced with the "double threat" that working-class and immigrant populations are reproducing at a faster rate than wealthy, native-born white women, many in the eugenics lobby advocate fertility control for certain classes and races, while encouraging the "threatened" white elite to propagate. Separating contraception and abortion along class lines, the film contradicts contemporary experiences, as reviewers at the time point out: as long as birth control remains illegal, well-to-do women with ties to the medical establishment have access to under-the-table family planning advice, while poor and disadvantaged women, without such connections, must resort to unsafe, backroom abortions.

The film begins with Dr. Homer's trial for disseminating birth control information, a situation one reviewer found "plainly indicative of the Margaret Sanger case" currently making headlines across the country (Rev. of *Where Are My Children?*). Homer's objection that he is being tried for circulating "indecent literature" refers to the common practice of filing obscenities charges against family planning advocates. Sanger herself had been subject to a similar indictment. By foregrounding the criminal nature of birth control in this early trial sequence, *Where Are My Children?* also draws attention to its own status as a text engaging such a controversial, and potentially criminal, subject matter.

In his defense, Homer recounts stories of women he has seen in desperate need of reproductive control, each told in a brief flashback: a penniless woman whose children are exposed to disease and death; an unmarried woman who kills herself and her child after being rejected by her lover; and a couple whose violent alcoholism endangers their offspring.[1] But as an insert from Dr. Homer's birth control treatise reminds us, his aims, however progressive, adhere to contemporary arguments about eugenics that favor limited reproduction only within certain segments of the population: birth control, he writes, will help the "race" to "conquer the evils that weigh it down."

Scenes of Edith Walton and her friend Mrs. Carlo (Marie Walcamp), who is contemplating an abortion, are intercut throughout Homer's trial. Mrs. Carlo's unhappiness seems especially unwarranted when set against the destitute conditions Homer describes. Her misery, the juxtaposition insists, cannot be equated with the poverty, disease, violent abuse, and death suffered by other less-fortunate women and children. In addition to its implied criticism of Mrs. Carlo's "selfishness," the crosscutting also sets the women's whispered and secretive communications against the open discourse of the courtroom. Behind the visible network of male power and decision making, the film shows us, is a clandestine network of women. Even as male doctors, judges, attorneys, and jurors make decisions about human reproduction, decisions from which women are noticeably excluded, privileged women like Edith and her circle take recourse in a shadowy underground world of illegal abortion. Dr. Homer's conviction—by a jury of men, the title reminds us—comes just as Edith and Mrs. Carlo resolve to visit another doctor, Malfit, for an abortion. As long as contraception remains illegal, the juxtaposition implies, forward-thinking physicians like Dr. Homer will be convicted for helping women in need, while less scrupulous doctors like Malfit profit.

When Lillian, daughter of the Walton's housekeeper, becomes pregnant after a liaison with Edith's brother and then dies following an abortion with Malfit, the story is complicated further. If *Where Are My Children?* seems to advocate birth control for the impoverished, unhealthy, and abused women described by Dr. Homer, while simultaneously denouncing Edith's circle for their reliance on abortion, in Lillian's case the message is less clear. In its limited advocacy of birth control, the film does not promote reproductive freedom for consenting, unmarried adults, a case Margaret Sanger is indeed making at the time. Lillian's storyline nonetheless introduces the topic of female sexuality, albeit with a rather clichéd tale of a male predator and his gullible victim.

Lillian's situation appears at first to be set against those of Edith and her wealthy friends, for her sexual naiveté seems at odds with Edith's confident navigation of the abortion process. Yet, Lillian and Edith are also connected as two women who indulge their sexuality beyond the parameters of motherhood. Edith's desire to remain childless is associated with her brother's self-indulgent lechery and his seduction of inexperienced, underprivileged young women like Lillian. Two sides of the same coin, Edith and her brother are both "selfishly" interested in sexuality outside of reproduction. The brother's hedonistic and careless approach to indulging his desires is ultimately paired with Edith's own extravagances: smoking, drinking, socializing, and doting on her dogs all become metaphors for sexual excess. In Lillian's case, abortion (and death) are the tragic consequences of her unbridled desire, the "wages of sin," a title proclaims. Two forces threaten the social order, according to the film's eugenics-based logic: the "lower" elements of society (immigrants, the poor, people of color) and the "baser" elements of human sexuality. Both must be restrained if the culture is to flourish. So while the film reserves its harshest criticism for Edith and her circle, in many ways it also reinforces their own bourgeois hierarchy valorizing white racial "purity" and feminine sexual virtue.

At a time when disseminating contraceptive information remains a felony and when motion pictures are no longer protected by guarantees of free speech, *Where Are My Children?* encounters significant problems with censorship and regulation. After first voting to pass the film, the National Board of Review of Motion Pictures convenes a body of medical and sociological experts and upon their advice reverses its original decision and votes to reject the film. The Board argues that while depictions of abortion and contraception onscreen are appropriate in many instances, *Where Are My Children?* circulates medical misinformation by conflating the two issues and suggesting that Edith's repeated abortions have left her infertile. Other commentators voice similar complaints. When *Where Are My Children?* plays in Portland, Oregon, members of the Birth Control League protest that the film's failure to distinguish between "birth control properly speaking and abortion" generates "misunderstanding and confusion" about their objectives. They point out that Sanger, who brought the term "birth control" into general usage, never intended to include abortion under that rubric, and that one of her chief reasons for advocating family planning was to reduce the number of abortions (Stamp, "Taking" 274–83).

Criticism of the film's political agenda or its "confusing" message appears to have little effect on its popularity and do nothing to curb Universal's enthusiasm for wide distribution. The studio releases the film without approval from the National Board of Review, and *Where Are My Children?* sets box office records in many communities across the country, becoming Universal's top moneymaker of the year. For the release Universal adds a preface to the opening titles, asking rhetorically whether a "subject of serious interest" ought to be "denied careful dramatization on the motion picture screen."

Despite its troubling confusion of abortion, contraception, and eugenics—or perhaps even because of this—*Where Are My Children?* stands as a landmark of Progressive-era filmmaking, a model of cinema vying to take on the challenge of presenting complex social issues through the lens of narrative cinema. Ultimately, *Where Are My Children?* aims to do much more that simply capitalize upon a topical, even sensational, issue like contraception; it asserts cinema's claim to participate in national debates on an equal footing with newspapers, magazines, and other forms of political commentary.

New Picture Personalities: *His Picture in the Papers* and *The Social Secretary*

As Weber and Griffith demonstrate cinema's newfound cultural status in different ways, writer Anita Loos and director John Emerson collaborate on a series of gender comedies, and in doing so make stars of Douglas Fairbanks and Norma Talmadge. Both actors become emblematic of the new male and female types created by cinema. Fairbanks was already a successful Broadway performer when he was signed to Triangle Pictures the previous year. *His Picture in the Papers* is Fairbanks's third feature for the studio and the first of several collaborations with Loos and Emerson. Talmadge makes several shorts and seven features, including *The Social Secretary*, during her eight months at Triangle this year, films which also make her a star.

His Picture in the Papers is a film simultaneously about masculinity and corporate America. Pete Prindle (Fairbanks) is the ne'er-do-well son of business magnate Proteus Prindle, who has grown rich marketing Prindle's 27 Vegetarian Varieties, which include such delicacies as Macerated Morsels, Perforated Peas, and Desiccated Dumplings. Restless sitting behind a desk at his father's company and even less enamored of its products, Pete prefers meat eating, boxing, alcohol, and women. Pursuing the latter, he falls in love with Christine Cadwalader (Loretta Blake), daughter of railroad tycoon Cassius Cadwalader, a prominent vegetarian and supporter of the Prindle's line. Like Pete, Christine rejects her father's dietary ways, along with the willowy fiancé her father has selected for her. Suspicious of his daughter's new suitor, Cadwalader agrees to let the two marry only if Pete secures a stake in his father's business. But in order to do so Pete's father dictates that he must earn his share in the company by marketing its wares. Pete then embarks on a campaign to get "his picture in the papers," failing spectacularly at first with a series of staged stunts, but succeeding in the end when he single-handedly thwarts a train wreck planned by a gang intent on destroying Cadwalader's railway empire.

Like many of his generation, Pete feels reigned in by corporate America, confined by desk, office, and time clock and perpetually infantilized in relation to his father and his family's business. His masculinity finds its expression outside the workplace, not within it. Corporate culture represents a loss of authenticity, a world where marketing has replaced anything genuine. Prindle's products are the ultimate marker of this—everyday food items renamed and repackaged, then sold back to consumers at a higher price. Lentils are no longer lentils, but Prindle's Life-Saving Lentils. National brand advertising in mass-market campaigns, lampooned through Prindle's Varieties, is a relatively new phenomenon. An impersonal consumer economy selling mass-produced goods through mass marketing is rapidly replacing an older agrarian economy where simple bartering and exchange amongst neighbors dominated. In the absence of real social contact, companies try to familiarize and humanize their relations with customers by creating recognizable brands and drawing them into a personal relationship with products through advertising campaigns. Food products lead the surge of national brand advertising, as convenience foods sold ready-to-eat in cans or jars, such as the Prindle's Varieties, become increasingly available (Ohmann 76–88). Pete's desire for steak, then, is more than a carnivore's rejection of vegetarianism; it expresses his longing for real, pure food, neatly encapsulated in the slice of rare, dripping beef he craves, visibly without any packaging, branding, or marketing.

Pete's authenticity and exuberance are contrasted with other models of manhood on display in the film. His father, though a wealthy captain of industry, effuses superficiality. He is a man who identifies completely with the marketing image he has created for himself, who makes no distinction between genuine family ties and business relations, and who values his children only insofar as they can support his company's bottom line. Cadwalader, the railroad tycoon, is Proteus's physical opposite—a petite man who appears all the more so when he stands alongside his outsized counterpart. Toward the end of the film, as threats against his life escalate, Cadwalader surrounds himself with four enormous bodyguards at all times, a visual reminder of the constraints Pete feels even on the lowest rungs of the corporate ladder. Thus, despite their wealth and power, neither Pete's father nor his future father-in-law can lay claim to the "natural" masculinity he represents. From Pete's own generation, Christine's effete, spineless fiancé, Melville—another vegetarian, naturally—represents complete capitulation to corporate control. Not only are his eating habits and working life defined by his submission to Proteus and Cadwalader; his sexual relationships are as well. Pete, on the other hand, resists corporate culture and consumer culture alike. He knows his own tastes (meat) and desires (Christine) without having them shaped by advertising or parental decrees. A character like Melville, who allows his actions to be dictated by other men, signals the way that corporate culture and marketing trends directed the needs, desires, even the very physical movements of many men. Pete breaks free of these restraints, literally and figuratively, his bounding motions the very emblem of his autonomy.

Pete Prindle is only one of many onscreen embodiments of what Gaylyn Studlar calls Fairbanks's particular brand of "optimistic performative masculinity" in the early years of his stardom (22). As a reviewer at the time noted, "Fairbanks represents physical agility and temperamental optimism, and it is really the latter that wins. His leaping and climbing feats would soon pall if he did not perpetually demonstrate that life is good and growing better" (qtd. in Studlar 16). In this climate Fairbanks's energetic onscreen persona seemed to effect a magical transformation, a change for which "many American men in routine-driven, sedentary, bureaucratized jobs yearned" (85).

It is instructive, then, that Pete succeeds in the end only after abandoning the publicity stunts he has staged—to no avail—and stepping in, quite unselfconsciously, to rescue Christine and her father from a train destined to be destroyed by Cadwalader's enemies. He succeeds, in other words, only when he stops trying to market an image of himself and instead performs a genuine act of heroism, single-handedly fighting off an entire gang of saboteurs. Reading the sequence at its most allegorical, one might say that Pete's natural athleticism saves corporate America trapped on a collision course with destruction. With this spectacular rescue Pete does finally succeed in getting "his picture in the papers," of course, but the concluding scenes do not emphasize how the ensuing publicity translates into higher sales of Prindle's 27 Varieties, as both Pete and his father had originally hoped. Rather, the ending underscores Pete's authenticity, athleticism, and daring. These traits, the film suggests, not his ability to generate media attention or fill corporate coffers, make him the rightful inheritor of his father's business and Christine's hand in marriage, and thus the true embodiment of modern masculinity, or, as *Photoplay* would have it, "biff-bang Americanism" (qtd. in Studlar 23).

"Ain't he the REEL hero?" an intertitle quips following Pete's final exploits, sending a wink to the audience that acknowledges Pete's heroism while also suggesting its cinematic construction, for he is only reproducing what audiences might already have seen countless times in railroad serials like *The Hazards of Helen*. Ultimately, the film suggests, it is cinema, unlike other forms of modern mass communication, that best captures Fairbanks's exuberant masculinity.

If modern masculinity finds its best expression outside an enfeebling corporate America in *His Picture in the Papers*, *The Social Secretary* suggests that the "feminization" of the workplace presents equal, but significantly different, challenges for women. A swift series of scenes at the opening of the film depicts the range of sexual harassment Mayme (Norma Talmadge) has faced in her secretarial jobs, demonstrating how women's entry into the clerical field in the early years of the twentieth century caused a confusing erosion of boundaries between home and work, public and private, professional and personal relations. Refusing to place herself in the hands of another lecherous boss, Mayme takes a position as social secretary to a wealthy woman, Mrs. Peabody de Puyster, disguising her good looks under a frumpy demeanor since Mrs. Peabody has advertised for a secretary who is "extremely unattractive to men," having lost a number of previous employees to marriage. In helping Mrs. Peabody de Puyster at home with her correspondence and social calendar, Mayme elects to return to an older model of women's employment. But in doing so she does not escape the confusing overlay of public and private, as she might have hoped, for she takes up residence in her employer's home, befriends the woman's daughter, Elsie, and ultimately courts her son, Jimmie. Moreover, Mayme's "work" soon evolves from simply managing Mrs. Peabody's social calendar to intervening in the social (and sexual) life of the family, as she sets out to derail Elsie's engagement to Count Limonittiez, intent only on gaining access to the family fortune.

Nor does the sexual harassment end when Mayme starts work in the Peabody household. Wasting no time, Jimmie immediately sizes up potential conquest in Mayme, asserting his class privilege to try and cajole sexual favors. He begins eyeing her as soon as she arrives at the family's exclusive town house, first inserting himself into conversations between Mayme and his sister, then ogling her from the margins of the frame, then later squeezing in next to her when they all go out in the car. He ultimately tries to assault her late at night in a lusty, drunken haze. The confusion of family and professional spheres overlaid with class privilege renders Mayme's work in the Peabody home ultimately more perilous than any office.

In the end Mayme becomes interested in Jimmie herself, and a further component of her "work" for the family soon involves reforming him, taming his self-absorbed hedonism into something approximating a good husband, decent worker, and suitable family heir. Mayme herself must also be domesticated, ironically tracing the same trajectory that all of Mrs. Peabody's former secretaries have followed—into marriage and out of the workforce. But Mayme gains the added bonus of upward mobility by marrying into her employer's family. She won't really have to leave after all, just shift roles from secretary to daughter-in-law.

Marriage, we realize, early in the film, is one of the only avenues of advancement open to her. Work certainly will not provide her with independence and financial security, as she had obviously hoped. In the Peabody home her own possibilities are set against those of two other contemporaries in the household: the debutante Elsie, whose "debut" suggests that she might very well be auctioned off to the highest bidder, and the Peabodys' silent, servile maid, who appears in the background of several shots. Framed by this limited horizon of possibilities, Mayme's best option is to marry for financial security. Interestingly, when Count Limonittiez tries virtually the same thing—courting Elsie after his business fails—the film looks disapprovingly on this arrangement, painting him as an exploitive gold digger rather than someone, like Mayme, merely seeking financial security and class mobility. Here the film inadvertently reveals its own sexual double standard.

Mayme's movement from workplace to home to marriage—what might be called her trajectory of domestication—is countered throughout the film by her status as an active heroine, someone who is not only an agent in her own narrative, but who also orchestrates the attention and energies of others. If the film remains skeptical about the limited options available to women in either the workplace or the home, Mayme offers an alternate model of active womanhood, and in doing so she embraces and foregrounds the performativity of the female roles circumscribed within the narrative.

Mayme is a constant object of surveillance. Prying eyes are upon her everywhere: sexual predators at work, gossiping housemates in the Stenographer's Home where she lives, Jimmie and his set when she begins living with the Peabodys, and finally a gossip columnist, Buzzard (Erich von Stroheim), who trails her every move hoping to get a whiff of scandal once she begins secretly courting Jimmie. Mayme counters this omnipresent surveillance by exerting her own control over space. By donning a disguise, she is able to control knowledge of who she really is and limit the licentious attention she receives. She also exerts a controlling viewpoint in the house—several scenes emphasize her sightlines through optical point-of-view shots—and through a kind of auditory control of the household as well, hearing Jimmie's drunken attempt to enter the house surreptitiously at night, then later eavesdropping on Mrs. Peabody's phone conversation with the Count. At Elsie's engagement party, Mayme orchestrates the Count's gaze to prove his infidelity, leading him through the house to stage an encounter on the bench outside for Mrs. Peabody's view. Becoming an active agent in the narrative, she turns a position of exploitation into one of empowerment.

Including a gossip columnist in the story acknowledges another arena in which boundaries between public and private are eroding, another arena in which private sexual behavior is now enacted on a public stage—not the workplace, but the stage of mass media. Buzzard's presence also acknowledges the role that movie stars, like Talmadge, play in the public consumption of private lives, as well as cinema's role as a purveyor of intimate views for its audience. Indeed, the film furnishes several glimpses of Mayme dressing and undressing by herself in front of her mirror, views that no diegetic characters are privileged to see.

Mayme's untroubled social mobility in *The Social Secretary* is a role that soon becomes common to Talmadge's screen persona and one, as Greg M. Smith documents, that mirrors her own offscreen life. She marries producer Joseph Schenk this year and the two form a business partnership that would later prove to be very lucrative. Fairbanks, too, builds on the persona created for him here by Emerson and Loos, emerging as the next decade's top star.

Cinema Sees Itself: *Behind the Screen* and *A Movie Star*

Even as feature films continue to dominate exhibition markets, comic shorts remain a regular element of theater programs. Charlie Chaplin, working at Mutual with increased freedom and creative control, begins a series of nuanced comedies that will define his mature comedic style. *Behind the Screen* shows Chaplin self-conscious about his own newly powerful role in the industry, as well as changes occurring across the industry as features prevail, bringing an increasingly rationalized and streamlined mode of production in their wake. If *Behind the Screen* lays bare the interior workings of a movie studio, Keystone's *A Movie Star* performs a similar analysis of the star system, by now the commercial nexus around which the entire industry operates. Spoofing Chaplin, his former Keystone colleague, Mack Swain takes on the role of movie star Big-Hearted Jack. While spoofing the industry, each film also asks us to look critically at our own role as viewers and fans.

In *Behind the Screen* the tramp finds himself working as an assistant to the head stagehand at a movie studio. Diminutive Charlie does all the work while his oversized boss (Eric Campbell) snoozes. The Tramp's constant motion back and forth across the frame is set against the large man's inertia as he moves enormous props single-handedly, slinging a pile of chairs and a piano over his back. Still, the Tramp's work goes unappreciated; the moment he sits down to catch his breath, he is chastised for laziness. Dissatisfied with the obvious inequities of their working situation, other disgruntled stagehands plan a strike, plotting to blow up the studio. A young woman (Edna Purviance), who has disguised herself as a male stagehand in order to get a foot in the studio door, overhears the strikers' plot and manages to quash their rebellion before it turns violent. Meanwhile, the Tramp and his boss are recruited to star in a pie-throwing comedy with predictable results.

As much about labor as it is moviemaking, the film provides a privileged view "behind the screen" through the eyes of those who are least privileged within the studio system—the lowly stagehands whose hard labor building and moving elaborate sets provides the backbone for everything else that happens. From this perspective, they do all the "real" work while the studio manager, directors, and camera operators are pushed to the margins of the frame. Performers appear to have the least interesting work of all, standing around in costume without much to do except orchestrate elaborately choreographed moves. The Tramp's comic mischief, performed in defiance of his abusive supervisors, foregrounds the issue of work, undermining productive labor by turning work into playful destruction (Musser, "Work" 50–54). The Tramp's mischief also finds an echo in the more organized, if still chaotic, strike planned by his fellow stagehands, a comment on the unrest felt by workers in the increasingly rationalized and hierarchical movie studios.

Gendered labor hierarchies also pervade the movie studio where men hold all positions of creative control, from manager to director to camera operator to stagehand. Performing onscreen—shown, from this perspective, to be the least interesting or creative occupation in the studio—is the only task for women, and limited at that to ceremonial roles in a heavy-handed costume drama and a love interest in the western. Although *Behind the Screen* begins with a rather typical depiction of a woman waiting outside studio gates in search of work, a common trope representing women's relation to cinema at the time, this view quickly shifts as the young woman sneaks into the studio, dons a pair of overalls, and excels at her job as a stagehand, making us question the allure of her original intentions.

Thus, in addition to shifting our gaze inside the studio to that of the lowly carpenters and stagehands, the film also shifts the accustomed image of women working there. At the end of the film the young woman is not recognized for her good looks, then rewarded with an acting contract, as we might presume. Instead, she embraces Charlie, still in her stagehand's overalls, as he winks at the camera. Will she stay on as a stagehand, hoping to move up the ranks of creative filmmaking labor "behind the screen," or will she continue to pursue stardom, now shown to be the least creative avenue within the studio? By playing with the usual narrative ascribed to would-be starlets in early Hollywood, the film points to other options for women akin to those already enjoyed by the likes of Lois Weber and Anita Loos. This greater mobility relies, the film implies, on a kind of play with traditional gender roles.

While studio labor is rigidly stratified along gender lines, in other ways the studio becomes an ideal locus for exploring gender and sexual identities, evinced by the young woman's budding romance with the Tramp. He begins flirting with her while she is in drag without realizing she is a woman, and she remains in full drag when they enjoy their first kiss. Upon discovering what he believes to be two gay men kissing, the Tramp's boss proceeds to mock them by skipping effeminately and lifting his rear in the air. What seems at the outset to be a predictable glimpse "behind the screen," by now a fan-discourse staple, turns out to be a portrait of labor unrest, queer sexuality, and fluid gender norms. Despite its cynicism about current filmmaking trends—pretentious historical epics, formulaic westerns, and infantile slapstick—*Behind the Screen* evokes the transformative potential of creative work. The best options for both the Tramp and the young woman appear to lie on the hidden creative side of the screen, rather than on its shimmering, translucent surface.

If *Behind the Screen* takes viewers into the studio, revealing hidden aspects of filmmaking labor through the eyes of the industry's lowliest workers, *A Movie Star* shows viewers that most familiar of spaces—the movie theater—while inviting us to see it, and our own experiences there, with new eyes. Mack Swain plays Big-Hearted Jack, a leading man from Thrill'Em Pictures who visits a local theater, sending his coterie of female fans into a frenzy. While Jack's onscreen self nearly loses his sweetheart to a handsome and charming newcomer, the star finds no lack of fawning attention from women in the theater, irritating men who have accompanied their wives and sweethearts there. Much of the film's humor derives from the transpositions stardom enacts. Rejected onscreen, Jack-the-movie-star becomes eminently desirable inside the theater. There the obviously inelegant, outsized Swain, his features embellished further by grotesque makeup and paste-on mustache, becomes a rather improbable matinee idol. Tables are turned in the end, however. Jack's character reunites with his sweetheart onscreen after he rescues her from an Indian attack, but his celluloid heroism deflates when his wife appears outside the theater and begins viciously pummeling him with her umbrella.

Big-Hearted Jack (Mack Swain) thrills female moviegoers watching him onscreen and irks their male companions in *A Movie Star*.

Jack's twists and turns mark out three distinct spaces—the screen, the theater, and the real world beyond—each corresponding to a facet of his identity as character, star, and man. Jack is emasculated both onscreen and in life, but in the liminal realm of the theater his star persona charms every woman present, as the theater becomes a physical marker for cinema's experiential delights. Reminding us of moviegoing's overlaid pleasures, several different compositions depict diegetic viewers' experiences of the cinema, as well as our own, using rear projection shots of the diegetic film showing in the theater, full-screen images of the film-within-the-film, and medium close-ups of viewers' reactions to the screen, each face illuminated by light reflected from the screen.

Within its sensual evocation of the moviegoing experience, *A Movie Star* foregrounds the hollowness of celebrity facades and Hollywood fantasies, along with our own willful investment in these conceits. It depends, in other words, on a mature star system now prevalent in Hollywood. By this time picture personalities are a mainstay of moviegoers' enjoyment, and fans' interests are increasingly shifting to hidden registers beyond the screen, to the closets, bedrooms, and kitchens of their favorite performers (deCordova 98–107). By playing on our own investment in the star system, the film shows how someone who is patently grotesque can become appealing solely because of his appearance in the movies and, moreover, that his onscreen exploits might be a far cry from his actual life as a badgered husband. Masculinity itself might be a construct, the film suggests, fabricated in equal part through onscreen fictions of the white man saving his sweetheart from "savage" others and fans' own willful blindness.

Fan culture, newly invested in the tensions between public and private life, involves, we see, an element of willful suspension of disbelief. It is no coincidence in this context, then, that Jack's fans are presented as doe-eyed matinee girls, blind to Swain's evident homeliness, with a few impressionable little boys thrown in for good measure. Fan culture has by now decisively shifted toward women, as Kathryn Fuller documents, but in this case the figuration of Jack's fans as either little boys or smitten, impressionable women derides and infantilizes movie fans (115–32). Only when reality intrudes in the final moments do Jack's female fans get their comeuppance—one even gets spanked with his wife's umbrella.

Big-Hearted Jack is equally invested in his own two-dimensional persona. Embracing the performativity of stardom, he poses alongside a poster of himself outside the theater, aware that he will not be recognized until he assumes the guise of his celluloid alter ego. After the screening, he again poses beside the poster handing out self-portraits in a composition neatly encapsulating the circulation and proliferation of star imagery. From screens to sidewalk ads to souvenir photos to live appearances, Jack's image is everywhere. The movie theater, site of cinema's optical delights, is also the primary locus of its commercial circulation. These two enterprises, the film reminds us, cannot be disconnected. If the movie theater is the pivot on which Jack's stardom turns—suspended between his roles as fictional character and real-life husband—it is also the pivot on which the star system depends, and with it the entire industry.

■ ■ ■

In this year of the "Master Film," cinema grapples with America's role on the international stage, with the continuing progressive agenda at home, and with the medium's own shifting cultural status—its ability to create "stars" and new screen personalities, its capacity to intervene in debates of national and international importance, its status as one of the most lucrative and influential industries in the country, and its role as *the* modern art form.

NOTE

1. Two shots described in the script of *Where Are My Children?* are missing from the second story in Homer's testimony, rendering it all but unintelligible in surviving prints. In the first shot, a woman on the bridge approaches a man, is shunned by him, and is then hustled off by a police officer; the following shot shows her drowned body floating alongside a baby's in the water. All that remains of this vignette is Homer's horrified response and his quick impulse to summon the officer. Though the script is not explicit, we can infer that the woman had conceived a child with a lover out of wedlock and when rejected by him felt compelled to kill herself and her child.

1917

Movies and Practical Patriotism

LESLIE MIDKIFFE DeBAUCHE

As the year begins, Americans have reason to worry that their country may become involved in the three-year-old European war. Still, there is no national consensus about the proper role for the United States to take in this conflict. Some advocate preparedness and increased aid to Britain and the Allies; others, especially in the Midwest and the West, are isolationists. On 1 February, Germany renews and expands its strategy of submarine warfare against the ships of neutral as well as combatant countries, leading President Woodrow Wilson to break diplomatic relations. He also asks Congress for permission to arm American merchant ships. Next, on 28 February, Wilson releases a telegram—intercepted and decoded by the British—from German foreign secretary Arthur Zimmermann to the German minister in Mexico. If Mexico allies with Germany, and the Central Powers prevail, its prize will be land Mexico lost in 1848, including parts of Texas, New Mexico, and Arizona. Suddenly, the war is urgent and very near.

Wilson calls a special session of Congress for 2 April. Eloquently if reluctantly, he pleads the case for America's entry into the war: "The world must be made safe for democracy." The Senate votes 82–6 in favor. The House of Representatives endorses the declaration of war by a count of 373 to 50. Jeannette Rankin, newly elected representative from Montana and the first woman to serve in the Congress, casts one of the "no" votes. On 6 April, the United States is at war. A president elected in part because "he kept us out of war" begins the job of raising an army, mobilizing industry, and enlisting the citizenry to cooperate on the home front.

In May Wilson signs the Selective Service Act, which institutes compulsory military service. The first draft registration is held in June, and African Americans are among those drafted. However, like the country, the military is segregated. Jim Crow laws are the order of the day, and the inferior training, equipment, and housing of black soldiers leads to dissatisfaction and even a race riot in Houston in August. Nineteen people die, including four white policemen. As a result, thirteen African American soldiers are executed immediately, six more soon after, and over fifty are sentenced to life in prison.

Industrial mobilization to meet the European war needs continues. A labor shortage in the North, as well as the desire of some manufacturers to try and tamp down the demands of labor unions, sparks the Great Migration of Blacks from the South. Hundreds of thousands of African Americans leave the South for better job opportunities in the northern factories, packing houses, and railroad yards in cities such as Chicago, Detroit, and Cleveland. Unrest follows as some whites fear "the Negro invasion," and in early July there is a race riot in East St. Louis, Illinois, where nine whites and forty African Americans are killed. Racial violence also occurs in Philadelphia and Chester, Pennsylvania, during the summer.

The Espionage Act passes Congress and is signed into law in May, making it a crime to obtain, transmit, or lose through negligence any information that might be used to the injury of the United States, or to intentionally "interfere with the operation or success of [U.S.] military forces or . . . promote the success of its enemies." The Trading with the Enemy Act enacted in October curtails trade or financial dealings with enemy nations, and establishes mechanisms for barring circulation of foreign publications deemed at odds with the interests of the United States or its allies. Postmaster General Albert Burleson revokes the mailing privileges of approximately forty-five newspapers.

Mobilization of industry and the citizenry are among the great achievements of the year. Right after Congress votes to enter World War I, Wilson appoints journalist and political supporter George Creel to head the Committee on Public Information (CPI). Conceived as a uniquely American way to inform the public about the war and the needs of government, the CPI aims to "devise machinery with which to make the fight for loyalty and unity at home and for the friendship and understanding of neutral nations of the world" (Creel 4). Creel's job to advertise and inform rather than to coerce and censor brings him in contact with those most able to spread the government's messages about buying war bonds and conserving food, for example, to a broad cross-section of its citizens: the American film industry.

For the course of the war, the film industry adopts the principle of what might be called "practical patriotism" (to use a term coined by a film exhibitor pronouncing that his theater's Liberty Bond sweepstakes enables patrons to enjoy amusement and perform a patriotic duty at the same time). Recognizing the advantages it might gain by cooperating in the war effort on the home front, the film industry finds ways to balance both profit and patriotism in its decisions about what sorts of movies to make and how best to distribute, publicize, and exhibit them.

A formal alliance between the film industry and the federal government is initiated and overseen by the industry's main trade association. One year old, the National Association of the Motion Picture Industry (NAMPI) quickly volunteers its help in May, providing all sectors of the film industry with a channel for its practical patriotism. In June *The Exhibitor's Trade Review* reports that a War Cooperation Committee has formed to "handle all matters in which the motion picture can be used to further the interests of the American Government in the world war" ("Industry" 173). NAMPI members come from all branches of the film industry: production, distribution, exhibition, and allied trades, and the men filling its leadership positions are prominent members of the business such as producers William A. Brady and Adolph Zukor, and William A. Johnson, editor of *Motion Picture News*. NAMPI assigns its members work with the federal government, including the Treasury Department, the Food Administration, the War Department, the U.S. Civil Service Commission, the Department of Labor, and the Department of Agriculture.

The aid the film industry provides, operating through its War Cooperation Committee, takes a variety of forms, including a series of slides that are produced to win compliance with the Second Food Pledge Card Drive in October. These are shown in theaters as part of the regular film program. Popular stars like Douglas Fairbanks campaign around the country speaking at rallies to sell war bonds for the Treasury Department. *The Chicago Tribune* reports, "He is trying to get subscriptions of $1,000,000 worth of bonds and has passed the halfway mark." Mary Pickford donates an ambulance to the Red Cross in June, and Four Minute Men, prominent local citizens, working from talking points developed in Washington, give speeches about war aims and home front needs during reel changes in movie theaters.

Film production also follows the dictates of practical patriotism. While the industry trade papers debate whether audiences want to see war-related movies, producers do not rush to exploit preparedness or war in their feature films to any great degree. Movies explicitly set during the war, such as *Draft 258* and *For the Freedom of the World,* are released, but they represent a small proportion of the films in distribution. The three to six months typical for scenario preparation and film production would allow topical films to be made, but producers limit neither the genres nor the variety of narrative content in their films.

Manifesting the popularity of certain actors and actresses as well as a star system at work, Paramount releases two features starring Billie Burke:

Arms and the Girl, a story about an American girl caught in Belgium when the war breaks out, and *The Mysterious Miss Terry*. Today's audiences know Burke better as the Good Witch Glenda in 1939's *The Wizard of Oz*. Mary Pickford is the most popular and best-paid actress. This year her films include *The Little Princess, The Poor Little Rich Girl, The Little American, Rebecca of Sunnybrook Farm*, and *A Romance of the Redwoods*. Only *The Little American* tells a war-related story. Irene Castle, famous as a ballroom dancer with her husband, Vernon, stars in *The Mark of Cain, Stranded in Arcady, Sylvia of the Secret Service*, and *Vengeance Is Mine*. She also plays Patria Channing in the fifteen-part serial *Patria*. Tapping Americans' fear of enemies within—fears heightened by the release of the Zimmermann telegram—it features both Mexican and Japanese characters as villains trying to overthrow the government. Burke, Pickford, and Castle are trendsetters, and in addition to watching them enact roles on the screen, audiences also watch to see how they dress. All three wear costumes designed by haute couturiere Lucile Duff Gordon, among others, and all three lend their names, images, and endorsements to the advertising of products such as Pond's Vanishing Cream, Pompeian Night Cream, and Oneida Community Silverware.

The industry continues to consolidate production and distribution. In the spring, twenty-four of the country's largest exhibitors form First National Exhibitors' Circuit in an effort to combat Paramount's growing monopoly by financing independently produced films and distributing them to hundreds of movie theaters. Charlie Chaplin releases several shorts through Mutual—*The Immigrant, The Cure*, and *Easy Street*—and then signs on with the First National. The deal is not for more money, but fewer films and more creative control. Social problem films, including *Enlighten Thy Daughter* and *Birth Control* (the latter directed by Margaret Sanger), are independently produced and speak to contemporary issues and anxieties. Sanger also publishes the first issue of the *Birth Control Review*, as well as *The Case for Birth Control*.

In addition to the movies, other arenas of popular culture are vibrant this year. Laura E. Richards and Maude Howe Elliot win the newly minted Pulitzer Prize for their biography of Julia Ward Howe, writer and author of "The Battle Hymn of the Republic." This song has particular resonance as the country mobilizes. Other popular authors include Mary Roberts Rinehart, whose stories are adapted for movies this year (*Bab's Burglar, Bab's Matinee Idol*, and *Bab's Diary*). Ring Lardner Sr. publishes a set of humorous short stories called *Gullible's Travels*. The eponymous story is about a trip to Palm Beach—the winter vacation destination of the rich and fashionable in the 1910s. Journalist, social critic, and satirist H. L. Mencken writes his controversial work of literary criticism, *A Book of Prefaces*, which is deemed to be pro-German, especially by those he attacks. Jazz played by black and white artists gains in respectability and is recorded for the first time. Wilbur Sweatman and his Jass Band create three records for Pathé, and The Original Dixieland Jazz Band, a group of white musicians, moves from New Orleans to New York City. They record "The Tiger Rag" among other songs this year. Gallery 291, opened by photographer Edward Steiglitz in 1905 and famous for introducing America to the modern art of Picasso, Cézanne, and Matisse, among others, closes. For its last exhibition, Steiglitz features drawings by his future wife, Georgia O'Keeffe. In the face of unsettled world events, Americans still follow the national game, baseball, and this proves to be a very good year for Ty Cobb, outfielder for the Detroit Tigers. He leads the American League in hitting singles, doubles, and triples, as well as in stolen bases. Cobb also stars in a feature film this year—a run-of-the-mill rural melodrama called *Somewhere in Georgia*—and fans could also see him in the five-reel documentary *The Baseball Review of 1917*.

The American Girl Defeats the Hun: *The Little American*

In March, Jesse Lasky, in charge of East and West Coast production for Famous Players–Lasky, contacts Cecil B. DeMille, his director-general in Hollywood, to confer about what sort of film narrative would be best for Mary Pickford, one of their company's most important stars. Referring to DeMille's screenwriter Jeanie MacPherson, he writes,

> I wonder if you and Jeanie couldn't write something typically American and something that would portray a girl in the sort of role that the feminists in the country are now interested in—the kind of girl who jumps in and does a man's work when the men are at the front. At any rate, some character and plot that would catch the national spirit that is rampant throughout the country at the present time.
>
> (qtd. in Higashi 145)

The film that results from this impulse of timeliness is *The Little American*. Production starts on 13 April and finishes on 22 May; the movie is running in theaters by early July.

The Little American plays like Allied propaganda. Pickford portrays Angela Moore, born on the Fourth of July, the ideal American girl. Angela is not only lively, beautiful, and stylishly dressed; she is modern and drives a car. Independent, she sails alone to France to help her ailing aunt in Vagny. Outspoken, she berates the commander of the U-boat that has torpedoed her ship, the *Veritania*—audiences would surely remember the

Lusitania sunk by Germany in 1915, killing 1,198 passengers and crew, among them 128 Americans. She is also compassionate and brave. Although she arrives to find her aunt has died, Angela remains in the chateau to nurse wounded French soldiers and later, fruitlessly, to try and protect her servants from rape.

Angela is loved by her German American neighbor Karl Von Austreim, "A Subject of the German Emperor," but also by Jules de Destin of the "Fighting Destins" of France. Both men bring her patriotic birthday presents, and even though Jules shows her that the red, white, and blue of the American flag are also the colors of France, she chooses Karl. Jules accepts her decision—"Bachelor buttons for me," he says as he puts a flower in his lapel. Karl gives her candies arranged in the shape of Old Glory, and a small cloth American flag. We watch as he teaches Angela's little brother Bobby to goosestep like a Prussian. He has just declared his love and his intention to remain in the United States when a German emissary arrives with an encrypted note ordering him to return home immediately and report for military service. He obeys.

DeMille and MacPherson create melodrama with national stereotypes in this film. Jules is noble, but his graceful surrender in the face of Angela's affection for Karl portends not a lack of will so much as the inability of France to defeat Germany alone. He meets her again when his men are attempting to defend their position in Vagny. Jules's right arm has been amputated, another loss he accepts with resignation and a cigarette. With the arrival of German troops imminent, he asks Angela "to render France a great service" and let one of his men pretend to be her butler in order to eavesdrop on the Germans and relay the positions of their cannons to the French gunners. The "butler" dies immediately when Karl's platoon fires on the house, a "Prussian calling card," to ensure compliance with their wishes. The stakes are raised higher after an old woman beseeches Angela, as an American, to save villagers condemned to death for "insolence." An intertitle reads, "Kulture, Prussians have their own methods for enforcing loyalty." This description makes use of another propaganda ploy, redefinition. When Germans speak of *kultur*, they mean art and music and literature, endeavors marked by a high degree of civilization and refinement. Allied propagandists turn the word inside out, causing it to denote violence, oppression, and a penchant for atrocity. Thus Angela watches helplessly as the German firing squad kills old men and young boys. This is intolerable and she responds—in the face of certain death—by spying for Jules and for France.

As Angela represents America and Jules France, so Karl embodies Germany. He behaves like a "splendidly drilled beast" and worse. Thinking that

Angela has died in the attack on the *Veritania*, he succumbs to the traits of the Hun: he follows orders he knows to be evil; he drinks to excess; and he attempts to rape Angela, mistakenly thinking she is a servant at the chateau his battalion has commandeered. After twice failing to save Angela from humiliation because he can't supersede the orders of his superiors, Karl finally snaps when she is caught spying, court-martialed, and condemned to death. After she looks at him with disgust, Karl exclaims that he is "done" and rips off his sword. He is found guilty of treason and both are marched outside to be executed. Angela begins to weaken and now Karl supports her. She notices the small American flag, Karl's birthday present, and she clutches it in her fist, giving her courage to face death with defiance. Fortuitously, at that moment the French guns fire a volley, knocking out the German weapons and causing the marauders to retreat. Angela and Karl are saved and stagger to the shelter of a bombed-out church collapsing underneath the crucifix. They are found by the "Dawn Patrol" the next day. Jules expresses anger at Karl, but Angela again makes her choice. She asks Jules to help Karl because she loves him. Again, Jules acquiesces and Angela is allowed to bring Karl back to the United States. The last image in the film is the Statue of Liberty.

The Little American reiterates the propagandist's story of America's duty to combat German barbarism, of the necessity for democracy to prevail over autocracy. Frequent descriptions of German atrocities include incidents of the murder of children by German soldiers, the mutilating of corpses, and the rape of women. *The Little American* may not show desecration of the dead, but the German soldiers step on and over the wounded Frenchmen lying on pallets in Angela's chateau. They also use statues as hammers, burn furniture, slice paintings out of their frames, and use the canvas to haul wood. Many of the stories in the Bryce Report will be discredited after World War I; nevertheless, they serve the purpose of swaying American attitudes to the Allies' cause. They also create a frame of reference for audiences watching this movie.

People going to see this film are familiar with images of Germans as barbarians. A year earlier, Louis Raemaekers had drawn a series of cartoons for *Century Magazine* with titles like "Kultur has passed here," showing a murdered mother and child. He also produces recruitment posters once the war starts. "Enlist in the Navy" portrays Uncle Sam wearing a doughboy's uniform lifting a cross whose beams read "Slavery" and "Barbarism" with one arm while the other aims a pistol at the kaiser. The cross threatens to crush a woman whose tattered clothes could only have been torn by brutish soldiers and whose streaming hair also bespeaks violation. These posters portray their own small melodramas in which good and evil, civilization and barbarism, America and Germany clash just as they do in *The Little American*. The film makes explicit the message that only with American grit will right prevail.

Demystifying the Movies: *A Girl's Folly*

It is her courage that puts the Little American's honor and life at risk, but in *A Girl's Folly*, it is the naiveté of the country girl that nearly brings about her fall from grace. The villain this time is not the barbaric Hun; instead, a jaded movie actor poses the threat, and the film relies on its audience's desire to peek behind the scenes at the work of film production. The film tells the story of Mary (Doris Kenyon), a girl living in rural New Jersey. She isn't like the other country girls who splash in streams, giggle, and move in a pack. Mary is solitary and reads romance novels in which "there came to him beside the fountain at which he sat, a woman whose walk was like the beginning of music." Sitting on a bench, she dreams of being this woman, and her imagination conjures a troubadour who materializes from the trees behind her and joins her after she scoots over to make room for him on her left. They talk, but the illusion is shattered and the singer literally disappears when Johnny Applebloom (Chester Barnett), the young, flesh-and-blood farmer who loves her, approaches and takes his place on her right. Then her mother arrives and all romance, fantastical or otherwise, is destroyed.

The bucolic opening scene fades and the setting shifts to a bustling film studio (in Fort Lee, New Jersey). Here we watch the mechanics of movie-making. An establishing shot reveals a large, barn-like building. Inside its walls, and in contrast to the relative emptiness, openness, and stillness of the country, there is a labyrinth of stages separated by walls. From a high camera height and extreme long shot we see directors at work, sets being built and dressed, cameras set up, stages themselves being rotated, and actors in costume. These images are familiar to film fans at the time. But, surprisingly, as the narrative progresses, we see that moviemaking is also monotonous and uncomfortable. An intertitle tells us that "Frequently 'movie' actors do not know the plot of the picture in which they are working." This lack of information doesn't really matter, though; actors simply replay their "types" from film to film or martinet directors order them to be "lively" or to die. Artistry is not shown to be part of the actor's job—only tedium and obedience. A battery of electric fans is positioned on the set to mitigate the heat of the klieg lights, and a movie star's black valet signs his

How stars prepare "personally autographed" fan photos, in *A Girl's Folly*.

"personally autographed" fan photos. One reviewer asks for this scene to be cut, presumably for reasons stemming from contemporary racial attitudes, as well as his worry about showing fans too much about how "the wheels go round" in a studio ("Bad Moral" 137). We also move beyond the sets and watch men in overalls tend large drums on which film is drying and a roomful of young women sitting at tables cutting film.

We meet Kenneth Driscoll (Robert Warwick), introduced via an art title that announces "Movie idol." These words are illustrated by the image of a heroically proportioned man, standing on a pedestal with three women kneeling at its base. Kenneth has a girlfriend of long standing, a theater actress named Vivian, but he is as bored with her as he seems to be by his work. He breaks studio rules—we see a sign prohibiting smoking framed in the shot as he smokes—and though, in the end, he will prove to be fundamentally decent, we hear him cynically tell a younger actor who has received a lock of hair from an adoring fan, "Just remember this—every heartache you cause a woman will boomerang." Of course, his path crosses Mary's, and as *The Exhibitor's Trade Review* apprises its readers, "the old familiar story of the traveling theatrical trouble and infatuation of a country lass for a handsome actor" ensues ("'Girl's Folly' Shows" 835).

The film company travels on location to the Kittatinny Mountains in New Jersey, and Mary interrupts a shot when she believes Indians are attacking. Thus she meets Kenneth. He suggests that she come with them when they decamp to the city because with her looks and his pull he can help her "make good" in the film business. Paralleling Kenneth's disaffection with his work, Mary has begun to find even her daydreams monotonous and she agrees to run away. At the studio, she is given the ingénue role but she exhibits no talent as an actress. Kenneth offers to set her up in an apartment in the city. She accepts, embarrassed to return home. After she sees an old charwoman, another failed actress, she tells Kenneth that she hates the country but loves new dresses. The moral direness of her situation is revealed on her first night in the new apartment. There is a party at which wine is served and she drinks too much. One of the young men exclaims that he will "dress up like a sky-pilot and marry the whole bunch." Mary's mother appears in the nick of time, however, bringing her daughter a birthday cake. Kenneth insists the partyers treat the widow respectfully, and Mary ultimately decides to return to the country. Kenneth also returns to his home to find the faithful Vivian waiting for him. The long-suffering Johnny Applebloom welcomes Mary when her train pulls into the station.

Maurice Tourneur and screenwriter Frances Marion deploy a narrative strategy of binary oppositions, an editing pattern of crosscutting, and intertitles to comment upon what is happening in the story. Thus, A Girl's Folly constructs a multivalent commentary on the romantic tales of the past and their modern-day replacement, the movies. As Mary reads her novel, she dreams of being a princess and living in a castle. When the movie company appears on the scene, it seems as if her dreams have come true. Kenneth, the matinee idol, is her prince; the movie set will be her castle. For audiences watching this film, the countryside where Mary lives, lit with sunshine, crossed by meandering streams, and peopled with innocent young girls, their faithful beaus, and Madonna-like mothers, might also seem to be a paradise. The film shows, though, that both idylls are easily punctured. In the country, Tourneur shows us insects and animals. While sitting and daydreaming on her front porch, Mary repeatedly swats away bugs. Silas Butterworth, the rube who works as "hired boy" for Mary's widowed mother, sleeps through an attack on his nose by a gigantic mosquito. Tourneur also intercuts an extended scene of Mary's three country friends trying to catch and drown a mouse that has scampered into their bedroom at night while she runs away to the train station to join Kenneth Driscoll and the movie company. This functions to parallel Mary with the mouse— vulnerable, nearly trapped, and fortunately escaping—but it also reinforces the reality of living in a farmhouse in the country: not only are there scenic vistas and peaceful streams, there are also annoying insects and invasive rodents. Likewise, life and work in a movie studio are exciting and lucrative but they are also mundane, hot, cluttered, and brimful of temptation.

The art titles in *A Girl's Folly* further nuance its "slender" story. Through word and image they convey a conventional moral judgment on the actions of these characters, but also by virtue of a sophisticated drawing style, they seem to wink knowingly at the audience. When we learn that actors often aren't given a scenario and don't know what is happening in the film, we see a hand moving the actor on a chessboard. When Mary fails as an actress and Kenneth offers to support her, but not, it is clear, to marry her, the intertitle portrays a small girl sucking her thumb next to a devil, and finally when Mary decides to return to the country with her mother, the intertitle repeats an earlier image of the boomerang catching a man in its orbit, but the text this time is different: "Thus doth the ever-changing course of things run a perpetual circle." Neither Mary nor Kenneth truly win in this movie. She is going back to owls, frogs, mosquitoes, mice, and shapeless dresses; he is destined to play cowboy roles he knows by heart and consigned to life with Vivian who dresses in black and sighs heavily.

The last shot of the film is awarded to two men working on the platform at the train station. As they watch the young couple and old widow walk into the distance, one man describes the scene as romantic. His buddy exclaims, "Romantick nothing!—That's movin' pictures."

Urbanizing the West but Saving Its Spirit: *Wild and Woolly*

In Douglas Fairbanks's second Artcraft film, directed by John Emerson with a scenario written by Anita Loos, we see an earnest young man, filled with pep and enthusiasm, playing a character who matches his star persona. The film opens with parallel editing that functions to create contrasts between the past romance of the Old West and its efficient and profitable but much less inspiring present. Fearless pioneers in wagon trains are replaced by locomotives. The dull, straight track of a trolley supersedes the zigzag path of a stagecoach down a mountainous road. Cowboys riding into town, guns blazing, lose pride of place to orderly traffic flowing in lanes on a downtown city street. This change has been brought about, in part, by Collis J. Hillington, "who helped make the West what it is today," the father of the film's main character. Hillington's name might well resonate with contemporary audiences. Only months earlier, the death of James J. Hill, the "Empire

Builder," owner of the Northern Pacific Railroad, made front page news in the *New York Times*. Hillington senior's name also resembles that of another railroad magnate, Collis P. Huntington, who built the Central Pacific network. Frederick Jackson Turner's famous essay "The Significance of the Frontier in American History," published in 1893, had argued that the West was a formative frontier that had imbued American citizens with individualism, democracy, and an adventurous spirit—the signature qualities of the nation (Wiebe 66). These are the same characteristics that Fairbanks manifests in his movies, including *Wild and Woolly.*

Fairbanks stars as Jeff Hillington, son of the railroad tycoon, who exclaims that he is "sick of this life." Trapped in his home, in his office, in New York City, he yearns for room to breathe, where "red blood runs free," and where "a six-shooter is a man's best friend." Jeff loves the "heroic West" of the dime novel and the picture-play: it is "rip-roarin'," "thunderin'," and "wide-spreadin'." So real is this chimera that the adjectival phrase "wild and woolly" becomes a noun, the name of the place he desires to live—the wild and woolly. Continuing the editing motif of juxtaposing scenes to highlight differences, Collis Hillington's breakfast is served by the family's butler. It is a time to eat and also to read the newspaper. Cut to Jeff. When we first see him, he is sitting cross-legged on the floor of his bedroom in front of a teepee. A campfire blazes; there is a tall cactus in the background and Indian blankets decorate the wall. Jeff is reading too, "Pell-mell the Yaquis dashed past the scout's place of concealment." Bounding up, he stands in front of a painting of cowboys busting broncos. Jeff imitates their stance, and, suddenly, the painting comes to life. Downstairs his father requests the butler to "tell that Comanche Indian we are due at the office in ten minutes." The narrative is set in motion when a trio of Arizona businessmen, products of the railroad's "march of progress," come to ask Collis Hillington to build a spur to connect their town, Bitter Creek, to what one reviewer identified as a borax mine ("Wild and Woolly"). Collis Hillington decides to send Jeff to Arizona to check out this prospect, and, with luck, to cure his obsession. He tells his visitors, "My son is a bit of a nut on the West." They experience this for themselves as Jeff offers each man a bite of tobacco. One takes out his cigarettes, another a stick of chewing gum.

An intertitle tells us that it is at the movies where "Jeff's dreams come true." Jeff's West, at least at the start of the film, is a matter of dressing up, interior decoration, and the consumption of popular culture. He demonstrates that he knows how to shoot a gun, twirl a lariat, and ride a horse, but the snake he shoots is a toy, the man he lassoes is the butler, and he could ride in Central Park whether or not he wore chaps and a cowboy hat.

In fact, Jeff delays setting out for Bitter Creek until his tailor can make him a fringed western outfit to match a picture of a cowboy that Jeff shows him. In contrast, Nell Larrabee, the daughter of one of the men who petitioned Jeff's father, really is western, but she wears a stylish riding habit as she waits for her horse to be brought to her. In Bitter Creek, when she refuses to take an automobile ride with Steve, the dishonest Indian agent, the scene is crosscut with one showing Jeff coming out of the movie theater where he has just watched "The Roundup." Looking at a film poster of a young woman galloping on a horse he says, "That's the kind of mate I am going to get."

Nell is also as adept at planning and implementing practical jokes. "Father, if we want favors from him, don't you think we ought to give him what he's looking for?" In contrast to Nell's quick thinking, the town responds by calling a meeting, setting up a blackboard, and, step by step, planning the "Program." Since Jeff is expecting to find the West of the 1880s, they oblige him by replacing signage so the Commercial Hotel becomes the Palace Hotel. They also nail ersatz slogans to the walls: "Guests bury their own dead" and "Gun-shy sleep on the prairie." Citizens of Bitter Creek don costumes and speak as if they had not been to school. One man tells Jeff that Nell's heart is true, although "she ain't had much book larnin.'"

This film is also true to contemporary narrative conventions in its depictions of race. Another sign hanging in the hotel states, "Good Injuns are Dead Injuns." All the villainous characters desire Nell, but the greatest threat to her is posed by the Hispanic character Pedro and the Native Americans, who, although they were originally enlisted by Steve, the Indian agent, have turned renegade. They kidnap Nell and encircle her, intending rape or murder. The Native Americans also drink to excess, are easily fooled, and have no qualms about making babies cry. (We see similar traits and behaviors attached to the Germans in *The Little American*.) Another striking scene occurs as Nell walks down a street in Bitter Creek. Jeff, worried for her safety in this Wild West town, hurries outside to protect her. Together, they pass a black mother and her two young daughters on a front porch. The woman sits, leaning against a column, dozing. These black characters are not dressed in 1880s garb like the white citizens of Bitter Creek. Either they are not included in the joke the town is playing on Jeff, or they have no need of costumes because their situation is no better than it was forty years earlier.

In the end, Jeff captures Steve, rescues Nell, provides the townsfolk with real bullets, and inspires them to defend their women and children like true western men. His riding and roping skills finally prove useful, and he shows himself to be a man of action. He apologizes for his foolishness and the trouble he has caused. "I've learned my lesson. So I guess I'd better go back east to my dad's office where I belong." But what lesson has he learned? That the West still needs rip-roaring vigilantes? That nonwhite men covet white women and those women need protection? That railroad tycoons and robber barons have given way to men in suits making decisions by committee?

The film ends, as did *A Girl's Folly*, acknowledging that the movie audience is in the know and has generic expectations. The satire for which Anita Loos is known surfaces again in the film's intertitles. Jeff makes his apologies and hops a train heading east. Mournfully, Nell wipes her eyes. Iris out, and the intertitle reads, "But wait a minute, this will never do! We can't end a western romance without a wedding. Yet—after they're married where will they live? For Nell likes the East and Jeff likes the West. So where are the twain to meet?" This question is not exactly answered because what we see, in the end, is Nell wearing the riding outfit in which she refused the auto excursion with Steve. In other words, she is dressed in modern attire. Neither is Jeff wearing western riding togs, even though we have seen him carefully outfit himself for his trip to Bitter Creek. Now, after learning his lesson, Jeff and Nell run down a grand stairway past two servants in livery, toward a doorway at the rear of the frame. The home looks like Park Avenue, but, when the door opens, their horses are waiting and they ride off into open country. Jeff Hillington wears a tie, coat, and jodhpurs. Even if he and Nell live in Bitter Creek, one assumes he will spend the day at an office in close contact with his father in New York.

This year, in addition to making movies, Fairbanks also publishes *Laugh and Live*. It is a motivational book that purports to respond to his fans' most frequently asked question: How can they make their lives as joyous as his appears to be? "People believe I am happy because my laughing pictures seem to denote this fact—and it is a fact!" *Laugh and Live* ends with an afterword written by George Creel. Creel, recall, is a journalist and the man Woodrow Wilson chose to head the Committee on Public Information during the war. Creel profiles Doug ("now that he is in the 'movies' we don't have to be formal"). He charts Fairbanks's life from boyhood in Denver through a course or two at Harvard, a trip to Europe with his buddies, stints as a clerk on Wall Street ("There are those who insist that he invented scientific management") and an actor on the stage. Creel's theme matches Fairbanks's: "It is the joyousness of the man that gets him over. It's the 100 per cent. *Interest* that he takes in everything he goes at that lies at the back of his successes. He does nothing by halves, is never indifferent, never lack-

Optimism incarnate: a portrait from Douglas Fairbanks's motivational book *Laugh and Live*.

adaisical." He is just the sort of American the Allies need two and a half years into the Great War and, more apropos, he fits exactly the requirements of the fully functioning classical Hollywood narrative style.

By 1917, it is conventional for the fictional character and the actor playing the part to share similar traits, and the audience also knows the rules of this efficient, entertaining game. Frederick Palmer, author of an early screenwriting text, advises that screenplays show action that results from "the outward expression of inward feelings" (qtd. in Bordwell 15). Fairbanks, seeking to motivate his readers, tells them almost the same thing: "More and more personality is coming into its own as man's greatest asset. . . . Personality is one's inner self outwardly expressed." Creel, sealing the bond between player and part, notes that Doug almost never uses a double to do his stunts, and that he spends any spare time he has learning new skills like bronco-busting. Realism, at least in the movies that Douglas Fairbanks makes, springs from "action and life." For Creel this is a sure-fire combination, not only for telling good stories but for living the right sort of American life. Sounding much like Jeff Hillington as he enthuses about the qualities of the West, Creel ends his piece praising Douglas Fairbanks: "And let no one quarrel with this popularity. It is a good sign, a healthful sign, a token that the blood of America still runs warm and red, and that chalk has not yet softened our bones" (Fairbanks 190).

Slapstick, Gender, and a New Silent Comedian: *The Butcher Boy*

This two-reel comedy, written and directed by Roscoe "Fatty" Arbuckle, opens as the "first half" of the bill at the American Theater, the New York Theater, and Proctor's 58th and 125th Street theaters in New York City in the spring. Among its small ensemble cast is a newcomer to movies, Buster Keaton. The former vaudevillian, recognized on the circuit for his acrobatic ability, will take pratfall after pratfall in this, his first film. Keaton and Arbuckle make a near perfect team: one is thin, the other is fat; one already shows beginnings of the stone face that will distinguish him from other silent comics while Arbuckle mugs, smiles, and winks at the audience. Keaton, even now, wears his signature flat straw hat, which provides the content for an early gag in the film; his opposite possesses an ill-fitting bowler that perches on his large, round head indoors and out. Arbuckle is absolutely the rascal in this story, as well as the improbable romantic lead, but Keaton, while sometimes the victim of the gag, proves quite resilient. Both men are agile, in fact, graceful physical comedians. This year alone they will make about half a dozen films together for the Comique Company in New York City, and they will continue to work together making shorts until 1920.

The Butcher Boy is a well-crafted little film. Its two reels neatly bisect the narrative and they illustrate how the gag and the chase can function in a silent, slapstick comedy. The film opens with an establishing shot of a general store. The setting is theatrical; we see three walls lined with goods from floor to ceiling. A rolling ladder is in place, ready for Arbuckle's character, Fatty the butcher boy, to glide around the store's perimeter, a most rotund "aviator." The store is bustling—everywhere gags are being set up. In an open office above the selling floor sits Almondine, the pretty love interest, animatedly talking on her phone, ready to receive the price of purchase and return both change and the wrapped item via a wire basket to Alum the head clerk, who is also Fatty's competitor for her affection. Near the back of the frame four older men sit around a barrel playing checkers. Centered in the foreground, a hen-pecked husband drapes himself over the molasses barrel catching the syrup as it drips off the spigot and licking his fingers. We meet the store manager, Almondine's father. A medium close-up introduces him chewing on a cigar, possessed of a stubby goatee that sticks straight out from his chin. Luke the dog barks at a black cat whose back arches in response to his threat.

The store springs to life as the stout wife yanks her husband off the molasses barrel and thrusts her packages at him. He drops them, of course, and she kicks him in the pants as he bends over to retrieve them. Meanwhile, Almondine places a parcel in a basket, which whisks down its wire track and clonks Alum in the head. The comedic rule of three operates here. His customer tries to help and only succeeds in causing the basket to knock him again. He stumbles back and gets caught up in the ropes that function to return the basket to Almondine. It is only after this opening business that we meet Fatty coming out of the cold storage vault in an area offscreen to the left of the main store. Now the fun really begins. The character Arbuckle plays is smart, sly, physically adept, and ultimately he is successful—Fatty gets the girl. The humor he generates is based on his size, shape, and the way he is costumed: his pants are too short, his hat is too small, and later he will disguise himself as a little girl—with long ringlets like Mary Pickford's. He uses his stomach to bounce people out of his way and his considerable backside to both insult authority figures and to shove them aside. Dialogue intertitles also make us laugh. One joke involves a woman who wants spicy, hot sausages. He accommodates her: "These hot sausages are nice and cold."

Fatty *acts* like he is uninterested in his job. Apparently unaware that he is leaning on the meat scale, he attempts to weigh the steak he has been trimming. Two times he cuts away the "excess." "This pound of beef sure is heavy." Then he notices what he is doing and uses his knife to push his arm off the scale. Still, we have seen Fatty doing some fancy knife work: in one fell swoop he whacks off the neck of a chicken carcass hanging on a hook poking him in the back. He deftly wields the butcher knife backward and forward as he slices the meat, and he pauses to split a hair that, dagger-like, falls and pierces the steak. Fatty also glances our way, twice, as he adds his considerable weight to the pound of steak. These nondiegetic moments signal that he is acting; he knows it; we do, too, and our pleasure is in his performance. Special effects are deployed to reiterate Fatty's proficiency at both his trades: carving meat and comedy. When he finally wraps his pound of meat and "all the trimmings" in butcher paper and ties it with string, the camera is cranked slowly so that he appears to be moving in double time. Such deliberation, focus, and skill belie the funny business with the scale. Fatty is not hapless. Before the melee that ends the first reel and motivates the action of the second, Fatty meets and bests Buster Keaton.

The gag that pits them against each other and has been set up since the film's beginning involves the leaky barrel of molasses. Keaton, a customer, enters the store carrying a small bucket because "Buster wants some molasses." Like the husband earlier, he too notices that the barrel drips and sticks his oversized shoe into the sticky dark puddle on the floor. Swiping his finger across the sole of his shoe he tastes the sweet syrup, starts to walk away, backs up, sticks his finger under the tap, and licks it clean. Then he approaches the counter where Fatty is working and begins his transaction. Unbeknownst to Fatty, he drops his coin into the bucket. Arbuckle scoops up the bucket and effortlessly jumps up on the counter, slides across, and hops to the floor on the other side. As he goes to fill the bucket, Buster advances on the checkers players and proceeds to interfere with their game.

You can imagine what happens next: Fatty demands payment; Buster explains. Fatty fishes in the bucket with his yardstick; Buster again pesters the checkers players. Fatty empties the bucket into Buster's hat, finds the coin, refills the bucket, and turns the straw boater over to hide the dark syrup that covers its insides. Buster puts on his hat, then tries to tip it in a gesture of goodbye. It sticks tight to his head. Fatty leans over the counter and tries to pull it off; Buster drops his pail and molasses pools around his impossibly long shoes. The hat finally separates from his head but now his foot is stuck to the floor. At last Fatty uses boiling water to "help" free

Buster, who tumbles backward and with a match on action somersaults out the door and onto the sidewalk.

The final, all-encompassing fight begins when Fatty notices Alum watching while he and Almondine "spoon in the spices." Provocatively, Fatty kisses her. The two clerks are arranged on either side of the store. Alum, screen right, has an arsenal of brooms; Fatty, on the left, is armed with paper bags of flour. As Alum starts to hurl a broom, Fatty's arm is faster, his aim is true, and he hits Alum in the face. Flour flies and quickly everyone is involved.

The free-for-all, caused by the rivalry between Fatty and Alum, has consequences. In the next scene Almondine is sent away to boarding school chaperoned by Mrs. Teachum. "Poor Fatty," the intertitle reads. The second part of the film builds to a grand chase inside the school. But first, the participants must assemble. Luke the dog and Fatty, disguised as a girl in a short, dropped-waist frock tied with a huge bow, arrive. Masquerading as Saccharine, Almondine's "little cousin," he enrolls. Next, Alum in a checkered dress and a wig of braids enters while Buster and a second clerk from

Fatty feeling awkward about being in Almondine's bedroom, in *The Butcher Boy.*

the store wait on the school lawn for Alum's call. They plan to kidnap Almondine. When Almondine, Fatty, and Alum are assigned to sleep in the same room, it's as if the starting gun fired signaling commencement of the race. In contrast to the fight in the first reel where projectiles are hurled back and forth and then up and down, the chase weaves in and out of various dorm rooms, the dining room, the hallway, the principal's bedroom, and finally her office. The characters run a figure-eight course. Finally, Buster, Alum and the other clerk are caught by Mrs. Teachum and held at gunpoint. Fatty and Almondine escape. Once outside, they notice a sign for the Reverend Henry Smith who lives next door. Fatty mimes putting a ring on his finger, proposes to Almondine, and she accepts. They both wink at the camera and the film ends with an iris-out as the two lovers, both wearing dresses, skip away to be married.

Comedy is a wonderful genre for glimpsing both the norms and the material culture of America. The general store is stocked with Sunshine crackers, Belfast Tea, and Horton's Ice Cream, as well as brand-name cigars and oatmeal. It is also the case that while Mrs. Teachum and the male characters in the film dress like comedy figures from vaudeville or the circus, Almondine and her classmates at boarding school wear the fashion of the day and at night are dressed in equally stylish pajamas. Fatty, as young Saccharine, resembles the child Mary Pickford plays this year in *Poor Little Rich Girl*. His long wig is set in curls; his coat is fur-lined; he dances similar steps; and he puffs out his cheeks in annoyance. Pickford's nemesis, a thinner little girl with glasses and braids, matches the description of Alum when he crashes Mrs. Teachum's school. "Saccharine" chastises Alum for his atrocious table manners: eating peas off his knife, bolting his food, and wiping his mouth with his hair ribbon. Still, after commenting on Alum's gluttony, he himself butters his bread with his fingers! This time Almondine, the real girl with proper manners, hands him a knife.

■ ■ ■

The year ends with the inauguration of the Rivoli, Roxy Rothapfel's newest picture palace in New York City. Located at Forty-ninth and Broadway, it looks from the outside like a Greek temple complete with Doric columns. Inside, it seats 2,400 people and the predominant hue is old rose, but the auditorium's great dome is fitted to cast light and change the room's color scheme. Music is provided by Dr. Hugo Reisenfeld's fifty-piece orchestra. The opening night program exhibits the film industry's preoccupations, especially its methods for responding to the Great War. The feature film is *A Modern Musketeer*, based on a short story called "D'Artagnan, of Kansas," but transformed to suit the talents and personality of its star, Douglas Fair-banks. It tells a story, as had *Wild and Woolly*, of a young man steeped in heroic fiction, pre-revolutionary France this time instead of the American West. In the surviving fragment of the film, the sole war-related moment occurs when a French chauffeur tells Ned, "With such wit the Yankees will make short work of the Boche." The villains of the piece include a greedy mother, a lecherous capitalist, and Chin-de-dah, a Hopi chief, all of whom desire young Elsie Dodge, "a sweet unspoiled flapper." It is set in the Grand Canyon instead of the battlefields of France. The war does enter the Rivoli's program through the live acts preceding the movie. The opening night is a special, invitation-only performance for the "movie world," but the *New York Times* reports that Colonel Edward House, an advisor to President Wilson on foreign affairs, is also in attendance ("Rivoli" 8).

Practical patriotism describes how the film industry balances the desire to grow and prosper with its wish to aid the government in this time of crisis. Filmmakers and theater managers adapt existing genres and practices to meet the challenge of running a business during a war. The industry continues to refine the star system, providing producers ways to distinguish their movies from those of other companies. Popular stars like Mary Pickford offer fans engaging roles in well-told stories, and they also participate in popular culture sharing their daily routines, their clothing and makeup choices, and their ideas on work and life with readers of magazines and newspapers. After April, they also encourage their followers to enlist in the war effort on the home front by buying Liberty Bonds. The industry realizes that profit lies in continuing to make the sorts of movies the public has shown it likes, including westerns, melodramas, and comedies; as the year progresses war films are added to the product mix, but they never dominate.

1918

Movies, Propaganda,
and Entertainment

JAMES LATHAM

The war remains far and away the most prominent and important news story. In some ways, however, this year in American life is as ordinary as any other. Most people and organizations go about their daily business as usual, with little fanfare, while some receive public attention. Edwin Armstrong, for example, is credited with developing an electronic circuit that dramatically improves radio reception. Emma Banister becomes the first female sheriff in Texas, and probably in the whole country. Newsworthy events range in interest from the international to the local, with obscure places sometimes gaining widespread attention, as when the small town of Codell, Kansas, is again hit by a tornado for the third consecutive year on 20 May. The news covers the usual kinds of curiosities, innovations, triumphs, and tragedies. In the area of transportation, for example, the first regular domestic airmail service begins, General Motors acquires Chevrolet, and a train crash in Nashville, Kentucky, kills 101 people and injures even more. Some noteworthy events will become more significant over time, for instance Babe Ruth leading the American League in home runs for the first time while his team, the Boston Red Sox, wins the World Series in what for eighty-six years would seem the last time.

American arts and culture continue to develop around the country on various levels, including their mass distribution, and receive varied recognition by the public and critics. The year's architectural innovations include the Hallidie Building in San Francisco, which becomes the first building to have an exterior wall made entirely of glass. In music, with the phonograph now an established mass medium, some 100 million records are sold worldwide, with Enrico Caruso and Al Jolson among the most popular artists. In literature, *My Antonia* becomes the final novel in Willa Cather's prairie trilogy, and possibly her greatest work. Booth Tarkington's new novel *The Magnificent Ambersons* will go on to win the Pulitzer Prize. And Edgar Rice Burroughs publishes *Tarzan and the Jewels of Opar*, another in his series of popular adventure novels. This popularity extends to the movies, with *Tarzan of the Apes* (released in January) becoming one of the year's top-grossing films.

Among the hundreds of films released this year, most come and go at local theaters with relatively little fanfare or lasting impact. Some of the year's more popular or critically notable films include *Mickey* (August, starring Mabel Normand); *Salomé* (October, starring Theda Bara); *The Forbidden City* (August, starring Norma Talmadge); Cecil B. DeMille's *The Whispering Chorus* (March), *Old Wives for New* (May), and *The Squaw Man* (December); *The Married Virgin* (December, with a young Rudolph Valentino); and *The Birth of a Race* (December). Fatty Arbuckle directs and co-stars with protégé Buster Keaton in some comedy shorts including *Out West* (January) and *The Cook* (September). Harold Lloyd stars with "Snub" Pollard and Bebe Daniels in over two dozen shorts, including *Kicking the Germ out of Germany* (July). Some of this year's other notable films are discussed below: *Stella Maris* (January); *Blue Blazes Rawden* (February); *Hearts of the World* (March); *The Blue Bird* (March); *The Kaiser, the Beast of Berlin* (March); *The Sinking of the Lusitania* (July); and *Shoulder Arms* (October). Familiar stars remain the commercial center of the industry, from Douglas Fairbanks, Mary Pickford, and Charlie Chaplin to Gloria Swanson, Larry Semon, Olive Thomas, Marguerite Clark, Pearl White, Sessue Hayakawa, and Tom Mix. Marion Davies appears in *Cecilia of the Pink Roses* (June), the first film backed by her lover, the media mogul William Randolph Hearst. Erich von Stroheim achieves notoriety as "The Man You Love to Hate" by playing evil Germans. Unlike stars, most directors work anonymously, though some, like D. W. Griffith, Thomas H. Ince, Cecil B. DeMille, and Maurice Tourneur, are touted as great artists. And some stars, like Chaplin and William S. Hart, begin directing their own films.

Their projects take shape amid a transition of power from the mostly East Coast–based studios of the Motion Picture Patents Company (the MPPC, or Edison Trust) to the Independent studios whose production facilities are increasingly located in Southern California. Following a Supreme Court antitrust ruling, the Edison Trust disbands. Member studios like Thanhouser, Selig Polyscope, and even the Edison studio go out of business or are absorbed by other companies. Edison releases its last feature in February: a war drama entitled *The Unbeliever* in which von Stroheim plays a brutal German officer who murders women and children. Studios that had fought the Trust increase their output and expand westward. Louis B. Mayer Pictures is incorporated, Warner Bros. opens its first West Coast studio, and Ince establishes a new studio in Culver City. Some stars form their own production companies, including Chaplin, who builds his own Hollywood production facility.

Increasingly, though never exclusively, cinema audiences include the urban middle class, for whom "movie palaces" are built and operated by the studios or entrepreneurs. In February, Sid Grauman opens his first downtown Los Angeles movie palace, the Million Dollar Theater. In October, Balaban and Katz open the luxurious Riviera Theater in Chicago. By providing audiences with clean, safe, comfortable, and stylish public spaces for watching films, such theaters enable exhibitors to charge higher ticket prices and cultivate social acceptance for themselves and the medium of cinema. Though these palaces always constitute a small proportion of theaters, they become a key element in Hollywood's growing wealth, power, and prestige.

While in some ways American life goes on as usual, it also is transformed by events of profound global and historical consequence. As the year begins, World War I has been raging for over three years, with American forces in the fray for eight months. In January, President Woodrow Wilson proposes his Fourteen Points, a blueprint for a lasting peace after the war's end (should the Allies prevail). After powerful German offensives into France in the spring, American troops consolidate with French forces and the Allies launch a series of successful counteroffensives in the late summer and fall. Military defeats, combined with the deteriorating morale of the suffering German civilian population and a navy mutiny, ultimately incapacitate the German war effort. In November, Kaiser Wilhelm II abdicates and immigrates to Holland, and armistice is finally declared to begin on the eleventh hour of the eleventh day of the eleventh month.

Throughout the year, war shapes life and death across the globe. More than a million American soldiers participate in a war that marks the introduction or modernization of technologies such as the submarine, machine gun, radio, and chemical weapon. These technologies transcend conventional limitations of space and time to deliver unprecedented destruction to distant military and civilian populations. By the end of the war, some nine million soldiers are dead, ranging from Germany's death toll of 1.8 million to the U.S. loss of nearly 49,000. Some six million civilian lives also are lost in Europe along with much of the infrastructure and social institutions that support them. Meanwhile, civilians in the United States experience the war less directly, though still powerfully, by hearing stories from loved ones or seeing them in newsreels, or by enduring domestic problems related to the war such as resource rationing and xenophobia. In the latter case, thousands of citizens around the country are threatened, arrested, and sometimes subjected to mob violence and even killed for being allegedly pro-German. This, along with rising anticommunism, prompts Congress to pass the Sedition Act of 1918, which forbids "disloyal, profane, scurrilous, or abusive language" and other actions deemed to be against the U.S. government. Further adding to the tragedies of this milieu, an influenza outbreak begins and soon becomes one of history's deadliest pandemics, killing as many as 50 to 100 million people worldwide. Despite its name, the Spanish influenza's first wave comes in the spring in U.S. military camps, where it goes mostly unnoticed. By the fall, it spreads around the country and the world—partly due to the war's close quarters, stress, and massive troop movements—and is especially lethal among healthy young adults. By February of the following year, it kills more than half a million Americans, far more than died in the war, including the romantic film star Harold Lockwood, whom a December fan magazine poll had ranked the second most popular male star, after Douglas Fairbanks ("Motion Picture").

John Collins, a Metro film director married to the studio's star Viola Dana, also dies; so do several exhibitors. The pandemic lasts until mid-1920 and disrupts society at all levels, including movie producers and theaters that already are struggling to recover from the war. Studios curtail production at a time when they need to boost it, theaters are closed for fear of spreading infection, and audiences generally resist public gathering places.

Once the United States formally entered the war in 1917, the mass media became fully engaged in it. Among the government's mobilization efforts was the formation of the Committee on Public Information (CPI), which conducted a massive multimedia campaign, modeled on British public relations, to promote the Allied war effort to international audiences as well as an American public whose isolationism and pacifism had delayed entry into the war. Throughout this year, the public is constantly exposed to promotional messages in newspapers, posters, speeches, and other forms. A relative newcomer to the mass media, cinema becomes integral to this campaign, participating in war as never before and perhaps since. The military, the American Red Cross, and the CPI itself produce some films, in the latter case including the features *Pershing's Crusaders* (May), *America's Answer* (July), and *Under Four Flags* (November). However, the film industry remains the chief source of movies—war-related and otherwise—with its established modes of production, distribution, and exhibition along with its increasingly global reach. The CPI coordinates the film industry to maximize cinema's effectiveness in the war effort in areas including film content, labor policies, taxes, and energy consumption. Through such work, the CPI not only shapes the immediate war effort, but also modern warfare itself as a campaign fought both in the media and on the battlefield.

Formally designated by wartime legislation as an "essential industry," the film business works to generate revenues as well as goodwill with the government and public. On an individual level, some film people enlist in the military or its domestic equivalents. Cecil B. De Mille, for example, becomes an honorary major, and Tom Mix is among some 200 members of the Fox studio to join a local home guard organization. Other movie people donate their resources to fundraising and recruitment efforts, as with the numerous actors who participate in parades, rodeos, concerts, pageants, and public speeches around the country. On a tour of the West Coast, cowboy movie star William S. Hart proclaims the need to "take the toot out of Teuton with the toe of Uncle Sam's boot" ("Film Trade"). On an organizational level, film studios produce and promote movies that deride Germany, praise America and her allies, and urge participation in the war effort. These movies range from feature films made by major studios and stars to shorts that include comedies and cartoons as well as serials, newsreels, industrials, advertisements, and training films. The overall production of war-related features reaches an average of about ten per month. By October, one series of newsreels, the weekly *Official War Review*, is screened in over half the country's movie theaters. Exhibitors participate in the war effort by collecting war taxes on theater admissions, closing regularly to conserve resources, and accommodating the "four-minute men" who give patriotic speeches during reel changes or at the end of programs.

While mostly maintaining a patriotic public front, the U.S. film industry is not entirely sanguine about participation in the war effort. Some producers are privately concerned about government interference in the film business, including censorship. Exhibitors also are concerned about government regulation as well as the sensibilities of their audiences, particularly regarding whether escapist entertainment that ignores the war or films that more directly engage with it better attract and serve the filmgoing public and the war effort. Exhibitors are concerned that overt propaganda might be unpopular because of its didactic or inflammatory content, as well as the pacifist or even pro-German sentiments of many filmgoers. This latter concern occurs amid a social context in which, by 1900, over a quarter of the American population is of German descent, and numerous communities around the country are predominantly German American. Even if these citizens mostly support the United States and oppose the German government, they still have family and ethnic ties to the old country and likely would have some resistance to films that criticize German people and culture.

The CPI and the film industry respond to such concerns in several ways, one of which is to persuade exhibitors and the public about the entertainment or informational value of war-related films. This includes intimidating exhibitors with admonitions to be patriotic, as with an *Exhibitor's Trade Review* ad that proclaims, "If you are a luke-warm American, a partisan of the Kaiser, or subsidized by the Imperial German Government, don't book *The Eagle's Eye*." Another approach is to appeal to different audience sensibilities by producing and distributing war-related films gradually over time and with varied genres, rhetorical tones, and degrees of direct reference to the war. This variability may be a conscious response to concerns about the reception of war films, but it also dovetails with the ongoing conditions and conventions of filmmaking that require time for films to be produced and distributed, and for new genres to develop, and which already tend to produce a range of films for a diverse filmgoing population. Consequently, films that are overtly war-related never form a dominant numeric proportion of overall wartime film offerings. However, while limited in proportion, war-related films also help to inform, entertain, and persuade mass audiences about the war, and sometimes are quite popular, from star vehicles to crude propaganda such as *To Hell with the Kaiser* (June). As such titles suggest, when war-related films criticize Germany it is mostly in terms of the government, especially political and military figures, rather than the ordinary German citizens with whom many Americans may sympathize.

Griffith Over There: *Hearts of the World*

Though war-related films are not as common as one might expect, they still are significant for their direct engagement with pressing social concerns of the day. Dramas about the war and the home front are among the most common war films, and, of those, *Hearts of the World* is especially significant, as much for its director as its content. D.W. Griffith probably is the single-most important American filmmaker of the silent era, whether for his early innovations in storytelling techniques, or his films that stir debate over cinema as an artistic and socially engaged medium, or his self-promotion of the director as author figure. The British government invites Griffith to make *Hearts of the World* due to his established stature and talent for filming battles. The film's ambitious production includes Griffith combining original scenes shot at the front and elsewhere in Europe with stock newsreel and other footage that is shot in Hollywood (constituting most of the film).

European footage is used in all three of Griffith's main releases of the year: *Hearts of the World* and the more modest *The Great Love* (August) and *The Greatest Thing in Life* (December). The international production of *Hearts of the World* is accompanied by international distribution, with three versions being released with intertitles identifying the characters as American, French, or British depending upon where the versions are shown. This sort of practice actually is not unusual in that film distribution always had been international, but, for an expanding American cinema, this is increasingly common.

Hearts of the World begins with a newsreel-like section showing Griffith preparing the film, including managing some filming at the front and meeting with war correspondents and the British prime minister, thus asserting the film's authenticity, authorship, and social significance. A fictional drama then follows, involving a French village where romance and family life are disrupted by the outbreak of war; the whole community is impacted as the men go off to the nearby battlefield. After German forces take the village, the character Marie (Lillian Gish), identified simply as "the girl," is traumatized by being put into forced labor and beaten. Later, in a powerful scene echoing recruitment poster imagery of allegorical female figures such as Liberty, Marie grips her bridal veil while searching the nearby battlefield for her fiancé, Douglas (Robert Harron). She finds him lying near death and consoles him with a long and ostensibly final embrace. After she returns home, some comrades revive Douglas, who also returns to the village. Marie and Douglas are reunited and, just as a German soldier is about to capture him, she intervenes; the Allies then recapture the village and rescue everyone. Dorothy Gish plays a romantic foil dubbed "the Little Disturber" and Erich von Stroheim has a small role as a German soldier. Overall, the story and characters are typical of Griffith's work, with outside forces of evil (usually men) victimizing a community of sympathetic ordinary folk, particularly women who are portrayed as needing to be protected by their male counterparts, though here it is the Lillian Gish character who saves the hero by stabbing the German soldier. The protagonists endure and ultimately prevail due to their determination and strong moral fiber.

Hearts of the World is well received by both audiences and critics. Indeed, it is among the most popular and prestigious American films of the wartime era. As a theater manager in Atlanta observes, "I have never seen such enthusiasm displayed in a playhouse. [The] people down here went wild. It was all we could do to keep many persons from standing in their seats" ("Many Thousands"). Likewise, a critic for the *New York Times* writes, "If the demonstrations by which those who saw the picture manifested their succession of emotions can be accepted as faithful indications, the motion picture succeeds in its ambitious aim" ("War Vividly Seen"). The film receives some mixed reviews, as with *Variety*'s 12 March description of the main romance storyline as "a fleshless skeleton upon which to hang a large number of brilliant war scenes." In addition to its authorship, subject matter, and reception, the significance of this film is further bolstered by the presence of the Gish sisters and Stroheim in the cast.

Patriotic Satire: *Shoulder Arms*

Though the war engenders drama, many comedies about it also are released at the time, usually mocking the enemy but sometimes also America, or at least some Americans. One such film is *Shoulder Arms*, another work that is significant not only for its content but also its director, Charlie Chaplin. A virtually unknown vaudeville performer before the war, in the mid-to-late 1910s Chaplin rises rapidly as a star and filmmaker.

Like all stars, Chaplin is vulnerable to the vicissitudes of public opinion. With his marriage in October to Mildred Harris, who is thirteen years his junior, this year marks the beginning of one ongoing concern the public would have with Chaplin, namely his marriages to much younger women that usually ended in bitter public divorce, in this case within two years. Chaplin also had been criticized in some quarters for inadequately contributing to the war effort. Consequently, in the year America enters the war he issues a press release saying that he had registered with the selective service but was rejected for being underweight. More substantively, he both makes war-related films and tours the country with Pickford and Fairbanks in support of fundraising and recruitment efforts. A publicity photo depicts him in New York City promoting Liberty Loans with Fairbanks. Chaplin is shown standing on his shoulders on the steps of the Sub-Treasury Building, across from the New York Stock Exchange, and beneath a statue of George Washington. Standing before a sea of some 50,000 people, the greatest movie stars of their time seem to signify the popularity and patriotism of both themselves and the film industry. They may signify the industry's active cooperation with government and business interests, and perhaps even the broader power of America's increasingly interrelated political, economic, social, and cultural systems. Given the poses of Chaplin and Fairbanks, this image calls attention to their physical dexterity and probably promotes Chaplin's most recent film, aptly titled *Shoulder Arms*.

Shoulder Arms is released in New York in October, two weeks before the end of the war, and then appears around the country during the following

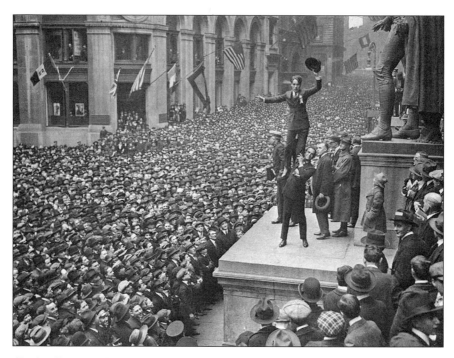

Charlie Chaplin and Douglas Fairbanks in Lower Manhattan in April 1918, promoting the Liberty Loan campaign.

months. Four other Chaplin films are released earlier this year: *A Dog's Life* (April), *Chase Me Charlie* (April), *Triple Trouble* (August), and *The Bond* (September). Another film, the behind-the-scenes *How to Make Movies*, is filmed but not released. Except for *Shoulder Arms*, these are mostly minor efforts. *A Dog's Life* is a typical Chaplin short about the tramp character and a stray dog getting into comical situations as they struggle to survive, though it is "longer and richer than any film he had previously attempted" and the dog is Chaplin's first sidekick to strongly parallel his tramp character—a scrappy social outcast who survives by his wits (Mast, "Chaplin" 119). *Chase Me Charlie* is compiled from previous Chaplin works; similarly, *Triple Trouble* consists of previous material shot but not used in other Chaplin films (*Work* [1915], *Police* [1916], and the unreleased *Life*). The storyline of *Triple Trouble* suggests a thinly veiled war-related film, with an inventor named Colonel Nutt who experiments with explosives and a foreign agent who tries to steal his work. The half-reel film *The Bond* promotes Liberty Loans as a form of human bond comparable to friendship and marriage.

Chaplin's major film of the year is planned and filmed as a five-reel feature, an unusual move at a time when comedies predominantly are shorts. Chaplin shoots enough footage for a feature, though he later removes several minutes including the ending of the film, which depicts an elaborate victory banquet in which the king of England cuts off a button from Charlie's uniform as a memento of his heroism. Perhaps this scene is cut for being disrespectful of the king or for promoting excess at a time of sacrifice. In any case, what remains is a three-reel film that not only enlists Charlie in the military but also humorously refers to the hardships of war, the fantasies of heroism, and, arguably, the hyperbole of wartime propaganda.

Chaplin stars as an ordinary if awkward recruit, first in boot camp and then at the frontline trenches in France. Following an introductory shot in which Chaplin apparently autographs the film as his own, the film depicts boot camp scenes with Chaplinesque gags such as his difficulties with marching in formation and the consternation this causes his drill sergeant. At the front, similar situations arise as there is constant danger, Charlie's quarters are flooded, and he is homesick. A package finally arrives for him but turns out to contain Limburger cheese. In a mocking gesture toward the atrocities of poison gas warfare, Charlie dons a gas mask and tosses the package over the top of the trench to the nearby Germans. Charlie then goes over the top himself and single-handedly captures several Germans, later saying, "I surrounded them." He then works as a spy behind enemy lines dressed as a tree trunk in scenes that further display Chaplin's talents as a physical comedian. After being saved by a French girl (Edna Purviance), he in turn rescues her and his sergeant buddy (Syd Chaplin, Charlie's brother) by impersonating a German soldier. In this process he miraculously captures the kaiser (also played by Syd), the crown prince, and Field Marshal von Hindenburg. After receiving a hero's welcome, he is awakened by his drill sergeant to discover that his heroism was all just a dream.

Shoulder Arms is very popular with audiences, furthering Chaplin's status as a star and filmmaker as well as allaying concerns about his patriotism. Released when the influenza pandemic is spreading, the film is so successful that a theater manager proclaims, "We think it a most wonderful appreciation of *Shoulder Arms* that people would veritably take their lives in their hands to see it" (qtd. in DeBauche 149). (DeBauche notes that the ad containing this statement ironically was published a week after the theater manager himself had died from the flu.) While this film dutifully mocks the Germans, it also is unusual for its criticism of army life, war, and propaganda. The film satirizes the discomforts and horrors of life in the trenches and the fantasies of an easy and total defeat over a powerful and evil enemy, while parodying the idealized American hero and film conventions such as the last-minute rescue (a staple of Griffith films). Such criticism is possible in this film partly because it is consistent with Chaplin's own filmic

tendencies to identify with the downtrodden and to comically flout authority figures and institutions of social power. It is possible because of Chaplin's skills at turning the most trying of circumstances into opportunities for
laughter, and for the broader disarming quality of comedy as a form that
often more readily challenges authority than the more "serious" form of
drama. And perhaps it is possible because the film is released so late in the
war, and for many audiences actually arrives afterward. The film probably
resonates with audiences who are weary of the war and its related rhetoric
and who seek a release from it while simultaneously engaging with it—safe
in the knowledge that Allied victory is likely or already had occurred.

Propaganda as Entertainment: The Kaiser, the Beast of Berlin

If *Shoulder Arms* mocks wartime propaganda, its target may be less the
earnest dramas like *Hearts of the World* than the shrill propaganda films
whose hyperbole could border on the comical, including *The Kaiser, the Beast
of Berlin*, *The Claws of the Hun* (June), and the early Raoul Walsh film *The
Prussian Cur* (September). During the previous period of official U.S. neutrality, American films about the war had been less common and strident in
their political rhetoric than films released afterward. After America formally
enters the war, German-ness, primarily in the form of the kaiser and his
regime, promptly is reconstructed as a bestial enemy that must be defeated
for the sake of humanity. German acts occurring at the moment or even
years earlier suddenly assume greater significance, especially those that can
be used to promote the Allied war effort. These acts include violence in the
form of the initial invasion (or "rape") of Belgium, the firing-squad execution of British nurse Edith Cavell (for helping hundreds of Allied soldiers
escape from German-occupied Belgium), and the sinking of the passenger
ship *Lusitania*. One-sided references in films and other media to such actual
events are accompanied by distortions or outright lies about German
malevolence, including tales of baby killing and other atrocities. While the
Allied media may distort events for their own purposes, the German media
and political leadership also can be tone deaf in their own public relations,
as with the Edith Cavell case. The kaiser himself also proves an easy target
for propagandists, with his militaristic personal appearance and sometimes
bellicose rhetoric, as when in 1900 he had declared that German troops
being sent to help defeat the Boxer Rebellion should "spare nobody, take no
prisoners. . . . Be as terrible as Attila's Huns" (qtd. in Gatzke 44–45). With
that one utterance, he provided the epithet that would most define Ger-

man-ness during World War I. Even in the months after the armistice in November, anti-German vitriol continues in war films just entering distribution, and in postwar films demanding vengeance or warning of a possible German resurgence. *Wanted for Murder* and *The Kaiser's Finish*, both released in December, are characteristic examples.

In this context, *The Kaiser, the Beast of Berlin* exemplifies the harsh rhetoric that appears in the most extreme propaganda films of the time. Less a conventional story than a series of charges against the kaiser and his regime, this film contrasts images of morally justified Allies with images of the kaiser as a lecherous warmonger whose regime kills babies, sinks civilian ships, and destroys churches at his bidding. The film provides audiences with a happy ending involving the kaiser being captured by Allied soldiers, turned over to the king of Belgium, and jailed by one of his former victims. As with *Hearts of the World*, this film depicts victims of German aggression, this time in Belgium. But unlike Griffith's or Chaplin's film, this one is much more concerned with the persona of the kaiser himself. It is an indictment of the purported greed, criminality, and violence of the kaiser and, by extension, his regime—but not the German people per se. Ads for the film refer to the kaiser's supposed insanity, monstrousness, vanity, aloofness, uncaring treatment of his men, and "admiration for pretty feminine hands" (Adv., 13 April). Rupert Julian plays the kaiser to great effect, with reviews in the trade and fan press hailing his performance as "a splendid bit of acting" and as so successful that "his entrance is greeted with spontaneous hisses" (Adv., 20 April; Adv., 1 June). In addition to playing the lead role, Julian also directs, co-writes, and produces the film as an independent production that is distributed through Universal. Not yet a star, Lon Chaney plays German Chancellor Bethmann-Hollweg in this film, one of nine in which he appears this year.

Accurately describing the content of *The Kaiser, the Beast of Berlin* poses a challenge, since there are no surviving prints of the film. However, the film received an extensive promotional campaign, yielding abundant images and descriptions that together provide a sense of the film's content, or at least how the producer and distributor meant it to be perceived and consumed by audiences. Advertisements tout the film as "an amazing exposé of the intimate life of the mad dog of Europe," and warn that "anyone who resents the message of this picture IS NOT A LOYAL AMERICAN" (qtd. in Campbell 100). Popular and trade newspapers report on the contents of the film, its promotion, and responses to it. An April news item in the trade press, for example, describes how the film's posters are eliciting violent responses toward the "bestial likeness" of the kaiser: "Patriotic citizens seem

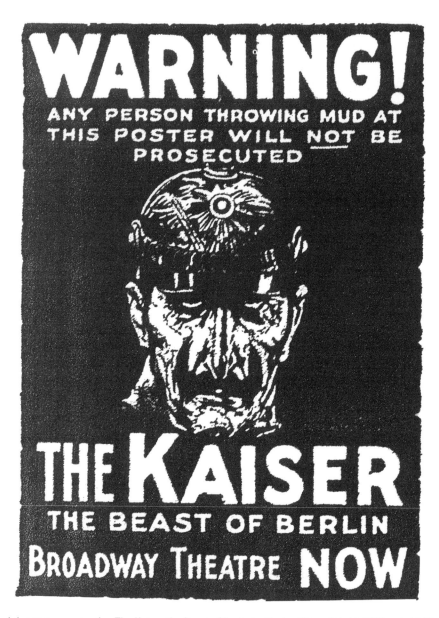

Advertising poster for *The Kaiser, the Beast of Berlin* in *Moving Picture World*, 30 March 1918.

to take a keen delight in making this face a target for missiles of every description" ("*Kaiser* Lithographs"). Indeed, advertisers for the film sometimes explicitly call upon the public to respond in this manner, as with a poster that simultaneously warns about the kaiser and promises that those who deface the image of him will not be punished. While promoting the film, such advertising also promotes the war effort by demonizing the enemy and providing the public with an indirect if playful way to combat him and win.

The extensive promotion of the film along with its contents and social milieu makes for a very successful popular reception. From Boston to Ohio to San Francisco, audiences reportedly come out in huge numbers, willingly paying premium admission prices, and sometimes appearing "as if on the verge of rioting" (Campbell 100). This latter behavior generally is in support of the film and its rhetoric, though some people dissent, if at some personal risk. For example, Rudolph Lahnemann of Fresno, California, apparently makes some disparaging remarks that are overheard and lead to his being indicted by a federal grand jury and eventually sentenced to five years in jail. Such incidents suggest that if America is fighting overseas for freedom, at home it does not always practice what it preaches.

Animated Documentary: *The Sinking of the Lusitania*

Along with features and star vehicles, movie programs also include short entertainment and informational films such as cartoons and newsreels. Some of these smaller films depict the war and related topics creatively, didactically, or, in the case of Winsor McCay's *The Sinking of the Lusitania*, with some of each. Released in July, this twelve-minute film sometimes has been described erroneously as the first animated propaganda cartoon, or the first one about World War I. Animated cartoons about the war in fact had been made since at least 1915, and their production and rhetoric increased thereafter along with that of other war-related films. In the months before the release of McCay's film, there are such cartoons as *The Peril of Prussianism* (January), *Me und Gott* (April), and *The Depth Bomb* (May). Among other producers, Pat Sullivan releases several animated shorts during the war, including two that apparently seek to capitalize upon the anticipation or popularity of *Shoulder Arms*, namely *How Charlie Captured the Kaiser* (September) and *Over the Rhine with Charlie* (December).

McCay's film is neither the first nor last animated cartoon about events related to World War I, nor is it the first film made about the German sinking of the passenger ship *Lusitania* off the Irish coast in May 1915, an act that had killed over 1,000 people, including 128 Americans, and edged a reluctant nation closer to war. In addition to coverage in other media, two feature films about this event appeared before McCay's film, both starring Rita Jolivet, an actress who actually had survived the *Lusitania* disaster. Little is known about *Her Redemption* (1916), but *Lest We Forget*, released in

January, is a drama in which the Jolivet character is captured by Germans and sentenced to death by firing squad (a likely reference to the Edith Cavell case). She escapes, only to find herself aboard the ill-fated ship but survive its destruction. Jolivet's real-life connection to the disaster not only provides a reason to make these films, but also helps to promote them and lend a degree of authenticity. McCay's film may have been created partly to tap into lingering interest in this particular subject as well as ongoing concerns about a possible direct German attack on the United States. Such concerns are heightened by ongoing submarine warfare and when, on 25 May, U-boats make their first confirmed appearance in U.S. waters.

What makes *The Sinking of the Lusitania* among the more interesting, accomplished, and unique films of its time is its hybrid form as an artful document. Unlike most documentaries it is animated, and unlike most animated cartoons it is not a comedy. And unlike many propaganda films of the time, its production values are exceptional, even noteworthy as one of the earliest films to use cel animation. As with *Hearts of the World*, the prologue of McCay's film depicts the author figure preparing the film, and likewise touts him as not only a great filmmaker but also "the originator and inventor of Animated Cartoons." While McCay certainly did not invent animation, he had already produced a number of groundbreaking works such as *Gertie the Dinosaur* (1914) and was an established Hearst newspaper comic strip and editorial cartoonist.

A powerful document with images drawn and edited to resemble a newsreel, McCay's animated film simultaneously informs, horrifies, and possibly entertains audiences with its spectacle. A self-described "historical record of the crime that shocked Humanity," the film depicts the ship being torpedoed, engulfed in flames and explosions, and sinking as passengers seek lifeboats and fall overboard to their deaths. The film culminates with a powerful scene of a mother and her baby drowning. While the film depicts the Germans as distant and dark silhouettes, the victims are portrayed with more humanity, including photographs of some prominent passengers who died, such as the millionaire Alfred Vanderbilt and "the world's foremost theatrical manager," Charles Frohman. Though clearly on the side of the Allies, and sometimes strident in its rhetoric, the film also makes gestures toward a more balanced journalistic tone, including its acknowledgment that there were public warnings that such an event could occur, and that these warnings had been ignored. Perhaps because it is not a feature film, there is not much of a documented popular or critical reception for *The Sinking of the Lusitania*, but it subsequently may be considered one of McCay's most accomplished works.

▰▰▰▰▰▰ Typical Western: *Blue Blazes Rawden*

The U.S. film industry contributes to and profits from the war effort with films about the war, but also continues producing its usual stories, genres, and star vehicles. In fact, though the war may impact everyday American life and nearly every genre, most films in most genres have little or nothing to say about the war. The western exemplified this tendency, with conventional character types, settings, and iconography that are mostly incompatible with the war. Only a few films even make an attempt, including *Western Blood* (April) and *Mr. Logan, U.S.A.* (September). Likewise, movie stars who are associated with certain genres or character types may dabble in films that are about the war but mostly maintain their screen personae in other films that are not. And when stars appear in war-related films, they retain familiar genre, story, or character traits. William S. Hart, for example, appears in ten westerns this year, including *The Border Wireless* (September), in which his cowboy protagonist encounters German spies sending radio messages across the border to Mexico as part of an assassination plot. At first glance this storyline may seem ludicrous, but it probably alludes to the Zimmermann telegram, which was intercepted, decoded, and publicized by the British in early 1917, and in which Germany made an overture to form a military alliance with Mexico. In the film, the Hart character's attempt to foil the assassination plot is challenged when the spies learn that he is an outlaw and hence reluctant to go to the authorities. Though in some ways unusual for Hart, this film is mostly consistent with his screen persona, including the theme of the "good badman," which appears in his more conventional westerns of the year, such as *Blue Blazes Rawden* and *Riddle Gawne* (August).

Blue Blazes Rawden is an example of a film that is noteworthy here not for its distinctive qualities, but for its ordinary ones. Though the work of a major star-director and supervised by a top-tier director-producer, Thomas H. Ince, the film is otherwise rather ordinary, neither addressing topical events nor boasting impressive production values nor receiving great promotion or reception. Instead, perhaps like most films, it is quite run-of-the-mill. Set mostly in a barroom in a remote northwest lumber town, the film stars Hart as a roughneck loner who challenges a similarly shady saloon proprietor at cards and for the attentions of his girlfriend. A gunfight ensues and Rawden wins, leading the victorious bad man to realize the consequences of his actions. When the proprietor's mother and brother arrive in town to determine what happened, Rawden tries to make amends by praising the man he killed and saying he died of natural causes.

However, the brother soon learns what really happened and shoots Rawden, wounding him. Rather than being vengeful, Rawden saves the boy from a lynching and admonishes him to maintain his mother's favorable illusion of her son. Rawden leaves town again as a loner, though reformed.

In many ways the story, characters, setting, and iconography of this film typify westerns of this period. Some elements, such as the lumber town setting, are unusual for Hart's films, though not radically so. The theme of the protagonist who embodies tensions between savagery and civilization, and ultimately chooses the latter, already was common in Hart's films, though not yet for the western genre, which tended to portray the West in more simplistic terms. In films like this, Hart provides a somewhat more realistic portrait of the West with more nuanced characters as well as relatively ordinary settings and action sequences. Unlike the action-oriented films of his main screen competitor at the time, Tom Mix, *Blue Blazes Rawden* is an example of Hart providing audiences with a somewhat more mature and thoughtful portrait of the Old West. It is not one of Hart's greatest films, but the everyday work of a distinctive artist grinding out mass entertainment from the Hollywood factory.

From today's perspective, one striking scene in this film is the near lynching of the character who shoots Rawden. It is powerful not so much in its dramatic intensity, but for its very ordinariness. In the 1910s, mob justice may be conventional in westerns and even in parts of America, but seeing it today calls attention to the violence of both the old West and "modern" society.

Double Pickford: *Stella Maris*

Mary Pickford appears in six films released this year, only two of which are explicitly war-related: *Johanna Enlists* (September) and *One Hundred Percent American* (October). Her four other films make little or no reference to the war: *Stella Maris*, *Amarilly of Clothes-Line Alley* (March), *M'liss* (May), and *How Could You, Jean?* (June). Most of these films contain Pickford's character type that had engendered and sustained her fame, namely the young girl or adolescent whose vitality, beauty, and charms enable her to overcome whatever challenges she encounters. Her characters often come from humble backgrounds and might get married or become wealthy but always remain true to themselves and others. Pickford's diminutive stature (only five feet tall), long curly blond hair, and lively onscreen persona endeared her to audiences who came to know her as "Little Mary" and "America's Sweetheart."

While continuing to play sweet and innocent youngsters, Pickford also diversifies her screen persona with roles that sometimes go against the grain. *Stella Maris* is one of the most striking examples of this effort. In an otherwise rather conventional melodrama, Pickford plays both the title character and Unity Blake, two very different women who each love the same man, a journalist named John (Conway Tearle). Stella is a rather typical Pickford character, an attractive, charming, and happy young woman who happens to be an invalid living a sheltered life with her wealthy foster parents. In many ways Unity is the opposite, a homely and impoverished orphan whose life as a maidservant is filled with sadness and drudgery. For Stella, John is a favorite frequent visitor and eventual suitor, while for Unity he is the estranged husband of Louise, the woman who adopts and abuses Unity until she goes to jail for beating her in a drunken rage. The kindly John then adopts Unity, who takes a liking to him. Years later, Stella is cured of her paralysis and becomes romantically attracted to John. She goes out into the world only to discover its hardships, including that John is married and his wife has just been released from jail. Taking revenge upon Louise and repaying John for his kindness, Unity breaks the love triangle by killing her tormentor and committing suicide, thus paving the way for a happy ending with Stella and John being united. Though the film is not overtly war-related, it does contain a few direct references, including a scene where an enlistment poster figures prominently in the background, and another where soldiers march off to war.

The film is frank in its treatment of alcoholism and child abuse, but what makes it especially distinctive is the dual roles played by Pickford. The title character is Pickford's usual type, but Unity really is the dramatic center of the film and the more interesting character to watch, both as a sympathetic victim and as a character played by Pickford. The role of Unity is risky for Pickford, given the character's pathetic life, unattractive physical appearance, and eventual murder-suicide. Pickford is transformed for this role through makeup, costuming, lighting, descriptive intertitles, and her own performance style, including a cringing posture, a twitch in her face, and earthy mannerisms. As noted in an April *Photoplay* review, "Miss Pickford's drudge is no mere matter of makeup; [she] realizes the character with all her mentality, and sustains it without the slightest lapse." The technical achievement of Pickford's transformation, along with several shots where she appears onscreen as both characters, even sometimes conversing with the other, are likely appeals for the film. Posters and publicity photos show these characters together, and the film itself almost seamlessly juxtaposes them.

Mary Pickford in her dual role in *Stella Maris*.

This film also is noteworthy for the contributions of screenwriter Frances Marion and director Marshall Neilan, both of whom were hand-picked by Pickford to collaborate on much of her best work. Marion initially encouraged Pickford to read the novel *Stella Maris*, which she then adapted for the film. As a close friend and collaborator, Marion wrote seventeen screenplays for Pickford. Neilan was an actor-director who had previously co-starred with Pickford; she had successfully persuaded him to focus solely on directing. Neilan subsequently directed additional stars who valued his talents in working with actors and capturing them effectively on film, including his wife, Blanche Sweet.

Stella Maris achieves success with audiences and critics, though perhaps more the latter than the former group. As with other efforts by Pickford to diversify her image, the public usually prefers the sweetheart, and in subsequent roles she mostly conforms.

Pursuit of Happiness: *The Blue Bird*

Fantasy films constitute a genre rather far removed from the war film as well as numerically more marginal. Only ten fantasy films are released this year. Though small in number, these films likely have strong appeal for the youth market, an audience that decades later becomes of primary importance to the film business. Films about Little Red Riding Hood and Santa Claus resonate for the youngest of film audiences, while other fantasy films also may appeal to somewhat older audiences, whether with the swimsuit imagery of Annette Kellerman in *Queen of the Sea* (September) or Willis O'Brien's animated prehistoric monsters in *The Ghost of Slumber Mountain* (November). Perhaps because of its content and marginal status during early film history, the children's fantasy film may be a genre where women can more readily find work in positions of creative power. This year at least, women hold top creative positions on two of the ten fantasy films, with Mollie Teschner writing *The Revolt of the Toymakers* (December) and Madeline Brandeis writing and directing *The Star Prince* (June). Of the ten films, however, *The Blue Bird* is the most historically significant due to its status as a film by Maurice Tourneur, with its associated quality production values and prestigious literary source (the 1909 symbolist play *L'Oiseau bleu* by Nobel Prize–winning playwright Maurice Maeterlinck).

At a time when most films are made more with an eye toward efficiency than aesthetics—more like *Blue Blazes Rawden* than *The Sinking of the Lusitania*—Tourneur is a proponent of cinema as an artistic medium comparable in expressive potential to painting, theater, and literature. His work can be regarded as reflective of the industry's increasing attempt to attract the growing middle-class film audience. Prior to working in film, Tourneur had developed extensive experience in the visual and performing arts, mostly by acting and directing in a French theater company that traveled around Europe and the United States. In 1914, after working a few years for the French film company Éclair, he was transferred to the United States, where he soon became a model auteur, directing and writing films that were consistently sophisticated in narrative and visual stylization. Tourneur's achievements were not single-handed; he benefited from a team of talented crewmembers, including editor Clarence Brown, cameraman John van den Broek, and art director Ben Carré. Tourneur's popular and critical success enable him to establish his own production company, whose first release is *Woman* (October). Five other Tourneur films are released this year: *Rose of the World* (January), *The Blue Bird* (March), *A Doll's House* (June), *Prunella* (June), and *Sporting Life* (September). Typical of Tourneur's output, these are mostly dramas and romances adapted from literary or theatrical works and lack the stars that he feels detract from narrative realism.

The Blue Bird is about two young peasant children, brother and sister, who are led by a fairy on a magical journey. Tyltyl (Robin Macdougall) and Mytyl (Tula Belle) selfishly refuse to give their pet dove to a poor sick girl next door, which causes the fairy, Berylune, to take them on a search for the meaning of happiness. The children have many magical encounters in faraway places, where they communicate with the spirits of animals and ordinary objects come to life. One of the spirits the children briefly encounter (and resist animating) is that of war. After witnessing many forms of happiness, they ultimately find their own by giving away their dove, now a blue bird, to the ill child.

Tourneur's film is impressive in its creative costuming, performance style, set design, lighting, special effects, and tinting. The orchestral score also is well crafted, including both original compositions and selections from the works of more than twenty composers. Some critics observe that this film is rather conventional in the more cinematic techniques of editing and camera work. However, the film's stylization does include techniques such as stop-motion animation and frame-within-the-frame staging that is creative in itself and may signal relations between film and other visual art forms that use framing, such as painting and theater. The ongoing presence within the film of the logo for the production company Artcraft (for copyright purposes) also signals the film's artistry.

The Blue Bird is a critical success upon its release and is considered by some critics to be among Tourneur's best works. A *Photoplay* review in May describes the film as "so beautiful, from beginning to end, that it fairly stings the senses, awakening in the spectator esthetic emotions so long dormant, so seldom exercised, that the flashing light of the awakening is almost a surfeit of joy." A review in the *New York Times* similarly observes that "those who have read 'The Blue Bird' and felt its charm will be exceptional if they do not get from the play at the Rivoli at least a very large part of what they got from the book, and if they are people whose imagination failed them before the printed page, they will get more" (*Blue Bird*). While the film may please critics, it is not a popular success. Despite the *Times* reviewer's observation that the audience was "delighted," the film fails at the box office.

■   ■   ■

In this year of momentous global events, American film participates more actively and effectively in the fabric of everyday life than ever before, and benefits handsomely from this participation. War enables the film industry to expand its distribution, revenues, and public standing as the movies engage with the war. Though most films only allude to the war subtly, if at all, they also serve the interests of institutions and individuals across the landscape by bringing images of the outside world to local theaters to inform, entertain, and persuade mass audiences.

1919

Movies and
Righteous Americanism

BEN SINGER

The decade ended with a turbulent year marked by both triumphalism and tribulation. World War I was finally over and Americans were full of jubilation, self-confidence, and hope. The country gloried in the recognition that American forces were a decisive factor in winning the war and, more generally, in the United States' new geopolitical status as the richest and most powerful nation in the world. The economy continued to thrive as America supplied the world with food, manufactured products, and raw materials, while European industry and agriculture lay in shambles. America's sense of ascendancy was not just material but moral as well. The Old World system of aristocracies and empires had just imploded in a frenzy of self-destruction; at the same time, the nascent Bolshevik experiment was mired in civil war. Mainstream America felt confirmed in the righteousness of its political system and way of life.

Despite such high spirits and hopes, the year also was marked by an extraordinary level of domestic unrest, involving terrorist bombings, political paranoia, labor strife, high demand-driven inflation, and race riots. In the wake of the Russian Revolution two years earlier, many officials genuinely believed that Bolshevik agitators, radical labor unions, and anarchists could ignite a socialist revolution at home. A wartime mentality lingered, segueing seamlessly from a war against the Huns to a war against "the Red menace." Yet the population was weary of constant upheaval and anxiety and yearned for a return to normalcy. In the cultural realm, normalcy entailed an impulse toward consumerism and popular amusement that helped create a boom year for the film industry.

On New Year's Day, Americans awoke to find headlines blaring news of terrorism. In Philadelphia the previous evening, bombs had destroyed the homes of the chief justice of the Pennsylvania Supreme Court, the city's police superintendent, and the president of the Chamber of Commerce. According to the police superintendent, the bombings were the start of terrorist plots planned to reach from one end of the country to the other . . . a reign of terror that means the general destruction of public build-ings and the homes of many wealthy men and influential officials. . . . This is a part of the plot which the Bolsheviki are starting on a nation-wide scale. . . . Outbreaks may be expected any day in any part of the country. . . . [These are] I.W.W. [Industrial Workers of the World] or Bolsheviki outrages, pure and simple.   ("Scent" 13)

The country endured another terrorist scare around May Day. Deadly mail bombs were sent to thirty-six federal officials, judges, politicians, and multi-millionaires. (After one exploded, maiming a senator's housekeeper, the rest were intercepted.) A month later, yet another audacious attack rattled the nation. Bombs again targeting government officials and judges deto-nated within minutes of each other in seven different cities, killing two and demolishing the home of the U.S. attorney general. A Red Scare now inflamed, the F.B.I. ramped up domestic surveillance programs and com-piled a list of some 60,000 suspected radicals. Agents conducted hundreds of raids, making thousands of arrests, searches, and seizures, typically with-out warrants (Faragher et al. 669; Hagedorn 219–25, 411–13).

The year saw 3,600 labor strikes, involving over four million American workers. Bolshevism was the pervasive scapegoat, but the root causes were less exotic: prices of food, goods, fuel, and housing had doubled in five years, outpacing blue-collar wages. In Seattle, more than 60,000 shipyard and other industrial workers went on strike over wages, effectively closing down the city for a week in late January. In September, 365,000 steel-workers across the country walked off the job. The strike—the largest to date—lasted four months and failed to win any concessions whatsoever (Faragher et al. 665; Hagedorn 59, 277, 346, 354, 428).

Along with labor unrest, major incidents of racial violence similarly drew attention to the failure of Progressivism to fully redress fundamen-tal social ills. Race riots erupted in twenty-six cities. A three-day clash in Washington, D.C., in mid-July left six people dead and over one hundred wounded. Just ten days later in Chicago, a stone-throwing fracas on a public beach escalated into five days of widespread rioting. By the time the police and 6,000 infantrymen managed to restore order, 38 men were dead, 537 injured, and more than 1,000 Blacks left homeless after racist mobs torched their homes (Faragher et al. 664–65; Hagedorn 304, 312–17).

Throughout the year, Wilson participated in the Paris Peace Confer-ence, pushing for principles of democracy, open agreements, free trade, and a treaty that would not punish Germany with enormous war reparations.

He championed with particular zeal the creation of a League of Nations as a mechanism to prevent future wars. Wilson failed to accomplish many of his goals due to resistance from Allied Powers, but he did succeed in establishing the League. However, in the bitterest possible outcome for the president, in November, the Republican-controlled Congress rejected ratification of the Treaty of Versailles and membership in the League of Nations. The primary rationale was straightforward: the League's covenant stipulated that an act of war against one member was an act of war against all members. Many feared that the League would entangle America repeatedly in overseas wars lacking vital national interest (Faragher et al. 667–68; Hagedorn 357).

Two hugely consequential constitutional amendments were in the news. The Eighteenth Amendment, establishing Prohibition, was ratified by the last of the required three-quarters of the states on 16 January, and would go into effect one year later. The Nineteenth Amendment, extending suffrage to women, passed Congress on 4 June, and proponents worked feverishly to achieve ratification before the 1920 presidential election.

Barriers of a different kind were broken in engineering. In April, an army flier made the first ripcord parachute jump out of an airplane. In May, a U.S. Navy flier made the first transatlantic flight, from Newfoundland to Lisbon with a stop in the Azores. The General Electric Company formed a subsidiary company called Radio Corporation of America (RCA) by buying out American, British, German, and French patents and assets. The nation's first dial telephones were introduced, and the pop-up toaster was patented.

Journalist John Reed published *Ten Days That Shook the World*, his eyewitness account of the Russian Revolution. Sherwood Anderson published his collection of midwestern short stories, *Winesburg, Ohio*. Music education received two large boosts when textile merchant Augustus Juilliard bequeathed $20 million for what would be renamed the Juilliard School of Music in New York and photography pioneer George Eastman endowed $3.5 for the creation of the Eastman School of Music in Rochester. Reflecting a national fad in spiritualism, over three million Americans bought "spook boards" (the most famous trademarked as the Ouija Board) in hopes of talking to "the other side." In baseball's World Series, seven members of the Chicago White Sox conspired to hand victory to the Cincinnati Reds in exchange for payoffs from underworld gamblers. So many individuals were involved in planning the fix and raising betting money that rumors soon swirled, leading to indictments the following year (Hagedorn 384).

■■■■■■■■■ Fights for Control in the Industry: First-Run Theaters and Star Power

The film industry thrived as theaters were packed with postwar pleasure-seekers willing to pay higher ticket prices for better films. Two giants continued to dominate the industry and battle each other: Adolf Zukor's Paramount, mostly distributing films from its Famous Players–Lasky studio, and First National Exhibitors Circuit, a consortium of about thirty major theater-chain owners banded together to combat Paramount's ever-growing power. Having seen First National woo away top talent (most notably Mary Pickford), move into production and distribution, and thwart its access to first-run theaters so crucial to its profits, Paramount launched a massive counteroffensive this year by plunging into the exhibition branch of the business. Armed with $10 million from Wall Street, Zukor bought or built first-class first-run theaters in every principal city. Other studios like Fox and Goldwyn similarly moved toward vertical integration (Hampton chap. 12).

Another new business model was spearheaded this year with the formation in April of United Artists by the industry's three biggest stars and top director: Mary Pickford, Charlie Chaplin, Douglas Fairbanks, and D. W. Griffith. Spurred by rumors that Paramount and First National might merge to create a mega-monopoly—something the stars realized would diminish their power in negotiations concerning salary and creative control—the "big four" decided to finance, produce, distribute, and promote their own movies rather than work as employees. Not only would they be able to craft films without front-office meddling, they would also be able to pocket the profit normally siphoned off by producers and distributors. Because Pickford and Chaplin were still under contract with First National, and Griffith with Paramount, United Artists released only three films this year, two successful comedy-adventures starring Fairbanks, *His Majesty, the American* and *When the Clouds Roll By*, and Griffith's *Broken Blossoms* (the rights for which the director had bought back from Paramount).

Pickford's three First National pictures were all major box office successes. *Daddy Long Legs*—the year's top grosser—*The Hoodlum*, and *Heart o' the Hills* followed similar formulas, showcasing Pickford's winning combination of spunky mischief-making, moral probity, pathetic humility, and colorful portrayal of social types (a rambunctious orphan girl, a ghetto toughie, and a hillbilly lass, respectively). The year's second biggest box-office hit was a surprise to everyone, since its cast included no stars. George Loane Tucker's *The Miracle Man* was an inspirational story focusing on a gang of crooks and the deaf, dumb, and nearly blind faith healer who gradually redeems them. Thomas Meighan, Lon Chaney, and the rest of the ensemble received rave reviews for their performances. The film (now, sadly, lost) prompted producers to rethink the prevailing wisdom that only stars sold tickets. Henceforth, directors became more prominent in publicity, and studios, eager to save money and cool down bidding wars for big-name talent, became receptive to so-called "All Star" films (meaning just the opposite—films with no eminent actors) (Hampton 216–18).

Still, stars remained the industry's focal point. After Fairbanks and Chaplin, dapper heartthrob Wallace Reid was the top male star, making eight features (five more than Fairbanks), all directed by James Cruze. (One of them, *Hawthorne of the U.S.A*, is analyzed below.) Japanese-born actor Sessue Hayakawa starred in nine features that enjoyed critical and commercial success, all made by his independent production company Haworth Pictures. Many films looked affectionately at the folksy foibles of rural Americana. Boyish-looking Charles Ray starred in nine features in which he plays basically the same character: a gangly, unaffected country youth who learns the hard away about the pitfalls of city life or the wiles of city slickers visiting small towns. Representative titles included *The Busher*, *The Egg Crate Wallop*, *Bill Henry*, and *Hay Foot, Straw Foot*. Jack Pickford (Mary's kid brother), an even more boyish boy-next-door type, specialized in the same sort of agreeable rural comedy-melodramas, including *Bill Apperson's Boy*, *Burglar by Proxy*, and *In Wrong*.

Director Maurice Tourneur earned critical plaudits for beautifully mounted thrillers *The White Heather*, *The Life Line*, and *Victory*. Erich von Stroheim directed his first film, *Blind Husbands*, in which he played his trademark type of vain Teutonic womanizer. African American filmmaker Oscar Micheaux also made his first film, *The Homesteader* (now lost), with an all-black cast. Adapted from his own novel, the story focused on the pathos of unrequited love between a white woman and black man, the disastrous consequences of the racially appropriate marriage the man forces himself to accept, and, after that relationship ends with the wife's suicide, the joyful discovery that the white woman is, in fact, of black ancestry.

Seeing Red: *Bolshevism on Trial*

Capitalizing on public concern about labor insurgency and Red infiltration in the wake of the Russian Revolution two years earlier, a number of films focused on well-meaning idealists who fall prey to radical demagoguery. In most examples, an earnest young woman joins a socialist group, hoping to make the world a better place, only to find that the leadership is corrupt and depraved. Socialism—the aspiration toward a society without gross disparities in material well-being—is repudiated not only as an impractical ideal, but also as a deception practiced by power-hungry hypocrites who are more interested in ravishing genteel white flesh than in helping the downtrodden. Following a long tradition of classical melodrama, evil is epitomized through attempted rape. This act, and the integrity of the rescuing hero, opens the woman's eyes to the perniciousness of radicalism and to the moral superiority of the American status quo (or some slightly tempered reformulation thereof). Another variant portrays a radical heroine who sees the error of her ways when mob violence threatens the lives of family members or sweethearts. Representative titles from this year included *The Red Viper*; *The World Aflame*; *The Uplifters*; *The New Moon*; *The Undercurrent*; *The Volcano*; *The Right to Happiness*; and *The World and Its Woman*.

One of the first and most prominent films in the cycle was *Bolshevism on Trial*, an adaptation of the 1909 novel *Comrades* by Thomas Dixon (best known for writing the novel upon which *The Birth of a Nation* was based). Shrewdly released on May Day (a workers' holiday associated with socialist rallies), the film's timing could not have been better: headlines were sizzling with news about the terrorist onslaught involving the three dozen mail bombs.

The film begins by introducing Colonel Henry Bradshaw, described, in terms that leave little doubt about the film's pro-capitalist stance, as "a brain worker whose inventions have increased the comfort of his generation; created work for thousands of employees; brought wealth to himself." Bradshaw is infuriated by news that Barbara Alden, the woman his son Norman wants to marry, has joined the Reds. Norman is more open-minded: "There's a lot that's wrong with our social system," he submits. "Maybe Barbara sees farther." Barbara is an earnest and empathetic young social worker based in the Lower East Side ghetto. Cut-ins show us her notes as she prepares to speak at a socialist meeting that evening: "Who should feed and shelter the unfit and the unfortunate? They cannot be left to starve and die. . . . Workers should unite to produce enough so that the surplus of the strong may be distributed to the weak." We also read a letter she writes to Norman: "I am sick with the misery I see all about me! I must do something."

Barbara visits a gravely ill mother of three in a squalid tenement. An intertitle reads, "Barbara's unconscious motive is a motherly sympathy for those unable to care for themselves." This narrational interjection is perplexing, since caring for others is hardly Barbara's unconscious motive—it's her *overt* motive. The characterization of her behavior as "motherly" presumably contains an editorial point: that Barbara's desire to aid the helpless is just a womanly weakness, an expression of women's instinctual impulse to care for offspring, and hence misdirected, even neurotic (what she really needs is to settle down and have a baby). Helping the miserable, by extension, is irrational. The rational solution is to let the unfit die off. This may sound outrageous today, but it accords with the philosophy of Social Darwinism influential at the time (as I discuss below). In any case, the sick mother dies quietly, in long shot, as Barbara attends to her. Barbara's sorrow is accentuated in a medium close-up as she says a prayer for the dead, her hands on her heart and her eyes gazing beseechingly toward heaven.

A large audience gathers in Socialists' Hall to hear about a plan to lease an island resort off the coast of Florida and turn it into a communist utopia. The man behind the scheme is a sour, maniacal-looking "professional agitator" named Herman Wolff. Surveying the audience, the camera lingers on a cluster of seven or eight wizened men with long beards, extras chosen for their prototypically Jewish appearance—reinforcing the period stereotype that most radicals are Jewish immigrants. Inspired by Barbara's impassioned speech, Norman pledges to finance the endeavor. Outraged, his father kicks him out of the house. As a precaution, however, the colonel asks two employees to join the colony: Tom Mooney, a brawny chauffeur "very handy with his knuckles," and a faithful Indian named Saka, a friend from family hunting expeditions. Two hundred people move to the fancy resort on the otherwise unpopulated island.

After the first order of business—replacing the American flag with a red one—Norman is voted Chief Comrade. An early sign of trouble appears when all members of the cooperative are asked to fill out a slip indicating occupations for which they are suited. "Leading woman—musical comedy," writes one woman. A dumpy old maid puts down, "Artists model—I am known for my svelte figure." Most of the men indicate a high management position. No one volunteers to wash, cook, plow, build sewers, or weave cloth, so Norman announces that jobs will be assigned by the Central Committee. There are to be no wages in this utopia—it is share and share alike.

Discontent soon percolates. Engine-room workers pull a blackout until Norman pays them to reconnect electricity. The head cook tells the Central Committee he won't work for nothing, especially given the haplessness of his untrained staff. Those kitchen workers, in turn, complain that they deserve more than he does, since he just stands around bossing everybody about. Then the vegetable gardeners gripe that the kitchen staff has it easy compared to their toil. Grievances spread like wildfire and the colony clamors for new leadership. Wolff engineers a special election that ousts Norman and places himself in power. He wastes no time turning the colony into a totalitarian dictatorship, with a private police force to crush any opposition. Wolff decrees that the island will serve as the launching pad for global revolution; that religion is forbidden; that marriage is nonbinding; and that the state will raise all children. Finally, he declares "absolute freedom"—a thinly veiled term for free love (a form of depravity that anticommunist propaganda from the period frequently cited as an earmark of Bolshevism). The crowd gets visibly aroused: men begin touching women; women gesture flirtatiously. Norman and Barbara are appalled.

When Wolff demands that Norman transfer over the lease to the island, on the pretext that "private property is wrong" (but really so that Norman cannot call in U.S. law enforcement), Norman refuses and is promptly imprisoned. Wolff and his flunkies predict that he will meet a "natural death" and his friends will soon "go missing." Tom alerts Saka (living by himself in the woods) and instructs him to row to the mainland and telegraph the colonel. The obligatory attempted rape scenario now unfolds. Wolff announces to Barbara, "I mean to make you the consort of a great revolutionary leader—myself." When she recoils, he seizes her and tries to take her by force. Norman (freed by Tom's handy knuckles) breaks in and rescues Barbara in the nick of time, knocking the villain out cold. A navy frigate promptly arrives with the colonel on board. As the relieved colony cheers, the colonel shakes his son's hand heartily and welcomes a shame-faced Barbara into the family. Soldiers arrest Wolff, whose real name, it turns out, is actually Androvitch (succinctly signaling the nation's seamless shift from a war against the Huns to a war against the Reds). The commander informs Wolff that he has been under surveillance for over a year (the film thus endorsing the Justice Department's aggressive program of domestic surveillance), and was allowed to carry out this scheme only at the request of Colonel Bradshaw, who knew it would teach Norman and Barbara an invaluable lesson. The final shot shows Norman vigorously tearing down the Red flag and hoisting up the Stars and Stripes.

Dixonian propaganda is generally hard to defend, but in all fairness, given that the novel *Comrades* predated the Russian Revolution by eight years and Stalinism by over two decades, Dixon's prescience regarding the specter of totalitarian tyranny was nothing short of remarkable. Moreover, while it goes without saying that *Bolshevism on Trial* is a work of unabashed propaganda, one is surprised by how well executed it is. With its ripped-from-the-headlines subject, its journeyman director (Harley Knoles), and maiden-voyage producer (Mayflower Photoplay Corp.), one expects it to be a lowbrow sensational melodrama made on the cheap. It was released, however, as a "special" (with higher rental prices and longer runs) by Select Pictures, a solid medium-priced distributor co-owned by Zukor and Lewis J. Selznick. Further, Mayflower Photoplay proved itself to be a class act—the phenomenally successful film *The Miracle Man* was its next production. Critics were surprised by *Bolshevism on Trial*'s intelligence as a disquisition on the vagaries of human nature as they impinge on competing political ideologies. Its indictment of socialism ultimately hinges on the critique that it is simply too idealistic, ignoring inevitable human failings such as laziness, naiveté, obtuseness, selfishness, hypocrisy, megalomania, and lechery.

Curiously, for a tract so keen to repudiate socialism, the film seems to go out of its way to underscore the problems and sentiments that motivate this belief system. Barbara's humanitarian statements, amplified by the disturbing scene showing the sick mother's death, would seem to validate socialism's impulse to ameliorate the poverty and misery of "the unfit and the unfortunate." Given that it accentuates this social problem and rejects any socialist remedy, we very much expect to see the film propose an alternative solution assuring capitalism's greater humanitarian efficacy. One could easily imagine a coda showing the colonel endowing a state-of-the-art charity hospital for the Lower East Side to be run by Norman and Barbara. But nothing of this sort materializes. The film's argument appears entirely negative: socialism is evil. It never makes even a perfunctory attempt to suggest that capitalism offers a better way to alleviate suffering.

Why not? Why would *Bolshevism on Trial* shine a light on poverty and misery and then simply ignore the issue? I daresay such questions probably would not have puzzled most contemporary spectators. They would have recognized that the film expressed a familiar current in conservative thought of the period. While historians emphasize Progressivism as the era's prevailing sociopolitical movement, another contender—a form of radical individualism based on principles of Libertarianism and Social Darwinism—remained strong after its heyday in the Gilded Age before the turn of the century. This ideology held that in society, as in Nature (putatively), it is every man for himself, and only with universal competition and self-interest will society develop to its full potential. The writings of the influential Yale sociologist William Graham Sumner exemplify the philosophy most forcefully. Like many of his generation, Sumner believed that the principle of natural selection—survival of the fittest—governed the social world as in the natural world. Like it or not, life is a struggle for survival; the fit flourish while the weak perish. Trying to prevent poverty is therefore not only futile ("We might as well talk of abolishing storms, excessive heat and cold, tornadoes"), it is also unethical, because it props up the unfit at the expense of those who actually advance social progress (Sumner, "Reply" 54). "Poverty is the best policy," Sumner argued, because it allowed natural selection to winnow out the unfit (Sumner, *What* 13).

While no one would dare voice this notion openly today, it remained prominent in the marketplace of ideas throughout the 1910s. The Red Scare gave it a shot in the arm, since socialism tampers with the natural order of things by equalizing material well-being irrespective of merit. It expropriates rewards earned by the diligent, thrifty, and intelligent and gives them to those lacking such virtues. According to Sumner, socialism thus "favor[s] the survival of the unfittest, and accomplish[es] this by destroying liberty" (Sumner, "Challenge" 25). *Bolshevism on Trial* embraces this discourse. In reply to Barbara's exhortation that "the unfit and the unfortunate . . . cannot be left to starve and die," the film coolly replies, "Yes they can—and, in fact, should be."

Survival of the Fittest Revisited: *Male and Female*

Cecil B. DeMille's *Male and Female* was the year's third biggest box-office success—and another indication of the commercial viability of the "All Star Cast," since neither of the leads—Thomas Meighan and Gloria Swanson—as yet commanded top-dollar salaries. It was DeMille's name that emblazoned advertisements. The film is an adaptation of a 1902 play entitled *The Admirable Crichton* by J. M. Barrie (most famous today as the author of *Peter Pan*, written two years later, in a decidedly different vein). The film adaptation alters the play in a number of significant ways. One simple change is the title: worrying people would misread "Admirable" as "Admiral" and mistake the film for a war picture—the commercial kiss of death after the armistice—DeMille opted for a title that was not only simpler, but sexier as well. "Undoubtedly the change of title . . . will be alluring enough to the picture fans to draw them in," *Variety* predicted (Rev. of *Male and Female*).

Another thought-provoking narrative dealing with questions surrounding the status of the individual within large-scale social systems, the film fashions a social-philosophical position that, compared with *Bolshevism on Trial*, is much closer to mainstream American Progressivism. The key difference is not that *Male and Female* takes a kinder, gentler posture toward the plight of the miserable (the issue simply does not present itself), nor that the film is more receptive toward a socialist model of common welfare (on the contrary, the film accepts that hierarchies and inequalities are inevitable), but rather that it rejects the conservative premise that fitness and well-being are necessarily correlated. As long as society is structured by divisions of class and caste, survival of the fittest cannot be said to operate in society just as it does in nature.

Male and Female's rebuttal against Sumnerian conservatism goes as follows: unlike nature, society does *not* (at least not necessarily or principally) distribute its rewards based on relative fitness. An aristocrat is able to live in luxury even if he is dimwitted and decadent. A common laborer will find it virtually impossible to ever enjoy such luxury, no matter how intelligent and industrious he may be. Luxury or hardship, dominance or subservience, are not manifestations of relative merit so much as arbitrary perpetuations of preexisting class boundaries. Class identities are solidified within lifespans and extended across generations as a result of differences in opportunity, differences in environmental peril, ideological mystification, and the dead weight of tradition.

Male and Female is a critique of this state of affairs and a reflection on what, if anything, can be done about it. Granted, the film's Progressive message—that purely hereditary structures of privilege and disadvantage are pernicious, since they inaccurately gauge individual merit—is not exactly controversial. It is what one would expect from a Hollywood film. What makes the film notable, however, is its unusual defeatism in acknowledging just how heavy the weight of social tradition really is. Established social barriers, the film shows, are not only baseless, they are also intractable—too entrenched for the protagonists to contravene. With this concession, *Male and Female* deviates markedly from the conventions of romantic melodrama operative in the vast majority of relevant Hollywood narratives, in which true love conquers all social and familial obstacles in the end. True love does not win out here.

The story begins with an upstairs/downstairs glimpse at the household of England's Earl of Loam—consisting of the vacuous Lord Loam; his two vain and haughty daughters, Lady Mary (Swanson) and Lady Agatha; a supercilious cousin, the Honorable Earnest Woolley; and Mary's fiancé, the insipid skirt-chaser Lord Brocklehurst. We see the sybaritic aristocrats lounging in bed, luxuriating in rose-water baths, being served breakfast in their rooms, and so on. A large staff of servants is supervised by the majordomo Crichton (Meighan), a man of uncommon intelligence and aesthetic sensibility. He is adored by Tweeny, a sweet, uncultured young scullery maid. The interest is not reciprocal, however, because Crichton loves Lady Mary from afar, admiring her intelligence and refinement despite her imperious manner. He never acts on his feelings due to his mindfulness of social and professional decorum and his awareness that Lady Mary would be horrified by such effrontery.

That fact is confirmed when Lady Eileen Duncraigie visits Mary and asks her opinion about "a friend" who is in love with her chauffeur and wants to marry him; could they ever be happy? Mary's reply is an instant and emphatic "No." Pointing to a pair of exotic birds, she asks, "Would you put a Jack Daw [common crow] and a Bird of Paradise in the same cage? It's kind to kind—and you and I can never change it." Lady Eileen confesses that she is that "friend." A series of omniscient insert shots shows the chauffeur waiting outside, slouching against the car with a witless expression on his face, spitting on the ground, chewing on a toothpick, and generally looking like a vulgar gold digger. Mary is appalled and upset. After Eileen leaves, she lashes out at Crichton, "Rather democratic you servants are getting!" He looks pained but responds with composure: "One cannot tell what may be in a man, my Lady: If all were to return to Nature tomorrow, the same man might not be master—nor the same man servant—Nature would decide the matter for us!"

The film's core problems are thus in place: are established social hierarchies grounded in substantive, intrinsic differences among the classes—like crows versus birds of paradise—or are they essentially baseless and arbitrary? And if one concludes the latter, as the viewer knows the film must, does it make any difference? Can anyone ever opt out of the dominant order of social stratification, however indefensible it may be?

The dramatic elaboration of these questions unfolds when, during a yachting expedition in the South Seas, all the aforementioned characters (minus Brocklehurst, and plus a young minister) are shipwrecked on a deserted island. The aristocrats take it for granted that the master-servant hierarchy will obtain. They sleep late, demand breakfast be served, and so on. Crichton, on the other hand, understands that in raw nature, outside of civilization, fitness for survival is the only relevant differential. Hereditary titles are utterly meaningless. He takes charge, forcing Woolley to help haul fresh water and ordering Tweeny to tend the fire instead of assisting Lady Mary's beauty regimen.

Lord Loam puffs out his chest and proclaims that since he was born a peer, naturally, he is the leader. Crichton ignores him and requests Mary's gold lace shawl for use as a fishing net. She refuses indignantly and Loam demands an apology ("or take a month's notice"—an absurdity that makes Crichton grin). The aristocrats storm off, Tweeny and the minister in tow, to make their own camp. Utterly hapless, by nightfall they are huddled together shivering, shelterless, hungry, and terrified of predators. Crichton, meanwhile, has built a sturdy lean-to and sits comfortably by a roaring campfire enjoying a hearty seafood soup. One by one, the aristocrats defect,

Lady Mary surrenders to the new order: Thomas Meighan and Gloria Swanson in *Male and Female*.

following their noses. Mary holds out the longest, but eventually hunger, cold, fear, and isolation force her to acquiesce to the new social order based on survival fitness. With a mixture of humility and humiliation, she requests a bowl of soup and hands Crichton her shawl—a gesture of surrender made all the more suggestive in that, as they both register, the act exposes her skimpily clad body as if part of her submission.

Months pass. Crichton is the uncontested alpha male, commanding deference and solicitude just like a king. The others are his eager and willing subjects, waiting on him hand and foot. The alternative to the established social hierarchy that the film presents is thus *not* a world free of social divisions. While cooperative, the new social order is by no means egalitarian. A new hierarchy has replaced the old one. This is not a target of criticism, however. The film does not proselytize for a society without disparities of power and reward—that is, socialism. It does not indict hierarchies per se, so long as they reflect actual differences in individual merit. This qualification was already intimated in the grossly unflattering shots of the chauffeur. The point was not that Mary's classist bigotry was legitimate, but that *some* hierarchies are perfectly justified. Crichton reigns due to his demonstrated prowess as a hunter, his bravery as a protector, his ingenuity as an engineer, and his general stature of manliness. The audience takes pleasure in his righteous ascendancy.

The succinct inversion of power is accentuated in a scene in which Mary serves Crichton a meal in his separate throne room, staged precisely so as to visually match an earlier scene in which Crichton-as-butler waited upon Lady Mary. Now Mary too is infatuated with Crichton, along with Tweeny. So eager is she to serve and please him that one evening, after her father eats figs Crichton had requested specially, she hurries into the jungle to pick more, mindless of the danger. Alarmed when he finds out, Crichton rushes out and finds her being attacked by a leopard. After he kills the beast, Crichton and Mary finally embrace and profess their love for each other. Returning to the group, they announce their wedding will be the next day.

During the wedding, just as the couple is about to finish exchanging vows in front of the minister, Tweeny spots a ship on the horizon. Everyone is ecstatic and races out except the couple, who are left devastated standing at the altar. Mary implores Crichton not to light the signal bonfire. He hesitates, but then, crestfallen, dutifully triggers the flame. Navy sailors and officers arrive, and the old social order immediately snaps back in place. Lord Loam, the assumed leader, takes credit for all the structures and inventions created by Crichton. Back in London, masters and servants resume customary modes of luxury and subservience. Crichton endures the humiliation of serving drinks to Lord Brocklehurst as he romances Lady Mary, while she endures heartache and social entrapment. Swanson and Meighan masterfully convey the anguish, longing, and dejection of their characters through eyelines and nuances of body language and facial expression.

Eileen Duncraigie calls again, this time wearing drab, threadbare clothes that contrast starkly with Lady Mary's evening gown and ornately bejeweled headdress. Eileen is miserable—disowned by her family for marrying the chauffeur, rejected by his family, shackled to an unemployed loser. Mary avers that none of that would matter if she really loved him: "I know because I, too, love someone—and am willing to give up *everything* for him." Crichton walks in and overhears. The viewer waits for the music to swell and Crichton and Mary to rush into each other's arms, but it does not happen. Crichton discretely shakes his head, signaling that no such denouement is tenable. Eileen, likewise, shows Mary the hole in her glove finger and the coarseness of her cheap coat and says, "Don't believe the storybooks, Mary—Love *isn't* everything! There is Heredity—and Tradition—and London!" Mary insists that true love trumps all that. Fearing that Mary might decide to give everything up for him, Crichton whisks in a bewildered but delighted Tweeny and informs Lady Mary that they will marry and sail for America as soon as possible. Even as he says this, Crichton and Mary lean into each other with plaintive longing as if about to kiss, but he checks himself and stiffens with resolve. Mary, head and body drooped in sorrow, slowly ascends a flight of stairs, escorted by Brocklehurst. On the top step, she pauses hesitatingly for several seconds. Will she run down the stairs and throw herself at Crichton, compelling the romantic coupling they (and viewers) yearn for? After a brief moment of suspense, she continues to walk slowly away.

The film concludes with a bittersweet coda consisting of two brief vignettes. In the first, we see Lady Mary with Lord Brocklehurst in a mansion garden; she emotes a mixture of dignified tristesse and gentle acceptance of her comfortable but passionless fate. In the second, Crichton and Tweeny are together on a bucolic farm out west with mountains rising majestically in the background. They beam health and happiness and, by all indications, are very much in love.

Male and Female is a surprising film with respect to its emotional tone and narrative trajectory. It is fair to say that most spectators, familiar with the conventions of romantic melodrama, strongly anticipate that Crichton and Lady Mary will, in the end, realize that their love is more powerful than social barriers. But the film is unexpectedly pessimistic in this central romantic and sociological strand. We learn that no amount of romantic idealism is able to eclipse social reality. The dead weight of society is simply too heavy to throw off. So habituated are we to romantic triumph that, when it is withheld, the film seems bleak and clinical, more sociological treatise than drama of the heart. This is, I believe, what *Photoplay*'s reviewer tried to express: "It is a typical DeMille production—audacious, glittering, intriguing, superlatively elegant, and quite without heart. It reminds me of one of our great California flowers, glowing with all the colors of the rainbow and devoid of fragrance."

Nevertheless, fragrant or not, for such a pessimistic film, *Male and Female* ends on a surprisingly upbeat note. The film is *not* a tragedy. Crichton ends up joyfully productive and in love. One might be inclined to dismiss this happy ending as merely cosmetic, a tacked-on and emotionally superficial cop-out motivated by Hollywood convention and commercial expedience. It is undoubtedly true that DeMille deemed it inadvisable to produce an emotional downer. Nevertheless, the final image of Crichton and Tweeny happy and robust in God's country is more than just an optimistic veneer over a defeatist film. It is, rather, an encapsulation of the motif of righteous Americanism that we saw in *Bolshevism on Trial* (and will shortly see in *Hawthorne of the U.SA.*, below). The European caste system is morally diseased beyond hope of remedy. Too entrenched to change and too unjust to live under, the only solution is to turn one's back on the putrid structure altogether. America shines forth as a new world ostensibly unburdened by ingrained social barriers, where material well-being is rewarded solely on the basis of individual virtues of industry and thrift, not class or caste. It is one of America's most cherished myths.

"American Presumption and Bad Manners": *Hawthorne of the U.S.A.*

If *Bolshevism on Trial* is a validation of Americanism via an object lesson of socialism run amuck, and *Male and Female* is a parallel validation via an indictment of aristocracy (and, by extension, plutocracy—rule by a wealthy elite) and its corollary caste system, *Hawthorne of the U.S.A.* manages to weave both critiques together in a much lighter, and more ostentatious, self-congratulatory fantasy. The film epitomizes American swagger, echoing the mainstream public's sense of postwar ascendancy, while at the same time perhaps overcompensating for nagging doubts raised by a year of extraordinary domestic turbulence.

Touring Europe with his sidekick Rodney Blake, a happy-go-lucky young American named Anthony Hawthorne (Wallace Reid) breaks the bank at a Monte Carlo casino, winning two million francs. When a reporter asks his name and title, he replies "Hawthorne—citizen of the U.S.A. And that's got every king in Europe backed off the map. . . . If I had my way, I wouldn't leave a king in the deck" [of cards]. Hawthorne's anti-monarchist rant delights Colonel Radulski, who thinks he may have found someone to bankroll a revolution in his country, the sleepy kingdom of Bovinia.

Speeding through Bovinia's tiny capital, Hawthorne's cap flies off and he stops to retrieve it. He discovers a lovely young woman sitting alone in a walled garden. It is mutual love at first sight, and they plan to meet again at twilight. The Americans check into the run-down central hotel. Seeking a hiding place for his luggage bag full of gold coins, Hawthorne discovers a sliding panel opening into the adjacent room, where a cadre of revolutionaries happens to be meeting. Radulski, a wild-eyed anarchist named Nicht (overtly coded as Jewish), Prince Vladimir of neighboring Austrovia (scheming to annex Bovinia), and others are conspiring to get their hands on Hawthorne's casino lucre. Hearing his name bandied about, Hawthorne closes the panel, strides next door, bribes the guard to gain entrance, and confronts the group. They soon persuade him that the king is a brutal tyrant who has impoverished his people, and the casino money is needed to secure a bloodless coup by winning over the army, which hasn't been paid for months. Unaware that they plan to assassinate the king, and thinking that the girl he met has been victimized by the monarch's greed and neglect (he visualizes her tattered shoes), Hawthorne agrees to finance the overthrow.

The king, we soon find out, is actually a kindly old man who is almost as broke as everyone else (he has to bum cigarettes from his guard). Prince Vladimir, pursuing his annexation scheme, requests the hand of his daughter, Princess Irma, promising to secure loans for Bovinia in return. Seeing no other way to alleviate his country's poverty, the king agrees. When he breaks the news to his daughter in the royal garden at twilight, she is horrified because she detests Vladimir and loves the American. She acquiesces, however, out of duty to her country. When the king leaves, Hawthorne (who has heard everything from behind a bush) declares his love, but Irma sorrowfully explains that even if Vladimir were out of the picture, she would never be allowed to wed a commoner.

U.S. senator Ballard, a big cigar-chomping Teddy Roosevelt type, arrives at the hotel with his daughter Kate. (Eager to court Kate, Hawthorne's pal Blake had wired the senator claiming the hotel's spa would do wonders for his rheumatism.) As the royal carriage drives past the hotel, the anarchist Nicht tries to assassinate the king and princess. Hawthorne knocks out Nicht before he can shoot again, and, hearing soldiers busting down the door, races back into his room through the secret panel. Prince Vladimir attempts to collect Hawthorne's money, but the American refuses: "Not one cent for murderers!" As a crowd rushes in, the prince fingers Hawthorne as the would-be assassin. Marching off to jail, Hawthorne asks the senator to deliver the large potted bush on his table to the princess as a token of his affection.

While soldiers ransack the American's room looking for the money bag, Vladimir strong-arms the king into signing Hawthorne's death warrant. Hawthorne is nonchalant; he has hidden a wad of cash in his cap and has no trouble bribing the guards escorting him to his execution. Just then, the revolution explodes. The terrified king prepares to flee, but Hawthorne arrives and confidently declares, "I'll handle this revolution." He and the senator calmly enjoy a cigar, relaxing with their legs up on the king's desk. A mob of angry soldiers and citizens bursts in, led by Prince Vladimir presenting a statement of abdication. As the king begins to sign, Hawthorne tears it up and addresses the crowd: "You know why I'm here—to boost business—to pay the troops—to make you rich. . . . If you'll cut this revolution bunk, I'll put money into this burg. What can his double-crossing nibs do for you?" "What can I do?" Vladimir retorts. "I can pay you here and now!" He brings forward Hawthorne's bag, which his soldiers have found, and opens it up to start passing out gold coins. To his horror, all it contains is potting soil. Hawthorne calls for the potted bush he sent to the princess. After leading the crowd in three cheers for the king, the Americans proceed to dole out the money hidden under the bush.

An epilogue shows how "Hawthorne awakens slumbering Bovinia . . . and transforms it with Yankee gold and ginger" (i.e., pep). Panoramic views of the city before and after drive the point home. The "Before" view shows the city's main boulevard so dead that a group of children sits right in the middle of the street playing a game, and only a few pedestrians can be seen ambling along, with not a single automobile or carriage in sight. The "After," a year later, shows the street bustling with hundreds of pedestrians and dozens of cars. A major construction boom has added dozens of buildings, including two massive resort hotels in the hills overlooking the city. By far the most prominent new structure is a huge cathedral towering over downtown (a not-so-subtle repudiation of atheistic Bolshevism).

The hotel lobby is also completely transformed, abuzz with dozens of guests and a hyperactive nine-piece all-black American jazz band. The staff now speaks in American slang and wears flashy American-style clothes. Royalty evidently no longer rules neighboring Austrovia, since Vladimir now works in the lobby café as a waiter. Hawthorne gets a kick out of tossing petty change onto his tray and watching his obsequious response. One final reform completes Bovinia's American makeover. The king (who also has picked up some stateside lingo) informs Hawthorne: "Today Bovinia junks all royalty and titles. Get me?" Now that Bovinia is a republic, the lovers are free to marry. The film's final shot shows Hawthorne proposing and the former princess happily accepting.

It would be hard to imagine a more self-satisfied fantasy of national superiority. *Hawthorne of the U.S.A.* conveys the arrogance of an America enjoying its enviable position as the only solvent and thriving Western industrialized nation. Hawthorne throws his money around with no small measure of condescension—circumventing authority twice through bribery; tipping Prince Vladimir in a humiliating way; asserting that his money "can handle this revolution"; promising that his infusion of investment capital will single-handedly generate a bustling Bovinian economy and stave off radicalism. The appearance of Senator Ballard is utterly gratuitous—he

Bovinia before and after "Yankee gold and ginger" in *Hawthorne of the U.S.A.*

serves no narrative purpose whatsoever—but his presence gives Hawthorne's actions an official imprimatur, reinforcing the tacit idea that Hawthorne stands in for American foreign policy and, more broadly, the government-bolstered power of American economic colonialism. The confidence encapsulated in his character stems to a large degree from a genuine conviction that America's supremacy is not just coincidental: it stems, rather, from its formidable system of entrepreneurial capitalism and democracy, coupled with quintessentially American qualities of energy, initiative, and can-do gumption. Americanism is antithetical to old Bovinia's bovine ways, but if Europe will only take the United States as its role model—vanquishing radicalism, relinquishing monarchism, opening its doors to American business—prosperity is guaranteed.

As reflective of the postwar mentality as *Hawthorne of the U.S.A.* may be, one should note that the film is based on a play (with the same title, written by J. B. Fagan) that ran on Broadway in 1912, well before the war. An up-and-coming stage actor named Douglas Fairbanks played Hawthorne—an experience undoubtedly shaping the persona of hyper-dynamic red-blooded Americanism that he later would adopt on screen. (The connection presumably also explains why much of the scenario of *His Majesty, the American*, written by Fairbanks, virtually replicates Fagan's play.) Evidently, American bravado was robust even before victory in the Great War gave Americans something more to crow about. A *New York Times* critic had observed, "It is the kind of play that foreigners alone would take seriously, finding therein an example of American presumption and bad manners" (Rev. 3). Being a Paramount release, the film almost certainly played internationally. One wonders how effective the film might or might not have been abroad as an instrument of democratic-capitalist propaganda and American boosterism. Whatever the case, it surely flattered mainstream America's ego at home—a satisfying dose of self-affirmation in a year of unusual upheaval and readjustment.

Cramming in Every Possible Bit of Beauty: *Broken Blossoms*

D. W. Griffith's *Broken Blossoms* is so universally spoken of in terms of fine art—by the filmmaker, by period critics, and by scholars today—that it would be virtually unthinkable to approach it solely as a social text. In its conception and promotion, the film overtly—more overtly than any other film of the year, if not the decade—invites recognition and appreciation as a work of lofty aesthetic aspiration. Even so, Griffith also viewed the film as a rejoinder to the spirit of ascendant Americanism I have been under-scoring. Citing the tension between Wilsonian internationalism and Amer-ican ethnocentrism, Griffith stated in *National Magazine* that one goal of the film was

> to help riddle the fallacious notion that Americans are superior to those they call "foreigners." Too many Americans labor under the delusion that they are the greatest people in the world and that all others are "foreigners." Now I believe that so long as we Americans speak out with shallow contempt of [other cultures], so long as we imagine that we alone represent all the hero-ism and beauty and ideals of the world first, so long will the efforts of such idealistic leaders as President Wilson [fail]." (qtd. in Lennig, *"Broken"* 2)

A small, intimate film shot in only eighteen days, *Broken Blossoms* tells a simple melodramatic story of good and evil. Virtue is embodied by an inno-cent waif (Lillian Gish) and a wistful "yellow man" (Richard Barthelmess) whose sympathy and platonic tenderness toward the girl brings a fleeting moment of happiness into her wretched life. Evil is incarnated in the waif's abusive father, the boxer "Battling Burrows," whose brutality culminates in his beating his daughter to death in a fit of racist rage upon hearing she "has taken up with a Chink." In a departure from the pervasive "yellow peril" xenophobia of the day (see Kepley), *Broken Blossoms* proclaims that the pro-tagonist Cheng Huan embodies Christian values of gentleness, humility, and compassion far more purely than the ostensibly Christian "barbarous Anglo-Saxons, sons of turmoil and strife." By associating virtue and spiri-tual beauty with a lowly ethnic outsider and violence with Western "civi-lization," Griffith repudiates the self-righteousness of the dominant culture. This remonstrance (so different from the bigotry of *The Birth of a Nation*, yet entirely consonant with *Intolerance*'s critique of authoritarian hypocrisy) takes on special relevance in the context of American postwar arrogance and ethnocentrism.

The film's moral high-mindedness was part of an overall project to create a prestige production evincing an aura of high class. Griffith's moti-vation was as much commercial as it was didactic or artistic: he wanted to establish a new upscale market sector, expanding cinema's reach into the class of an urban, well-to-do audience still primarily attending legitimate theater. Tapping that audience, Griffith believed, was the key to longer engagements and higher ticket prices. Before submitting the film for gen-eral release through United Artists, Griffith mounted high-profile runs in New York and other major cities. Exhibition was enhanced by a fancy alle-gorical dance prologue, an exotic balalaika orchestra, and an arrangement of multicolored spotlights hitting the screen to intensify and variegate the

A tonalist transition in *Broken Blossoms*, original tinted blue.

film's already richly hued tinting. In an audacious move (and a brilliant one for publicity), Griffith set ticket prices at $3 for the best seats (equivalent to $35 today)—matching the most expensive tickets of any live-drama Broadway theater, and roughly 25 times more than a normal movie admission.

Such rarefaction is only viable if a film is able to prompt audiences to perceive it as a work of art rather than ordinary entertainment. *Broken Blossoms* clearly pursued that goal. "We were out to cram into that picture every possible bit of beauty," Griffith stated with ironic artlessness (qtd. in Lennig, "*Broken*" 10). The primary cramming strategy was to emulate works in other visual arts already exalted as instances of beauty. *Broken Blossoms* borrowed its look from a movement in art photography known as Pictorialism. Influenced by the hazy, muted, semi-abstract style of Tonalist painting (best exemplified by the moody Nocturnes of James McNeill Whistler) and anxious to distance themselves from the quick-and-easy Kodak, pictorialist photographers favored fuzzy, low-contrast, low-detail images that they created using high-diffusion lenses, engulfing shadows, and complicated printing techniques using malleable pigments and gums that allowed various sorts of tonal and textural manipulation.

This influence is most apparent in four moody nautical transitions that strongly evoke Tonalist paintings. The shots blur the boundaries between hand-created and machine-rendered imagery. It is nearly impossible to discern whether or not they are paintings or highly worked real-world footage (an ambiguity pictorialist photographers also aimed for). "We tried to make the whole thing a series of moving paintings," Griffith stated. These transitions are indeed a kind of moving painting: conceived by cinematographer Karl Brown, they are actually painted landscapes composed of flats (like stage scenery) with moving miniature boats (Lennig, "*Broken*" 3).

To achieve similar visual effects cinematographically, Griffith hired a still photographer named Hendrik Sartov, who had developed a special telephoto lens with a "single element—actually a spectacle [eyeglass] lens—that was full of every kind of aberration known to glassware; stopped down to a certain point these aberrations not only gave a wonderful soft-focus quality, but also cast an indescribable sparkle to highlights such as catchlights in the eyes and on the lips" (Karl Brown, qtd. in Lennig, "*Broken*" 3). These optic effects—amplified by twilight, ambient fog, chiaroscuro, gauzes, edge-blurring mattes, fade-outs, and low-contrast developing—give many shots in *Broken Blossoms* a softness and delicacy never before seen in film. Beyond delicate aestheticism, the look perfectly captures the setting (a misty waterfront area in foggy London) and conveys aspects of subjective psychology and spiritual nuance essential to the story—the opium-induced haze of Cheng Huan's mind; the spiritual elevation of his early Buddhist idealism; his evanescent memories of youth; the angelic ethereality of the waif; the nonworldly quality of the yellow man's transcendent love.

Critics far and wide immediately hailed *Broken Blossoms* as a masterpiece. Its innovations in what would become known as "the soft style" won praise, as did Griffith's rare willingness to take the commercial risk of making a tragedy. The film did extremely well in its big-city first runs, but box office performance in its subsequent general release was unremarkable at best, as trade journals had predicted. *Harrison's Reports* zeroed in on the likely cause: "An hour and a half spent in a graveyard among skull and cross bones would not make one feel as gloomy and depressed as that length of time spent watching *Broken Blossoms*." Nevertheless, the reviewer conceded, "It is a piece of art."

■ ■ ■

Griffith's experimentation with a form of art cinema stood outside the mainstream of this year's releases. As in any other year, probably most films were unprepossessing genre entertainments that only tangentially reflected

current events or participated in serious sociopolitical and intellectual discourses of the day. Nevertheless, this was an exceptional year, marked by
an unusual sense of both international triumph and domestic uneasiness,
and punctuated by major events that invited reflection on fundamental
questions of social organization. At least some filmmakers approached these
questions head on, crafting narratives that dealt with the implications of
social hierarchy from various perspectives informed by Social-Darwinist
conservatism, progressive reformism, democratic-capitalist individualism,
and anti-socialism. At the same time, filmmakers drew attention to the aesthetic aspects of cultural hierarchy as they amplified overt artistry in a bid
for the respect and revenue of "higher-class" audiences.

SOURCES FOR FILMS

Many films from this decade are difficult to find. Some titles are only available in film archives. Some may be acquired for personal use, but only from small companies that distribute "collector's copies" on VHS or DVD-R. Typically mastered from video copies of battered and "dupey" 8 mm or 16 mm prints, these copies are often well below normal commercial standards. Quite a few silent films have been released by commercial distributors, but individual titles, particularly short films, can be difficult to locate when they appear on multi-title DVDs that vendors or libraries might catalog using only the overall title.

This guide will aid readers in locating sources for the films that are examined in detail in this volume. DVDs, like books, may go out of print over time, but the information below will nevertheless assist in the placement of interlibrary loan requests should a title become otherwise unavailable. A good source of information about the availability and quality of silent films on DVD and VHS is *www.silentera.com*

All the companies and organizations listed below have web sites that can be located easily by typing their full names into any Internet search engine. For companies whose titles appear multiple times within the following list, we have abbreviated the full names as follows:

> Grapevine = Grapevine Video
> Image = Image Entertainment
> Kino = Kino International
> Milestone = Milestone Films
> NFPF = National Film Preservation Foundation
> Thanhouser = Thanhouser Company Film Preservation

For titles discussed in this volume that do not appear in the list below, the reader may assume that the film has survived (unless the discussion indicates otherwise) but is available only in a film archive. Specific information about the location and preservation status of virtually all surviving films from this era may be found in the FIAF International Film Archive Database, an online database available from Ovid (www.ovid.com) via library subscription.

FILMS AND SOURCES

Alias Jimmy Valentine (1915) is on VHS on *The Origins of the Gangster Film* (Library of Congress & Smithsonian Video).

The Ambassador's Daughter (1913) is on DVD on *Edison: The Invention of the Movies* (Kino).

Behind the Screen (1916) is on DVD on *The Chaplin Mutuals*, Volume 2 (Image)

The Birth of a Nation (1915) is on DVD from Kino.

The Blue Bird (1918) is on DVD from Kino.

Blue Blazes Rawden (1918) is on DVD-R from both Reel Classics and Sinister Cinema.

Bolshevism On Trial (1919) is on VHS from Nostalgia Family Video.

Broken Blossoms (1919) is on DVD from both Kino and Image.

The Butcher Boy (1917) is on DVD on *Arbuckle and Keaton, Volume One: The Original Comique/Paramount Shorts, 1917–20* (Kino).

The Cheat (1915) is on DVD from Kino.

A Child of the Ghetto (1910) is available on DVD from the National Center for Jewish Film.

The Confederate Ironclad (1912) is on DVD on *Treasures from American Film Archives* (NFPF/Image).

The Cry of the Children (1912) is on DVD on *The Thanhouser Collection*, Volume 2 (Thanhouser).

The Evidence of the Film (1913) is on DVD on *The Thanhouser Collection*, Volume 5 (Thanhouser).

The Exploits of Elaine (1915) is on DVD-R on *Pearl White Films* (Sunrise Silents); only selected installments are available.

A Fool There Was (1915) is on DVD from Kino.

A Girl's Folly (1917) is on DVD-R from Reelclassicdvd, or in an abridged version on DVD on *Before Hollywood There Was Fort Lee, N.J.* (Image).

Hawthorne of the U.S.A. (1919) is on DVD-R from Grapevine.

Hearts of the World (1918) is on VHS from Terra Entertainment and laserdisc from Landmark Laservision.

His Picture in the Papers (1916) is on DVD from Flicker Alley.

The House with Closed Shutters (1910) is on DVD in a reissued version as an extra on *The Birth of a Nation* (Kino).

Intolerance (1916) is on DVD from Kino.

The Little American (1917) is on DVD from JEF Films.

Little Nemo in Slumberland (1911) is on DVD on *Winsor McCay: The Master Edition* (Milestone).

The Lonedale Operator (1911) is on DVD on *Treasures from American Film Archives* (NFPF/Image).

Mabel's Dramatic Career (1913) is on DVD on *Slapstick Encyclopedia* (Image).

Male and Female (1919) is on DVD from Image.

Manhattan Trade School for Girls (1911) is on DVD on *Treasures III: Social Issues in American Film, 1900–1934* (NFPF/Image).

Matrimony's Speed Limit (1913) is on VHS on *America's First Women Filmmakers* (Library of Congress & Smithsonian Video).

A Modern Musketeer (1917) is on DVD from Flicker Alley.

A Movie Star (1916) is on DVD on *Slapstick Encyclopedia* (Image).

The New York Hat (1912) is on DVD on *D. W. Griffith's Biograph Shorts* (Kino).

Perils of Pauline (1914) is on DVD from Grapevine; only selected installments are available.

Ramona (1910) is on DVD on *Treasures III: Social Issues in American Film, 1900–1934* (NFPF/Image).

Regeneration (1915) is on DVD from Image.

Shoulder Arms (1918) is on DVD on *Charlie Chaplin: The First National Collection* (Image).

The Sinking of the Lusitania (1918) is on DVD on *Winsor McCay: The Master Edition* (Milestone)

The Social Secretary (1916) is on DVD-R on *Norma Talmadge Double Feature* (Grapevine).

Stella Maris (1918) is on DVD from Milestone.

The Stenographer's Friend (1910) is on DVD on *More Treasures from American Film Archives* (NFPF/Image).

Suspense (1913) is on DVD on *Unseen Cinema* (Anthology Film Archives/Image) and *Saved from the Flames* (Flicker Alley).

Swords and Hearts (1911) on DVD as an extra on *The Birth of a Nation* (Kino).

Tillie's Punctured Romance (1914) is on DVD on Image.

Traffic in Souls (1913) is on DVD on *Perils of the New Land: Films of the Immigrant Experience, 1910–1915* (Flicker Alley).

Twelfth Night (1910) is on DVD on *Silent Shakespeare* (Milestone/Image).

Where Are My Children? (1916) is on DVD on *Treasures III: Social Issues in American Film, 1900–1934* (NFPF/Image).

White Fawn's Devotion (1910) is on DVD on *Treasures from American Film Archives* (NFPF/Image).

Wild and Woolly (1917) is on DVD from Flicker Alley.

WORKS CITED
AND CONSULTED

Abel, Richard. *Americanizing the Movies and "Movie-Mad" Audiences: 1910–1914*. Berkeley: U of California P, 2006.

Abrams, Hiram. "How I Keep 12,000,000 Customers Sold." *System* Aug. 1918: 199–204.

Addams, Jane. "Why Women Should Vote." *Ladies' Home Journal* Jan. 1910: 22.

Rev. of *Alias Jimmy Valentine*. *Moving Picture World* 6 March 1915.

"All War Pictures Fakes." *Moving Picture World* 3 Oct. 1914: 50.

Altman, Rick. *Silent Film Sound*. New York: Columbia UP, 2004.

Anderson, Robert. "The Role of the Western Film Genre in Industry Competition, 1907–1911." *Journal of the University Film Association* 31.2 (1979): 19–26.

"Art and Pictures United by Belasco." *Motion Picture News* 30 May 1914: 48.

Arvidson, Linda [Mrs. D. W. Griffith]. *When the Movies Were Young*. New York: Dover, 1969.

"Attacks Five-Cent Film Shows." *Los Angeles Times* 11 July 1910: II8.

"Bad Moral and Tells Secrets, But Will Get Money." *Wid's* 1 March 1917: 137.

Balides, Constance. "Character as Economics: Fordism, the Consuming Housewife, and *The Cheat*." *Celebrating 1895: The Centenary of Cinema*. Ed. John Fullerton. Sydney: John Libbey, 1998.

Balio, Tino, ed. *The American Film Industry*. Rev. ed. Madison: U of Wisconsin P, 1985.

Banks, Vera J., and Calvin L. Beale. "Farm Population Estimates 1910–70." *Rural Development Service Statistical Bulletin* no. 523. *http://www.eric.ed.gov*. Accessed 10 April 2008.

Bazin, André. *What Is Cinema?* Volume 1. Trans. Hugh Gray. Berkeley: U of California P, 1967.

Bean, Jennifer. "Technologies of Early Stardom and the Extraordinary Body." *camera obscura* 48 (2001): 9–56.

Bernardi, Daniel, ed. *The Birth of Whiteness: Race and the Emergence of U.S. Cinema*. New Brunswick: Rutgers UP, 1996.

Bigsby, Christopher, ed. *The Cambridge Companion to Modern American Culture*. Cambridge: Cambridge UP, 2006.

Black, Ernestine. "Lois Weber Smalley." *Overland Monthly* 68 (Sept. 1916): 198–200.

Blaisdell, George. "*Traffic in Souls*." *Moving Picture World* 22 Nov. 1913: 849.

Blanke, David. *The 1910s*. Westport, Conn.: Greenwood, 2002.

"*The Blue Bird* a Hit on Screen." *New York Times* 1 April 1918: 9.

Rev. of *The Blue Bird*. *Photoplay* May 1918.

Bordwell, David. "The Classical Hollywood Style, 1917–1960." In David Bordwell, Janet Staiger, and Kristin Thompson, *The Classical Hollywood Cinema: Film Style and Mode of Production to 1960*. New York: Columbia UP, 1988.

Bowers, Q. David. *Nickelodeon Theatres and Their Music*. Vestal, N.Y.: Vestal Press, 1986.

Bowser, Eileen. *The Transformation of Cinema, 1907–1915*. New York: Charles Scribner's Sons, 1990.

Brewer, Susan. *To Win the Peace: British Propaganda in the United States during World War II*. Ithaca: Cornell UP, 1997.

Brewster, Ben. "*Traffic in Souls:* An Experiment in Feature-Length Narrative Construction." *Cinema Journal* 31.1 (1991): 37–56.

Rev. of *Broken Blossoms. Christian Science Monitor* 27 May 1919.

Rev. of *Broken Blossoms. Harrison's Reports* 1, no.11 (1919).

Brooks, Peter. *The Melodramatic Imagination: Balzac, James, Melodrama, and the Mode of Excess.* New Haven: Yale UP, 1976.

Brownlow, Kevin. *Behind the Mask of Innocence: Sex, Violence, Prejudice, Crime: Films of Social Conscience in the Silent Era.* Berkeley: U of California P, 1990.

Bush, W. Stephen. "The Single Reel—II." *Moving Picture World* 4 July 1914: 36.

———. "The Social Uses of the Motion Picture." *Moving Picture World* 27 April 1912: 305.

Butsch, Richard. "Bowery B'hoys and Matinee Ladies: The Re-gendering of Nineteenth-Century American Theater Audiences." *American Quarterly* 46.3 (Sept. 1994): 374–405.

Byington, Margaret F. *Homestead: The Households of a Mill Town.* New York: Charities Publication Committee, 1910.

Campbell, Craig. *Reel America and World War I: A Comprehensive Filmography and History of Motion Pictures in the United States, 1914–1920.* Jefferson, N.C.: McFarland, 1985.

Cashman, Sean Dennis. *America Ascendant: From Theodore Roosevelt to FDR in the Century of American Power, 1901–1945.* New York: New York UP, 1998.

———. *America in the Age of the Titans: The Progressive Era and World War I.* New York: New York UP, 1988.

Cherchi Usai, Paolo, ed. *The Griffith Project.* Vol. 4: *Films Produced in 1910.* London: BFI, 2000.

———. *The Griffith Project.* Vol. 5: *Films Produced in 1911.* London: BFI, 2001.

———. *The Griffith Project.* Vol. 6: *Films Produced in 1912.* London: BFI, 2002.

———. *The Griffith Project.* Vol. 7: *Films Produced in 1913.* London: BFI, 2003.

Rev. of *Civilization. Photoplay* Aug. 1916: 135–37.

Condon, Charles R. "A Six-Reel Keystone Comedy." *Motography* 14 Nov. 1914: 657.

Cooper, John Milton, Jr. *Pivotal Decades: The United States, 1900–1920.* New York: W. W. Norton, 1990.

Crafton, Donald. *Before Mickey: The Animation Film, 1898–1928.* Chicago: U of Chicago P, 1993.

———. "Pie and Chase: Gag, Spectacle, and Narrative in Slapstick Comedy." *Classical Hollywood Comedy.* Ed. Kristine Brunovska Karnick and Henry Jenkins. New York: Routledge, 1995. 106–22.

Creel, George. *How We Advertised America.* New York: Harper & Brothers, 1920.

"A Declaration of Personal Independence. Away with Meddlers." Promotional herald accompanying the release of *Intolerance,* 1916. Excerpted on the DVD release of *Intolerance,* Kino Video, 2002.

DeBauche, Leslie Midkiff. *Reel Patriotism: The Movies and World War I.* Madison: U of Wisconsin P, 1997.

deCordova, Richard. *Picture Personalities: The Emergence of the Star System in America.* Urbana: U of Illinois P, 1990.

de Koven Bowen, Louise. *Safeguards for City Youth at Work and at Play.* New York: Macmillan, 1914.

Dorr, Rheta Childe. *What Eight Million Women Want.* Boston: Small, Maynard & Co., 1910.

"The Drama of the People." *The Independent* 29 Sept. 1910: 713.

Dyer, Richard. "Into the Light: The Whiteness of the South in *The Birth of a Nation.*" *Dixie Debates: Perspectives on Southern Cultures.* Ed. Richard H. King and Helen Taylor. New York: New York UP, 1996. 165–76.

Adv. for *The Eagle's Eye*. *Exhibitor's Trade Review* 16 Feb. 1918: 873.

"Educated Classes and the Moving Picture." *Moving Picture World* 9 April 1910: 545.

Erenberg, Lewis. *Steppin' Out: New York Nightlife and the Transformation of American Culture, 1890–1930*. Westport, Conn.: Greenwood, 1981.

Fabian, Ann. "History for the Masses: Commercializing the Western Past." *Under an Open Sky: Rethinking America's Western Past*. Ed. William Cronon, George Miles, and Jay Gitlin. New York: W. W. Norton, 1992. 223–38.

"Facts and Comments." *Moving Picture World* 21 Nov. 1914: 1047.

Fairbanks, Douglas. *Laugh and Live*. New York: Britton Publishing Company, 1917.

Faragher, John, et al. *Out of Many: A History of the American People*. Vol. 2. 3rd ed. Upper Saddle River, N.J.: Prentice-Hall, 2000.

"Fearful Fly Seen on Sheet." *Los Angeles Times* 17 Nov. 1910: I7.

"Feature Producers Affiliate." *Moving Picture World* 30 May 1914: 1268–69.

"Film Trade a Great Help to Loan." *Moving Picture World* 11 May 1918: 831–32.

"Films for Commuters." *New York Times* 29 Dec. 1910: 16.

"Films Thrive Here on Quintuple Lines." *Los Angeles Times* 16 Oct. 1910: II1.

Fleener-Marzec, Nickieann. *D. W. Griffith's "The Birth of a Nation": Controversy, Suppression, and the First Amendment As It Applies to Filmic Expression, 1915–1973*. New York: Arno Press, 1980.

Flexner, Eleanor, and Ellen Fitzpatrick. *Century of Struggle: The Woman's Rights Movement in the United States*. Enlarged ed. Cambridge, Mass.: Harvard UP, 1975.

Fort Lee Film Commission. *Fort Lee, Birthplace of the Motion Picture*. Chicago: Arcadia, 2006.

Fuller, Kathryn. *At the Picture Show: Small-Town Audiences and the Creation of Movie Fan Culture*. Washington, D.C.: Smithsonian Institution P, 1996.

Gaines, Jane. *Fire and Desire: Mixed-Race Movies in the Silent Era*. Chicago: U of Chicago P, 2001.

Gatzke, Hans W. *Germany and the United States: A "Special Relationship?"* Cambridge, Mass.: Harvard UP, 1980.

Rev. of *A Girl's Folly*. *Motography* 3 March 1917: 479.

Rev. of *A Girl's Folly*. *Moving Picture World* 3 March 1917: 1369.

"*A Girl's Folly* Shows Secrets of Picture Making—Old Plot and Good Cast."

Exhibitor's Trade Review 24 Feb. 1917: 835.

Grieveson, Lee. *Policing Cinema: Movies and Censorship in Early Twentieth-Century America*. Berkeley: U of California P, 2004.

———. "Stars and Audiences in Early American Cinema." *Screening the Past* (Fall 2002): 1–27.

Griffith, D. W. *The Rise and Fall of Free Speech in America*. Los Angeles, 1916. Excerpted on the DVD release of *Intolerance*, Kino Video, 2002.

Gunning, Tom. "Crazy Machines in the Garden of Forking Paths: Mischief Gags and the Origins of American Film Comedy." *Classical Hollywood Comedy*. Ed. Kristine Brunovska Karnick and Henry Jenkins. New York: Routledge, 1995. 87–105.

———. *D. W. Griffith and the Origins of American Narrative Film: The Early Years at Biograph*. Urbana: U of Illinois P, 1991.

———. "From the Kaleidoscope to the X-Ray: Urban Spectatorship, Poe, Benjamin, and *Traffic in Souls*." *Wide Angle* 19.4 (1997): 25–63.

———. "Systematizing the Electric Message: Narrative Form, Gender, and Modernity in *The Lonedale Operator*." *American Cinema's Transitional Era: Audiences, Institutions, Practices*. Ed. Charlie Keil and Shelley Stamp. Berkeley: U of California P, 2004. 15–50.

Hagedorn, Ann. *Savage Peace: Hope and Fear in America, 1919*. New York: Simon & Schuster, 2007.

Hall, Ben M. *The Best Remaining Seats: The Story of the Golden Age of the Movie Palace*. New York: Crown Publishers, 1961.

Hampton, Benjamin B. *History of the American Film Industry*. 1931. New York: Dover, 1970.

Harris, Neil. *Cultural Excursions: Marketing Appetites and Cultural Tastes in Modern America*. Chicago: U of Chicago P, 1990.

Harrison, Louis Reeves. "The 'Bison-101' Headliners." *Moving Picture World* 27 April 1912: 320–22.

———. *The Indian Massacre. Moving Picture World* 9 March 1912. 854–55, 857–58.

———. "Nineteen-Fifteen." *Moving Picture World* 2 January 1915: 43.

———. "*Ramona.*" *Moving Picture World* 4 June 1910: 933.

Rev. of *Hawthorne of the U.S.A.* [play]. *New York Times* 7 Nov. 1912: 3.

Rev. of *Hearts of the World. Variety* 12 March 1918.

Hendrick, Burton J. "Oxygenizing a City." *McClure's Magazine* Aug. 1910: 373–87.

Higashi, Sumiko. *Cecil B. DeMille and American Culture: The Silent Era*. Berkeley: U of California P, 1994.

"House Fly Actors Make Their Debut on the Stage." *Moving Picture World* 12 March 1910: 375.

"How Fast Mankind Is Getting Acquainted." *Life* 28 July 1910: 146.

Howe, Irving. *World of Our Fathers*. New York: Touchstone, 1976.

"In the Motion Picture Swim." *Los Angeles Times* 1 Feb. 1910: II14.

"The Indian and the Cowboy (By One Who Does Not Like Them)." *Moving Picture World* 17 Dec. 1910: 1399.

"Industry Subscribes Over 2 Million to Liberty Loan." *Exhibitor's Trade Review* 23 June 1917: 173.

Inglis, William. "Morals and Moving Pictures." *Harper's Weekly* 30 July 1910: 12–13.

Jameson, Fredric. "Reification and Utopia in Mass Culture." *Signatures of the Visible*. London: Routledge, 1992. 9–34.

Jenkins, Henry. *What Made Pistachio Nuts? Early Sound Comedy and the Vaudeville Aesthetic*. New York: Columbia UP, 1992.

Rev. of *Joan the Woman. Photoplay* March 1917: 113–16.

Jump, Herbert A. "Moving Picture Statistics in New Britain, Conn." *Moving Picture World* 31 Dec. 1910: 1541.

Adv. for *The Kaiser, the Beast of Berlin. Moving Picture World* 13 April 1918: 162–63.

Adv. for *The Kaiser, the Beast of Berlin. Moving Picture World* 20 April 1918: 438.

Adv. for *The Kaiser, the Beast of Berlin. Photoplay* 1 June 1918: 94.

"*The Kaiser* Lithographs Spell Ruin for Billboards." *Moving Picture World* 20 April 1918: 411.

"Kathlyn the Intrepid." *Photoplay* April 1914: 46.

Kauffman, Reginald Wright. *The House of Bondage*. New York: Moffat, Yard, & Co., 1911.

Keene, Jennifer D. *Doughboys, the Great War, and the Remaking of America*. Baltimore: Johns Hopkins UP, 2001.

Keil, Charlie. *Early American Cinema in Transition: Story, Style, and Filmmaking, 1907–1913*. Madison: U of Wisconsin P, 2001.

———. "Transition through Tension: Stylistic Diversity in the Late Griffith Biographs." *Cinema Journal* 28.3 (1989): 22–40.

Keil, Charlie, and Shelley Stamp, eds. *American Cinema's Transitional Era: Audiences, Institutions, Practices*. Berkeley: U of California P, 2004.

Kelly, Kitty. "How Sennett Makes Keystone Comedies." *Chicago Tribune*. 15 April 1915: 10.

Kepley, Vance. "*Broken Blossoms* and the Problem of Historical Specificity." *Quarterly Review of Film Studies* 3.1 (Winter 1978): 37–47.

Kern, Stephen. *The Culture of Time and Space, 1880–1918*. Cambridge, Mass.: Harvard UP, 1983.

Koszarski, Richard. *An Evening's Entertainment: The Age of the Silent Feature Picture, 1915–1928*. New York: Charles Scribner's Sons, 1990.

Laemmle, Carl. "Doom of Long Features Predicted." *Moving Picture World* 11 July 1914: 185.

Lang, Arthur J. "Cashing in on Europe's War." *Motion Picture News* 28 Nov. 1914: 25.

"Latest Film Snapshots Local and Worldwide." *Cleveland Leader* 2 March 1913: M11.

Lawford, C. W. "The Moving Picture vs. the Reformers." *Moving Picture World* 1 Oct. 1910: 741–42.

Lears, T. J. Jackson. *Fables of Abundance: A Cultural History of Advertising in America*. New York: Basic Books, 1995.

———. *No Place of Grace: Antimodernism and the Transformation of American Culture, 1880–1920*. New York: Pantheon, 1981.

Lee, Betty. *Marie Dressler: The Unlikeliest Star*. Lexington: U of Kentucky P, 1997.

Lennig, Arthur. "*Broken Blossoms*, D. W. Griffith, and the Making of an Unconventional Masterpiece." *Film Journal* 1.3–4 (Fall-Winter 1972): 2–15.

———. "Myth and Fact: The Reception of *The Birth of a Nation*." *Film History* 16.2 (April 2004): 117–41.

Levine, Lawrence W. *Highbrow/Lowbrow: The Emergence of Cultural Hierarchy in America*. Cambridge, Mass.: Harvard UP, 1988.

Lindsay, Vachel. *The Art of the Moving Picture*. New York: Macmillan, 1915.

———. "Photoplay Progress." *New Republic* 17 Feb. 1917: 76.

Rev. of *Male and Female*. *Photoplay* Dec. 1919.

Rev. of *Male and Female*. *Variety* 28 Nov. 1919.

"A Mammoth and Novel Publicity Plan." *Motion Picture News* 17 Jan. 1914: 21.

"Many Thousands See Griffith Film." *Moving Picture World* 28 Sept. 1918: 1912.

Mast, Gerald. "Chaplin." *World Directors*. Vol. 1, *1890–1945*. Ed. John Wakeman. New York: H. W. Wilson, 1987.

———, ed. *The Movies in Our Midst: Documents in the Cultural History of Film in America*. Chicago: U of Chicago P, 1982.

McMahan, Alison. *Alice Guy Blaché: Lost Visionary of the Cinema*. New York: Continuum, 2002.

Miles, Dudley. "The Civil War as a Unifier." *Sewanee Review* 21 (Jan. 1913): 188–97.

"Miss Mary Pickford." *Moving Picture World* 24 Dec. 1910: 1462.

"The Motion Picture Hall of Fame." *Motion Picture Magazine* Dec. 1918: 12.

Mottet, Jean. *L'invention de la scene Americaine: cinema et paysage*. Paris: Harmattan, 1998.

Mould, David H., and Berg, Charles M. "Fact and Fantasy in the Films of World War One." *Film History* 14.3 (Sept. 1984): 50–60.

"Moving Picture Hypnosis." *New York Times* 14 Aug. 1910: 8.

"Moving Picture Shows." *Christian Observer* 11 May 1910: 5.

"Moving Pictures." *Health* 5 July 1910:151.

"Moving Pictures Sound Melodrama's Knell." *New York Times* 20 March 1910: SM7.

Münsterberg, Hugo. *The Photoplay: A Psychological Study*. 1916. New York: Dover, 1970.

Musser, Charles. "On 'Extras,' Mary Pickford, and the Red-Light Film Filmmaking in the United States, 1913." *Griffithiana* 50 (1994): 149–75.

———. "Work, Ideology, and Chaplin's Tramp." *Resisting Images: Essays on Cinema and History.* Ed. Robert Sklar and Charles Musser. Philadelphia: Temple UP, 1990. 36–67.

Mutual Film Corporation v. Industrial Commission of Ohio. 236 U.S. 230 (1915): 244.

"New Hero for Matinee Girls." *Los Angeles Times* 6 Feb. 1910: II3.

Oberdeck, Kathryn. *The Evangelist and the Impresario: Religion, Entertainment, and Cultural Politics in America, 1884–1914.* Baltimore: Johns Hopkins UP, 1999.

"Object to Film Profanity." *New York Times* 13 Dec. 1910: 1.

O'Dell, Paul. *D. W. Griffith and the Rise of Hollywood.* New York: A. S. Barnes, 1971.

Ohmann, Richard. *Selling Culture: Magazines, Markets, and Class at the Turn of the Century.* London and New York: Verson, 1996.

"150 Trapped, 7 Hurt in a Downtown Fire." *New York Times* 3 July 1910: 1.

Paranagua, Paulo Antonio. "Ten Reasons to Love or Hate Mexican Cinema." *Mexican Cinema.* London: BFI, 1995. 1–13.

Park, Robert E. "The City: Suggestions for the Investigation of Human Behavior in the Urban Environment." *The City.* Ed. Robert E. Park and Ernest W. Burgess. 1925. Chicago: U of Chicago P, 1967. 1–46.

"Pathé Will Issue Film Daily." *Motion Picture News* 13 June 1914: 68.

Pearson, Roberta. *Eloquent Gestures: The Transformation of Performance Style in the Griffith Biograph Films.* Berkeley: U of California P, 1992.

Peiss, Kathy. *Cheap Amusements: Working Women and Leisure in Turn-of-the-Century New York.* Philadelphia: Temple UP, 1986.

Rev. of *Perils of Pauline. Motion Picture News* 4 April 1914: 56.

"Pictures in Church Before the Sermon." *New York Times* 12 Sept. 1910: 9.

"Pictures to Soothe Insane." *New York Times* 23 Feb. 1910: 3.

Pratt, George C. *Spellbound in Darkness: A History of the Silent Film.* Greenwich, Conn.: New York Graphic Society, 1973.

Quinn, Michael Joseph. "Early Feature Distribution and the Development of the Motion Picture Industry: Famous Players and Paramount, 1912–1921." Ph.D. dissertation, U of Wisconsin–Madison, 1998.

"The Real Perils of Pauline." *Photoplay* Oct. 1914: 59–64.

Rev. of *Regeneration. Moving Picture World* 2 Oct. 1915.

"Review of Special Feature Subjects." *New York Dramatic Mirror* 24 April 1912: 27.

Richardson, Bertha June. *The Woman Who Spends: A Study of Her Economic Function.* Boston: Whitcomb & Barrows, 1910.

"The Rivoli, Newest Film Palace, Opens." *New York Times* 29 Dec. 1917: 8.

Robertson, J. H. *The Story of the Telephone.* London, 1947.

Roosevelt, Theodore. "The Recent Prize Fight." *Outlook* 16 July 1910: 550.

Ross, Steven J. *Working-Class Hollywood: Silent Cinema and the Shaping of Class in America.* Princeton: Princeton UP, 1998.

Ryan, Mary. *Cradle of the Middle Class: The Family in Oneida County, New York, 1790–1865.* Cambridge: Cambridge UP, 1981.

Sargent, Epes Winthrop. *Moving Picture World* 26 Aug. 1911: 525.

"Scent Nation-wide Terrorist Plot." *New York Times* 1 Jan. 1919: 13.

Schickel, Richard. *D. W. Griffith.* London: Pavilion, 1984.

Schlereth, Thomas J. *Victorian America: Transformations in Everyday Life, 1876–1915*. New York: HarperCollins, 1991.

Seabury, William Marston. *The Public and the Motion Picture Industry*. New York: Macmillan, 1926.

"Selig-Hearst Pictorial Announced." *Motion Picture News* 7 March 1914: 26.

Sennett, Mack, with Cameron Shipp. *King of Comedy*. New York: Doubleday, 1954.

Silva, Fred. *Focus on The Birth of a Nation*. Englewood Cliffs, N.J.: Prentice-Hall, 1971.

Simmon, Scott. *The Films of D. W. Griffith*. Cambridge: Cambridge UP, 1993.

———. *The Invention of the Western Film: A Cultural History of the Genre's First Half-Century*. Cambridge: Cambridge UP, 2003.

———. Program notes to *Treasures from American Film Archives*. DVD. Washington, D.C.: National Preservation Foundation, 2000.

Singer, Ben. "Feature Films, Variety Programs, and the Crisis of the Small Exhibitor." *American Cinema's Transitional Era: Audiences, Institutions, Practices*. Ed. Charlie Keil and Shelley Stamp. Berkeley: U of California P, 2004. 76–100.

———. *Melodrama and Modernity: Early Sensational Cinema and Its Contexts*. New York: Columbia UP, 2001.

Slossin, Edwin E. *Great American Universities*. New York: Macmillan, 1910.

"The Smalleys Have a Message to the World." *Universal Weekly* 10 April 1915.

Smith, Andrew Brodie. *Shooting Cowboys and Indians: Silent Western Films, American Culture, and the Birth of Hollywood*. Boulder: U of Colorado P, 2003.

Smith, Greg M. "Silencing the New Woman: Ethnic and Social Mobility in the Melodramas of Norma Talmadge." *Journal of Film and Video* 48.3 (Fall 1996): 3–16. Available online at http://www2.gsu.edu/~jougms/Norma.htm.

"Special Film Reviews." *Motion Picture News* 7 Feb. 1914: 35.

Spengler, Oswald. *Der Untergang des Abendlandes: Umrisse einer Morphologie der Weltgeschichte*. Munich: Beck, 1923.

Stamp, Shelley. "'It's a Long Way to Filmland': Starlets, Screen Hopefuls, and Extras in Early Hollywood." *American Cinema's Transitional Era: Audiences, Institutions, Practices*. Ed. Charlie Keil and Shelley Stamp. Berkeley: U of California P, 2004. 332–51.

———. *Movie-Struck Girls: Women and Motion-Picture Culture after the Nickelodeon*. Princeton: Princeton UP, 2000.

———. "Taking Precautions, or Regulating Early Birth Control Films." *A Feminist Reader in Early Cinema*. Ed. Jennifer Bean and Diane Negra. Durham, N.C.: Duke UP, 2002. 270–97.

Storey, Walter. "Limits of Censorship" (letter). *New York Times* 1 Oct. 1910: 12.

Studlar, Gaylyn. *This Mad Masquerade: Stardom and Masculinity in the Jazz Age*. New York: Columbia UP, 1996.

Sumner, William Graham. "The Challenge of Facts." (n.d.; ca. 1880s). *The Challenge of Facts*. New Haven: Yale UP, 1914. 15–52.

———. "Reply to a Socialist" (1904). *The Challenge of Facts*. New Haven: Yale UP, 1914. 53–62

———. *What Social Classes Owe to Each Other*. New York: Harper & Brothers, 1883.

Tedlow, Richard S. *New and Improved: The Story of Mass Marketing in America*. New York: Basic Books, 1990.

"A Theatre with a 5,000,000 Audience." *World's Work* May 1910: 12876.

Thompson, Kristin. *Exporting Entertainment: America in the World Film Market, 1907–1934*. London: BFI, 1985.

Tilden, Freeman. "If Shakespeare Lived Today." *Puck* 21 Sept. 1910: 7.

Rev. of *Tillie's Punctured Romance. Motion Picture News* 14 Nov. 1914: 40.

Rev. of *Tillie's Punctured Romance. New York Dramatic Mirror* 4 Nov. 1914.

Tönnies, Ferdinand. *Community and Association.* Trans. Charles P. Loomis. 1887. London: Routledge and Kegan Paul, 1955.

"Turned to Arson by Moving Pictures." *New York Times* 15 July 1910: 16.

"Unwarranted Wholesale Condemnation." *Moving Picture World* 11 June 1910: 982.

Uricchio, William, and Roberta E. Pearson. *Reframing Culture: The Case of the Vitagraph Quality Films.* Princeton: Princeton UP, 1993.

U.S. Bureau of the Census. "Census of Population and Housing." http://www.census.gov/prod/www/abs/decennial/index.htm. Accessed 10 April 2008.

———. "Estimated Population of the United States: 1790 to 1957." *Historical Statistics of the United States: Colonial Times to 1957.* Washington, D.C., 1960. 7.

———. "Index of Average Daily Wages in All Industries . . ." *Historical Statistics of the United States: Colonial Times to 1957.* Washington, D.C., 1960. 90.

———. "Motor-Vehicle Factory Sales and Registrations, and Motor-Fuel Usage: 1900 to 1957." *Historical Statistics of the United States: Colonial Times to 1957.* Washington, D.C., 1960. 462.

———. "Population of the 100 Largest Cities and Other Urban Places in the United States: 1790 to 1990." http://www.census.gov/population/www/documentation/twps0027.html. Accessed 10 April 2008.

———. "Thirteenth Census of the United States—1910." http://www2.census.gov/prod2/decennial/documents/00168442_TOC.pdf. Accessed 10 April 2008.

———. "Urban/Rural and Inside/Outside Metropolitan Area." *http://www.census.gov.* Accessed 10 April 2008.

"Villa at the Front; 'Movies' Sign Him Up." *New York Times* 7 Jan. 1914: 1.

Wakeman, John, ed. *World Film Directors.* Vol. 1, *1890–1945.* New York: H. W. Wilson, 1987.

"War Vividly Seen in Griffith Film." *New York Times* 5 April 1918: 13.

"Western Types Are in Vogue." *Los Angeles Times* 2 Dec. 1910: II5.

Rev. of *What's His Name. Motion Picture News* 7 Nov. 1914: 39.

Rev. of *What's His Name. Moving Picture World* 7 Nov. 1914: 792.

"What's Offered This Week in the Local Show Shops." *Minneapolis Journal* 2 June 1912: 8:8.

Rev. of *Where Are My Children? Moving Picture World* 29 April 1916: 817.

Wiebe, Robert H. *The Search for Order, 1877–1920.* New York: Hill and Wang, 1966.

Rev. of *Wild and Woolly. Moving Picture World* 17 June 1917: 1836.

Wilinsky, Barbara. "Flirting with Kathlyn: Creating the Mass Audience." *Hollywood Goes Shopping.* Ed. David Desser and Garth S. Jowett. Minneapolis: U of Minnesota P, 2000. 34–56.

Wing, Ruth, ed. *Blue Book of the Screen.* Hollywood: Pacific Gravure Co., 1924.

"Wisconsin Manager Quickly Puts End to Boycott with Newspaper Declaration." *Motion Picture News* 27 July 1918: 588.

Rev. of *Zudora. Motion Picture News* 14 Nov. 1914: 39.

Zukor, Adolph. "Pleasing Most of the People Most of the Time." *System* Oct. 1918: 4.

CONTRIBUTORS

RICHARD ABEL is Robert Altman Collegiate Professor of Film Studies in the Department of Screen Arts and Culture at the University of Michigan. Most recently he edited the award-winning *Encyclopedia of Early Cinema* (2005), published *Americanizing the Movies and 'Movie-Mad' Audiences, 1910–1914* (2006), and co-organized the Ninth International Domitor Conference at the University of Michigan (2006). Currently he is co-editing *Early Cinema and the "National"* (2008) and completing research for *Menus for Movie Land: Newspapers and the Movies, 1911–1915*.

EILEEN BOWSER is internationally known as a film archivist and as a film historian. She was for many years curator of the film collection of the Museum of Modern Art. She is the author of *The Transformation of Cinema 1907–1915*, *D. W. Griffith* (with Iris Barry), *The Slapstick Symposium* (editor and contributor), *The Movies* (with Richard Griffith and Arthur Mayer), *Film Notes, Biograph Bulletins* (editor), *Carl Dreyer*, and other publications.

LESLIE MIDKIFF DeBAUCHE is a professor in the Division of Communication at the University of Wisconsin–Stevens Point. Her first book, *Reel Patriotism: The Movies and World War I*, was published in 1997. She is currently at work on a history of the American Girl, a popular character type in fiction of the 1910s who played an important role in the film, fashion, and advertising industries of her day.

LEE GRIEVESON is a Reader in Film Studies and the director of the Graduate Programme in Film Studies at University College London. He is the author of *Policing Cinema: Movies and Censorship in Turn-of-the-Century America* (2004) and co-editor, with Peter Kramer, of *The Silent Cinema Reader* (2003).

CHARLIE KEIL is the director of the Cinema Studies Institute and an associate professor of history at the University of Toronto. He is the author of *Early American Cinema in Transition: Story, Style and Filmmaking, 1907–1913* (2001) and co-editor, with Shelley Stamp, of *American Cinema's Transitional Era: Audience, Institutions, Practices* (2004). His next project is an anthology, co-edited with Daniel Goldmark, on humor in studio-era animated films.

ROB KING is an assistant professor in the Cinema Studies Institute and Department of History at the University of Toronto. He is the author of *The*

Fun Factory: The Keystone Film Company and the Emergence of Mass Culture (2009) and co-editor, with Richard Abel and Giorgio Bertellini, of *Early Cinema and the "National"* (2008).

JAMES LATHAM teaches in the Semester in Los Angeles program for the University of Texas at Austin. He holds a Ph.D. in Cinema Studies from New York University, where his dissertation research was on early Hollywood promotion. He has published articles in *The Velvet Light Trap, Film & History*, and *Post Script*.

SCOTT SIMMON, a professor of English at the University of California–Davis, is curator of the National Film Preservation Foundation's Treasures from American Film Archives DVD series. His book *The Invention of the Western Film* received the Theatre Library Association Award for 2003; he is also the author of *The Films of D. W. Griffith* and co-author of *King Vidor, American* (1988), *Film Preservation 1993* (1993), and *Redefining Film Preservation* (1994).

BEN SINGER is an associate professor of film in the Department of Communication Arts at the University of Wisconsin–Madison. He is the author of *Melodrama and Modernity: Early Sensational Cinema and Its Contexts* (2001) and *Alexander Bakshy: Modernism and the Space of Spectatorship* (2009).

SHELLEY STAMP is the chair of the Department of Film and Digital Media at the University of California–Santa Cruz. She is the author of *Movie-Struck Girls: Women and Motion Picture Culture after the Nickeloeon* (2000) and co-editor (with Charlie Keil) of *American Cinema's Transitional Era: Audiences, Institutions, Practices* (2004) and a special issue of *Film History* on "Women and the Silent Screen" (with Amelie Hastie). Her current book project, *Lois Weber in Early Hollywood*, is supported by a Film Scholars Grant from the Academy of Motion Picture Arts and Sciences.

INDEX

Page numbers in italics indicate illustrations.